9.5.78

POPULAR LITERATURE

A History and Guide

POPULAR LITERATURE

A HISTORY AND GUIDE
From the beginning of printing to the year 1897

Victor E. Neuburg

THE WOBURN PRESS

This edition published 1977 in Great Britain by
THE WOBURN PRESS
Gainsborough House, Gainsborough Road,
London E11 1RS, England
by arrangement with Penguin Books

and in the United States of America by
THE WOBURN PRESS
c/o Biblio Distribution Center
81 Adams Drive, Totowa, New Jersey 07512

ISBN 0 7130 0158 5

Printed in Great Britain by
Billing & Sons Ltd., Guildford, London and Worcester

CONTENTS

ACKNOWLEDGEMENTS

So many have helped – often unknowingly – with the making of this book. Without Barbara Gilbert's enthusiasm and competence I should have been overwhelmed at an early stage. My daughter Caroline has been ever critical and always ready to assist. Brian Alderson, Stanley Brett, Denis Crutch and Chris Needham were all helpful in one way or another. Pamela Bater, a colleague, answered many requests for help. Thank you to Martha Vicinus, who read the manuscript and made perceptive suggestions. I offer especial thanks to my wife, whose forbearance in the face of book-buying and my unsociability when writing was remarkable and sustained. Finally, students at the School of Librarianship, the Polytechnic of North London, and at State College, Buffalo, were critical and iconoclastic. I am grateful to them too.

V.E.N.

LIST OF ILLUSTRATIONS

INTRODUCTION

What I want to do in this book is to define popular literature, to trace its development in England from the beginnings of printing to the year 1897, and finally to provide a critical survey of sources available for its study. I have not attempted to discuss the growth of newspapers or periodicals. Both are related to my theme, but seem to me to require entirely separate treatment. Any attempt to be comprehensive in a book of this size would result in a superficiality which I hope, by taking a more narrow view, to have avoided.

It is more than thirty years since a French historian, Lucien Febvre, urged a change in the direction of historical studies, so that what he described as 'l'histoire des mentalités collectives' should be given greater prominence. By this phrase he meant the assumptions, beliefs, feelings and modes of thought of men and women in the past. Only during the last ten years or so, however, have serious efforts been made in this country to look with sympathy and understanding at the world of the inarticulate. In the continuing process of its exploration it becomes increasingly clear that the study of popular literature has an important role to play, for it can throw light upon what the relatively unlettered members of society were really like – how they thought and felt, their attitudes and values, the way they looked at life.

Similar claims for popular literature were made over one hundred years ago by J. O. Halliwell, who wrote:

A student who is anxious to obtain that extensive knowledge of the habits, customs, and phraseology of our ancestors, without which the humour of Shakespeare and his contemporaries can only be imperfectly appreciated, will do well to turn his attention to the ancient literature of the cottage, and make himself acquainted with the tales that were familiar 'as household words' to the groundlings of the Globe or the Blackfriars . . . Let us ask, where would a reader turn for explanations of the jocular allusions in a modern farce or extravaganza. Certainly not to the works of Faraday or Mrs Somerville, but oftener to the ballads of Seven Dials.[1]

At the time of its writing this claim went unheeded; but today we are inclined to look at it very much more sympathetically, in the realization that it is no longer valid to see working men and women of the past within the framework of what their 'betters' thought or assumed they believed. If we are to discover them on their own terms, then we have something to learn from what they read for pleasure. Put another way, popular literature offers us a window – and it is certainly no more than this – upon the world of ordinary men and women in the past. The view is both partial and qualitative. It will yield no data that can be quantified. At best we shall get something of the 'feel' of this world which lies beyond our grasp; at worst we shall lapse into a formless antiquarianism. The risk is worth taking, for however we qualify this view of the past, it does seem an exceptionally fruitful method of penetrating the mental universe of people.

At its simplest, popular literature can be defined as what the unsophisticated reader has chosen for pleasure. Such a reader may, of course, come from any class in society, although the primary appeal of popular literature has been to the poor – and, by the end of the eighteenth century, also to children. Generally this literature has comprised non-establishment, non-official publications; but it has also included the religious tracts which one group in society thought that another group ought to read for its own good – and these were distributed in extremely large numbers. Then, too, in the nineteenth century there was an increasing

1. *A Catalogue of Chapbooks, Garlands and Penny Histories in the Possession of James Orchard Halliwell Esq.* (for private circulation, London, 1849), Preface, p. ii.

amount of cheap 'improving' literature, which comprised for the most part cheap editions of the classics, including the Penny Poets; and these became in a very real sense equally 'popular', as the concept of self-help grew.

The study of popular literature in England today is scarcely accepted as an academic activity. In France, where, we are told, they order things better (in some respects at least), this is not true, and in the last ten years or so a number of scholarly studies in this field has appeared. It may well be that the sociologists have to some extent pre-empted things in this country, and while television programmes, newspapers – the 'mass media' – are subject to varying kinds of scrutiny, such investigations so far have generally lacked an historical perspective. Such a perspective will not, of course, provide some magic ingredient by which everything will be understood, but it will, I believe, add significantly to our understanding of both past and present.

Since the existence of printed material presupposes that someone will read it, it is necessary to speculate briefly about the ways in which men and women came to terms with the printed word in such numbers as to make a mass reading public an actuality.

Central to my argument is the assumption that mass literacy is a powerful force in society, and that there was a mass reading public in this country by the end of the eighteenth century. Let us look at these two important issues.

The growth of the working class, with its increasing involvement in politics at a number of levels, would have been impossible in this country without the ability to read. Long after the demagogue and the orator have finished their speeches, long after the crowds have dispersed, long after the spoken word has slipped from memory, the written word remains. One of the earliest mass movements in modern British history, Methodism, relied a great deal upon the personal charisma of John Wesley and George Whitefield. Nevertheless, Wesley saw clearly the need to follow up the spoken exhortation with something more permanent, and a continuing concern of his long working life was with the provision of cheap books, and with the encouragement of the writing of books by Methodists, by means of which men might be converted.

Indeed, one of the characteristics of popular movements in England since the eighteenth century has been the amount of ephemeral printed matter they produced. The first in the field was, in fact, the Society for Promoting Christian Knowledge, which, soon after its foundation in 1698, was circulating specially written tracts amongst the sailors of Admiral Benbow's fleet, the soldiers of Marlborough's army, innkeepers in London, hackney coachmen. In making their appeal through the printed word they were following a more secular tradition of balladry and popular fare which had fairly deep roots in society. The Methodists followed their example; so, too, did the various radical societies of the late eighteenth century, and in the years which followed there could have been no social movement which did not propagate its ideas through pamphlets or newspapers. The assumption that people could be reached and influenced by means of the printed word seems to have been widely held; and some confirmation of this comes from two books which look at the problem from very different standpoints. W. H. Reid, whose *The Rise and Dissolution of Infidel Societies* was published in 1800, took a sour view and held that mass literacy was unsettling and, in part at least, responsible for the spread of what he called infidelity. In his *James Watson, a Memoir* (undated, c. 1879), W. J. Linton demonstrates how Watson provided a wide range of cheap publications on Chartism, freethinking, Owenism and so on, and saw the ability to read as the means by which working men could shape increasingly the world they lived in.

Here are two views of literacy;[2] and the point I wish to stress is that the ability to read, and its effects upon society, provided the subject for discussion.

Closely connected with the notion of literacy is the method by which it is achieved. Generally the growth of literacy has been a a

2. Both books have been reprinted. See *Literacy and Society* (ed. Victor E. Neuburg, Woburn Press, 1971).

gradual process; and this was certainly the case in England, where the development of elementary educational facilities during the eighteenth century, together with the ready availability of chap-books, meant that by the time the nineteenth century began a mass reading public was in existence.

These two factors – literacy as a positive force in society and the progressive growth of the reading public during the eighteenth century – seem crucial to an historical approach to popular literature.

It is perhaps necessary to justify the date 1897 as a terminal point for this study. Like most dates used in this way, this one is largely a matter of convenience and as such open to question. The fact is – and clearly hindsight plays an enormous part here – that in this year, as the result of a prize competition run in its pages, the circulation of *Pearson's Weekly* reached one and a quarter million. Such a readership, approached also by similar journals like *Answers* and *Tit-bits*, meant that by the closing years of the nineteenth century the age of mass-produced literature was under way. The year 1897, then, symbolizes both a beginning and an end.

The period ending was one which had very largely been dominated by the cultural patterns of a rural society, one in which most people earned their daily bread in one way or another from some connection with the land. In saying this I am not, of course, denying that by 1897 the Industrial Revolution had already changed irrevocably, and often brutally, not merely the face of England but also the way of life of most of its working men and women. What I am arguing is that cultural change lags behind economic change, and that many of the industrial working men in Victorian times were quite often only one generation away from their rural past. Thus their capacity either to absorb or to create a new culture was limited both by the sense of psychic shock following upon fundamental changes in a way of life and by the unspoken wish to hold on to older values and ideas as something secure in a rapidly changing world where human relationships were increasingly dominated by the impersonal nature of the factory system. The extent to which cultural changes took place was infinitely variable, depending partly upon influences beyond the control of men and women who earned a living in the workshops of a new age.

Pearson's Weekly in 1897, then, highlights the fact that a change had been taking place in the kind of popular literature being produced, and throws into sharp relief the relationship between such literature and its public. If we trace the development of ballads, jestbooks, chapbooks, tracts, from the beginning of printing to that date, it must surely help us to see the way in which this mass reading public came into being, and how its taste gradually changed.

The problem, of course, is extremely complex. What, for instance, do we mean by literacy? Can we define it in terms merely of being able to read? Or is the ability to write a vital element in it? At its basic level, and seen from the standpoint of history, it seems to me that the ability to read is the fundamental point, and it seems certain that more people have, in general, been able to read than to write. I also conclude that an increase in the sheer volume of popular literature argues for an increase in the size of the reading public at the lower end of the social scale – and, again, it seems certain that such an increase did take place, notably during the eighteenth century, and with increasing impetus during the nineteenth.

All such evidence is to some extent nebulous and cannot be quantified; but this fact does not necessarily invalidate it. On the contrary, undue reliance upon computerized data can so easily be inhibiting to the understanding and the writing of social history. Is it, for example, possible to measure intellectual or moral climates? How are we to assess the strength or significance of attitudes and patterns of feeling? Of course the historian must know how to count, but there are some things he can never know. Despite this, the asking of questions is both a legitimate and an important activity, and I am aware that in writing an introductory survey of the development of popular literature I am, by implication at least, asking questions rather than providing a set of ı.eatly tabulated answers. If anyone disagrees with the kind of question that I pose, takes issue with such tentative conclusions as I draw, or finds anywhere a provocation that is rarely intentional, then I believe that the subject will be better served by discussion than by dogma. Even polemic is preferable, I think, to an arid dullness which can so easily clothe the give and take of argument in a cloak of respectability which grows inevitably threadbare and shabby while retaining an entirely spurious gentility.

ONE

FROM THE BEGINNING
OF PRINTING TO 1600

Lithe and lysten, gentylmen
    That be of frebone blode;
I shall tell you of a good yeman,
    His name was Robyn Hode.

Robyn was a proud outlawe,
    Whyles he walked on grounde,
So curteyse an outlawe as he was one
    Was never none y founde.

Robyn stood in Bernysdale,
    And lened him to a tree,
And by hym stode Lyttel Johan,
    A good yeman was he;

And also dyde good Scathelock,
    And Much the millers sone;
There was no ynche of his body,
    But it was worth a grome.

A Lytell Geste of Robyn Hode,
ed. J. Ritson (London, undated)

In a marchauntys house in London there was a mayd which was gotten with chylde to whom the mastres of the house came and chargyd her to tell her who was the father of the chylde. To whome the mayden answeryd forsooth nobody/why quoth the mastres yt ys not possyble but some mane must be the father thereof. To whom the mayd sayd/why mastres why may not I have a chylde without a man aswell as a hen to lay eggs without a cok. Here ye may se it is harde to fynde a woman without an excuse.

A Hundred Mery Tales, ed. H. Oesterley
(London, 1866)

THE earliest forms of printed popular literature were the broadside, the jestbook, narratives – usually but not always based upon themes from medieval romance – and, finally, almanacs.

The fact that early material can be so readily classified in this way should not mislead us as to the complexities of the subject. These spring mainly from the curious accidents of survival. The late Cyprian Blagden talked about the destruction of 'a very high proportion of the books which are produced in the greatest quantities'.[1] This means that to a great extent we must rely for our knowledge of popular literature upon hearsay, an entry in the Stationers' Registers, or at best upon a single imperfect copy of a book or a broadside which was once widely circulated.

A wide variety of subject matter is covered by the term 'broadside'. Besides the ballads and songs with which it is chiefly associated, broadside publishing also comprised proclamations, religious documents, handbills, advertisements. What these had in common was the fact that they were printed upon one side only of a flimsy sheet of paper. A superb collection of these publications, ranging over more than three centuries, is owned by the Society of Antiquaries, who published a catalogue of their holdings in 1866.[2] The earliest item is an 'Indulgence granted by Our Holy Father Pope Leo that nowe is to all such as shall contribute money towards the ransom of Sir John Pyllet, Knyght of the Holy Sepulchre of Christ, who, coming from Jerusalem, was taken prisoner by the Mauris and Infidels . . .' Undated, this broadside was probably issued in 1513, the year in which Pope Leo X, 'Our Holy Father . . . that nowe is', was elected.

In the same collection the earliest ballad is on Thomas Cromwell, who had fallen from grace in 1540. As the promoter of radical reform in the Church Cromwell had made many enemies who were not slow to rejoice when he lost the favour of Henry

1. 'The Distribution of Almanacks in the Second Half of the Seventeenth Century', in *Papers of the Bibliographical Society of the University of Virginia*, Vol. Eleven (1958), p. 107.
2. See Bibliography.

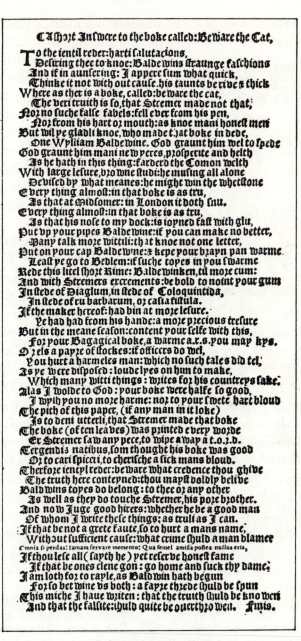

1. A sixteenth-century ballad

VIII. One of them was the anonymous author of this ballad, which begins:[3]

> Both man and chylde is glad to hear tell
> Of that false traytoure Thomas Crumwell,
> Now that he is set to learne to spell.
> > Synge trolle on away.

> When fortune lokyd the in thy face,
> Thou haddyst fayre time, but thou lackydyst grace;
> Thy cofers with golde thou fyllydst a pace.
> > Synge, *etc.*

> Both plate and chalys came to thy fyst,
> Thou lockydst them up where no man wyst,
> Tyll in the Kynges treasoure suche thinges were myst.
> > Synge, *etc.*

> Both crust and crumme came thorowe thy handes,
> Thy marchaundyse sayled over the sandes,
> Therefore now thou art layde fast in bandes.
> > Synge, *etc.*

> Fyrste when Kynge Henry, God save his grace!
> Perceyvd myschefe kyndlyd in thy face,
> Then it was tyme to purchase the a place.
> > Synge, *etc.*

The ballad goes on to accuse Cromwell of interfering with the Church, and to hope that while he may suffer physical torment, his soul will be saved:

> Yet save that soule, that God hath bought,
> And for thy carcas care thou nought,
> Let it suffre pain, as it hath wrought.
> > Synge, *etc.*

The final verse is a tribute to King Henry VIII.

This ballad is typical of the comment upon men and affairs

3. I quote from the version printed in Thomas Percy, *Reliques of Ancient English Poetry*, ed. Henry Wheatley (3 vols., 1866), Vol. 2, pp. 17ff.

which was beginning to find its way into print at the close of
Henry VIII's reign. It was followed in the year of its publication
by eight surviving broadsides, several of which showed Protestant
sympathies. The series, preserved in the collection of the Society
of Antiquaries, illustrates the political and religious conflicts of
the time.

There were lighter themes. An undated broadside from the
reign of Edward VI was entitled 'A New Mery Balad of a Maid
that Wold Mary wyth a Servyng Man', and ended with an
exhortation:

> And for my sake all you that tipple pot or canne
> Drynke freely to the merie good serving man.

Then there was Thomas Churchyard's satire upon a contemporary, 'Davy Dycar's Dream', published in 1552, which gave
rise to a lively controversy with an opponent who called himself
'T. Camel'. Thirteen separate publications of this are extant in
the same collection.

It was, however, not until 1557, when the Company of
Stationers of London received a charter giving it a virtual
monopoly of printing, that titles printed by members of the
company were entered in a register[4] quoting the printer's name,
the title of the publication and the appropriate fee. Until 1558 the
minimum was 4d., and a book was usually 6d. The register was
kept, of course, because of the need to have an accurate cash
account, but its value to posterity has been immense, for it provides in brief a view of the intellectual life of Englishmen in the
sixteenth and seventeenth centuries.[5]

The late Professor Hyder E. Rollins compiled an index to the

4. In fact some records in the first volume date from 1554. These were
probably transcribed from earlier records and comprise much miscellaneous
information.

5. See E. Arber (ed.), *A Transcript of the Registers of the Company of
Stationers of London: 1554-1640* (5 vols., London and Birmingham, 1875-
94); and G. E. B. Eyre (ed.), *A Transcript of the Registers of the Worshipful
Company of Stationers: from 1640-1708 A.D.* (3 vols., 1913-14).

ballad entries from 1557 to 1709.[6] It contains more than 3,000 titles; for the first twenty or thirty years ballads made up the bulk of the entries – indeed, until 1640 they probably took up more space than books or plays.[7] Naturally, not all of these ephemeral sheets have survived. They were read to pieces, or thrown aside when pleasure in them waned, and many of them are known today only by their titles; but it is clear that the broadside ballad formed the most considerable element in the printed popular literature of the late sixteenth and early seventeenth centuries.

Some two hundred sixteenth-century ballads are extant today, all except two or three of them in single copies. About one third of this number are in the library of the Society of Antiquaries, to which reference has already been made; the others have a curious history. Early in the nineteenth century they were first heard of as a loose bundle of ballads, wrapped in a sheepskin, in the hands of a housekeeper at Holmingham Hall in Suffolk. They were given or sold to a Mr Fitch, postmaster at Ipswich, and passed either directly or through a dealer into the collection of George Daniel, who lived in Canonbury Square, Islington. Eventually he sold about half of them to a bookseller and they were bought by Richard Heber, whose vast collection of books filled eight houses, but was broken up and disposed of in a series of sales held in 1834 and 1835. The ballads were purchased by W. H. 'Measure' Miller, so called because of his passion for the size of his books, and he formed the Britwell Court Library, which has been in process of disposal since 1919. A reprint of the ballads was presented by their then owner, Mr Sydney Christie Miller, to members of the Roxburghe Club in 1912.

George Daniel retained the other half of the ballads until his death in 1864, when they were bought by Henry Huth, whose son bequeathed them to the British Museum in 1910. They had been

6. See Bibliography, p. 276.

7. Unfortunately the Stationers' Company records are defective. There is a hiatus between 1570 and 1576, and the practice of registering ballad titles fell into disuse during the greater part of the reign of James I.

reprinted by Huth in 1867 for members of the Philobiblon Club, and were commercially reprinted by Joseph Lilly in 1867 and 1870.[8]

This digression into the bypaths of nineteenth-century book-collecting has been made to stress the role played by bibliophiles in preserving the most ephemeral and flimsy of sheets and books, many of which would otherwise have disappeared.

The name 'ballad' given to these broadsides is a reminder that, whatever the subject matter, most of them were intended to be sung. Usually the words were set to an air which would have been familiar to both seller and purchaser, and it does not take too great an effort of the imagination to see the broadside being sold by street vendors or pedlars. The titles hardly lent themselves to verbal repetition in order to attract buyers: 'A discription of a monstrous Chylde borne at Chychester in Sussex, 1562', 'A merye balade, how a wife entreated her husband to have her own Wyll', 'The Marchants Daughter of Bristow' - all these are typical titles which add credence to the notion that melody was a major factor in selling broadsides. 'A Spell for Jone' or 'A Paradox' are certainly briefer titles, but essentially the contents of these sheets were sung by the seller, and presumably by the customer too.

The ballads which follow, quoted from Lilly's edition, are typical. At this period it would be difficult to make a clear division between popular literature and some overspill from serious literature, for each borrowed from the other - an obvious example, perhaps, would be the work of Shakespeare. With this in mind, it will be seen that the first two ballads quoted were by writers who were able to make literary allusions derived from a classical tradition.

8. See Bibliography, p. 269. There is also an American facsimile reprint of Lilly's edition.

A NEWE BALLADE OF A LOVER EXTOLLINGE HIS LADYE

To the tune of Damon and Pithias

Alas, my harte doth boyle,
    And burne within my breste,
To showe to thee, myne onely deere,
    My sute and my request.
My love no toung can tell,
    Ne pen can well descrye;
Extend thy love for love againe,
    Or els for love I dye.

My love is set so suer,
    And fixed on thee so,
That by no meanes I can abstaine,
    My faythfull love to showe;
My wounded harte, theirfore,
    To thee for helpe doth crye;
Extend thy love for love againe,
    Or els for love I dye.

Although the gods were bent,
    With greedie mynde to slaye
My corpes with cruell panges of death,
    And lyfe to take awaye.
Yet should my faythfull harte
    At no tyme from thee flye;
Show love therfore for love againe,
    Or els for love I dye.

Although the sun were bent
    To burne me with his beames;
And that mine eyes, throw greous pangs,
    Should send forth bloudy streames;
Yet would I not forsake,
    But styll to thee woulde crye,
To showe me love for love again,
    Or els for love I dye.

Ye though ech sterre were tournd
    Untyll a fiery darte,

And were all ready bent with payne,
  To perce throwe-out my harte;
Yet coulde I not forsake
  To love thee faythfullye;
Extend thy love for love againe,
  Or els for love I dye.

Ye though eche foule were formde,
  A serpent fell to be,
My corps to flay with bloudy wounds,
  And to devower me;
Yet would I be thine owne,
  To love full hartelye;
Extend thy love for love againe,
  Or else for love I dye.

Ye though the lyon were,
  With gapinge gredye jawe,
Readye with rygorus raggye teeth,
  My fleshe to teare and gnawe;
Yet woulde I be thine owne,
  To serve most earnestlye;
Extend thy love for love againe,
  Or els for love I dye.

Ye though the fishes all,
  That swymes in surginge sease,
Should swallowe me with gredy mouth,
  Yet could thee not apease.
My earnest harte to thee,
  To love entyerlye;
Extend thy love for love againe,
  Or els for love I dye.

Ye though the earth would gape,
  And swallowe me there-in,
And that I should tormentyd be
  In hell, with every syn;
Yet would I be thy owne,
  To save or els to spyll;

Show me therfore lyke love againe,
Or els thou dost me kyll.

Finis, q M. Osb.

Imprinted at London, in Fletstrete, at the
signe of the Faucon, by Wylliam
Gryffith, 1568.

In the original sheet the first eight lines are set to music. First
published in 1563, this seems no better and no worse – although
quaintly archaic on the page – than the words of any twentieth-
century popular song.

The same is true of the following ballad, which was published
in 1569. The original sheet includes five woodcuts in a line at the
top. The entry in the records of the Stationers' Company reads:
'Received of Thomas Colwell for his lycense for pryntinge of a
ballett intituled the prayse of mylady marques iiiid'.

A PROPER NEW BALAD IN PRAISE OF MY LADIE MARQUES,

whose Death is bewailed to the Tune of New lusty gallant

Ladies, I thinke you marvell that
  I writ no mery report to you,
And what is the cause I court it not
  So merye as I was wont to dooe;
Alas! I let you understand,
  It is no newes for me to show;
The fairest flower of my garland
  Was caught from court a great while agoe.

For, under the roufe of sweete Saint Paull,
  There lyeth my Ladie buryed in claye,
Where I make memory for her soule
  With weepinge eyes once everye daye;
All other sightes I have forgot,
  That ever in court I ioyed to see,
And that is the cause I court it not,
  So mery as I was wont to be.

And though that shee be dead and gone,
 Whose courting need not to be tolde,
And natures mould of fleshe and bone,
 Whose lyke now lives not to beholde,
Me thinkes I see her walke in blacke,
 In every corner where I goe,
To looke if anie bodie do lacke
 A frend to helpe them of theyr woe.

Mee thinkes I see her sorowfull teares,
 To princelye state approching nye;
Mee thinkes I see her tremblinge feares,
 Leste anie her suites shulde hit awrie;
Mee thinkes she shuld be still in place,
 A pitifull speaker to a Queene,
Bewailinge every poore mans case,
 As many a time shee hath ben seene.

Mee thinkes I see her modeste mood,
 Her comlie clothing plainlie clad,
Her face so sweete, her cheere so good,
 The courtlie countenance that shee had;
But, chefe of all, mee thinkes I see
 Her vertues deutie daie by daie,
Homblie kneeling one her knee,
 As her desire was still to praie.

Mee thinkes I cold from morow to night
 Do no thing ells with verie good will,
But spend the time to speake and writte
 The praise of my good ladies still;
Though reason saith, now she is dead,
 Go seeke and sarve as good as shee;
It will not sinke so in my head,
 That ever the like in courte will bee.

But sure I am, ther liveth yet
 In court a dearer frinde to mee,
Whome I to sarve am so unfit,
 I am sure the like will never bee;

For I with all that I can dooe,
    Unworthie most maie seeme to bee,
To undoo the lachet of her shooe,
    Yet will I come to courte and see.

Then have amongste ye once againe,
    Faint harts faire ladies never win;
I trust ye will consider my payne,
    When any good venison cometh in;
And, gentill ladies, I you praie,
    If my absentinge breede to blame,
In my behalfe that ye will saie,
    In court is remedie for the same.

Finis, q^d W. ELDERTON.

Imprinted at London in Fletestreat
beneath the Conduit, at the signe
of S. John Evangelist, by
Thomas Colwell.

The next ballad is far from romantic. Undated, it belongs
approximately to the same period as the others, and besides
having Chaucerian overtones it represents an attitude to marriage
and human relationships which was common in the popular
literature of the time, faithless wives and cuckolded husbands
always being good for a laugh.

A MERRY NEW SONG HOW A BRUER MEANT TO
MAKE A COOPER CUCKOLD, AND HOW DEERE THE
BRUER PAID FOR THE BARGAINE

To the tune of, In Somer time

If that you list, now merry be,
Lend listning eares a while to me,
To heare a song of a Bruer bold,
That meant a Cooper to cuckold.

The Cooper walked downe the streete,
And with the Bruer chanc'd to meete:

He called, – Worke for a Cooper, dame;
The Bruer was glad to heare the same.

Cooper, quoth the Bruer, come hether to me,
Perchance I have some worke for thee:
If that thy doings I doe well like,
Thou shalt have worke for all this weeke.

The Cooper with cap and curtesie low,
Said, ready I am my tunning to show;
To doe your worke, sir, every deale.
I doe not doubt it doe it well.

Then, quoth this lustie Bruer tho,
If thou my worke doest meane to doe,
Come to me to morrow before it be day,
To hoope up these olde tubs out of the way.

And so to make up my merry rime,
The Cooper the next day rose betime;
To the Bruers gate he tooke his race,
And knocked there a great pace.

The Bruer leapt from his bed to the flore,
And to the Cooper he opned the dore;
He shewed him his worke without delay;
To the Coopers wife then he tooke the way.

The Cooper he called at mind at last,
His hatchet he had left at home for hast:
And home for his hatchet he must goe,
Before he could worke; the cause it was so.

But when he came his house somwhat nere,
His wife by fortune did him heare:
Alas! said she, what shift shall we make?
My husband is come, – you will be take!

O Lord! sayd the Bruer, what shall I doe?
How shall I hide me? where shall I goe?
Said shee, – if you will not be espide,
Creepe under this fat yourselfe to hide.

The Bruer he crept under the same,
And blundering in the Cooper came:
About the shop his tubs he cast,
To finde out his hatchet all in hast.

Then his curst wife began to prate, –
If thou let out my pig, ile breake thy pate!
A pig, said the Cooper, I knew of none;
If thou hadst not spoke, the pig had bin gone.

If it be a sow-pig, said the Cooper,
Let me have him rosted for my supper:
It is a bore-pig, man, said she,
For my owne dyet, and not for thee.

It is hard if a woman cannot have a bit,
But straightway her husband must know of it.
A bore-pig, said the Cooper, so me thinks;
He is so ramish, – fie, how he stinkes!

Well, sayd the Cooper, so I might thrive,
I would he were in thy belly alive.
I thanke you for your wish, good man;
It may chance it shall be there anon.

The Bruer that under the fat did lye,
Like a pig did assay to grunt and crie:
But, alas! his voice was nothing small;
He cryed so big that he mard all.

Wife, said the Cooper, this is no pig,
But an old hog, he grunteth so big!
He lift up the fat then by and by;
There lay the Bruer like a bore in a stie.

Wife, said the Cooper, thou wilt lie like a dog!
This is no pig, but a very old hog:
I sweare, quoth the Cooper, I doe not like him;
Ile knock him on the head ere ile keepe him.

O Lord! said the Bruer, serve me not so;
Hold thy hand, Cooper, and let me goe,

And I will give thee both ale and beere,
To find thy house this sixe or seaven yeare.

I will none of thy ale nor yet of thy beere,
For feare I be poisoned within seaven yeere!
Why, sayd the Bruer, if thou mistrust,
Hold here the keyes of my best chest;

And there is gold and silver store,
Will serve thee so long and somewhat more:
If there be store, quoth the Cooper, I say,
I will not come emptie-handed away.

The Cooper went and filled his hat;
The Bruer shall pay for using my fat!
The hooping of twentie tubs every day,
And not gaind me so much as I doe this way.

When he came againe his house within, –
Packe away, quod he, Bruer, with your broken shin;
And under my fat creepe you no more,
Except you make wiser bargaines before.

Finally, a ballad which was entered in the Stationers' Registers
for 1586 and which commemorated an actual happening. In their
treatment of sensational news, Tudor broadsides to some extent
anticipated the tabloid newspaper of the twentieth century, and
certainly exploited events in the same kind of way. It is also of
interest because, unlike most broadsides, which were published
in London, this one bore a Norwich imprint.

A PROPER NEWE SONET DECLARING THE LAMENTATION
OF BECKLES [A MARKET TOWNE IN] SUFFOLKE, WHICH
WAS IN THE GREAT WINDE UPON S. ANDREWES EVE LAST
PAST MOST PITTIFULLY BURNED WITH FIRE, TO THE
LOSSE BY ESTIMATION OF TWENTIE THOUSANDE POUND
AND UPWARDE, AND TO THE NUMBER OF FOURE SCORE
DWELLING HOUSES, 1586

To Wilson's Tune

With sobbing sighes, and trickling teares,
  My state I doe lament,
Perceiving how God's heavie wrath
  Against my sinnes is bent;
Let all men viewe my woefull fall,
  And rue my woefull case,
And learne hereby in speedy sort
  Repentaunce to embrace.

For late in Suffoclke was I seen
  To be a stately towne,
Replenished with riches store,
  And had in great renowne;
Yea, planted on a pleasant soyle,
  So faire as heart could wish,
And had my markets, once a weeke,
  Well storde with flesh and fish.

A faire fresh river running by,
  To profite me withall,
Who with a cristall cleered streame
  About my bankes did fall;
My fayres in somer welthely
  For to increase my store;
My medowes greene and commons great, –
  What could I wish for more?

But now beholde my great decay,
  Which on a sodaine came;
My sumptuous buildings burned be
  By force of fires flame:
A carelesse wretch, most rude in life,
  His chymney set on fire,
The instrument, I must confesse,
  Of God's most heavie ire.

The flame whereof increasing stil
  The blustering windes did blowe,

And into divers buildings by
  Disperst it to and fro;
So, kindling in most grievous sort,
  It waxed huge and hie;
The river then was frozen, so
  No water they could come by.

Great was the crye that then was made
  Among both great and small;
The wemen wept, and wrong their handes,
  Whose goods consumed all;
No helpe was found to slacke the fyre,
  Theyr paines was spent in vaine;
To beare theyr goods into the fieldes
  For safegarde they were fayne.

And yet, amid this great distresse,
  A number set theyr minde
To filtch, and steale, and beare away
  So much as they could finde;
Theyr neighbors wealth, which wasted lay
  About the streetes that time,
They secretly convayde away, –
  O most accursed crime!

Thus, from the morning nyne a clocke
  Till four aclocke at night,
Fourescore houses in Beckle's towne
  Was burnd to ashes quite;
And that which most laments my heart,
  The house of God, I say,
The church and temple by this fyre
  Is cleane consumde away.

The market-place and houses fayre,
  That stood about the same,
Hath felt the force and violence
  Of this most fearefull flame;
So that there is no Christian man
  But in his heart would grieve,

35

To see the smart I did sustaine
  Upon saint Andrewes eve.

Wherefore, good Christian people, now
  Take warning by my fall, –
Live not in strife and envious hate
  To breed each other thrall;
Seeke not your neighbors lasting spoyle
  By greedy sute in lawe;
Live not in discord and debate,
  Which doth destruction draw.

And flatter not yourselves in sinne,
  Holde not Gods worde in scorne,
Repine not at his ministers,
  Nor be not false forsworne;
For, where such vices doth remaine,
  Gods grace will never be;
And, in your health and happie state,
  Have yet some minde on me, –

Whose songes is changd to sorrowes sore,
  My ioyes to wayling woe,
My mirth to mourning sighes and grones,
  The which from griefe doth growe;
My wealth to want and scarsetie,
  My pleasure into payne,
All for the sinne and wickednesse
  Which did in me remaine.

If then you wish prosperitie,
  Be loving, meeke and kinde, –
Lay rage and rancour cleane aside,
  Set malice from your minde;
And live in love and charitie,
  All hatefull pride detest,
And so you shall with happie dayes
  For evermore be blest.

And thus I ende my wofull song,
  Beseeching God I may

Remaine a mirrour to all such
That doe in pleasure stay;
And that amongest their greatest mirth
And chiefest ioye of all,
They yet may have a heart to thinke
Of Beckles sodaine fall.

Finis, T. D.

At London:
Imprinted by Robert Robinson, for Nicholas
Colma[n], of Norwich, dwelling in S.
Andrewes church yard.

Four typical ballads. What of the authors? For the most part they were hacks of whom little or nothing is known, but there are two who are more than mere names and who were clearly in touch with a wide range of people: William Elderton, author of the second ballad quoted above, and Thomas Deloney, who wrote the fourth. If we take them as representative of their kind, it is not that they wrote more, or better, than others, but only that we know something about them.

Elderton was writing from 1559 to 1584. More than twenty of his ballads have survived, the earlier ones somewhat stiff and full of classical allusions, his later productions very much more vigorous. Scurrilous, on occasion indecent, with a reputation for drunkenness, Elderton of the 'ale-crammed nose' was the leading ballad-writer of his time. He died in 1592.[9]

Although he was not so definite a character as Elderton, more is known about Deloney, whose earliest known ballad was printed in 1586. Some six years later he was sufficiently well known to be described by Robert Greene as 'T. D. whose braines beaten to the yarking up of Ballads, might more lawfully have glaunst at the

9. There is a useful account of Elderton in C. H. Firth, 'Ballads and Broadsides', in *Shakespeare's England* (Clarendon Press, Oxford, 1916), Vol. II, p. 512.

quaint conceits of conny-catching and crosse-biting'.[10] Gabriel Harvey ,who wrote so often with what Virginia Woolf has called 'the pride of a self-made man', advised Thomas Nash '. . . to boast less with Thomas Deloney, or to atchieve more with Thomas More'.[11]

Clearly Deloney had something of a reputation amongst his contemporaries, and in 1596 he came into collision with the law. The occasion was the publication of 'a certain Balled, containing a Complaint of great Want and Scarcity of Corn within the Realm'. The Queen was brought into the composition and shown 'speaking with her People Dialogue wise in very fond and undecent sort'. It was felt by authority that the ballad might cause discontent among the poor.

'Abusive Ballads and Libels were too common in the City in Queen Elizabeth's Time, therein reflecting too boldly and seditiously upon the Government, particularly in case of Dearth', wrote Strype in his edition of Stow's *Survey of London*.[12] He went on to discuss particulars: 'The maker of this scurrilous Ballad was one Delonie, an idle Fellow, and one noted with the like Spirit, in printing a Book for the Silk Weavers: Wherein was found some such like foolish and disorderly matter . . .'[13] Alas, neither the ballad nor the 'Book for the Silk Weavers' is known to survive. This is a matter for some regret, for Deloney came from a Huguenot silk-weaving family, and what he had to say about the trade might have been very revealing. Certainly the novels he wrote show considerable familiarity with the life of travelling craftsmen and some of the districts connected with the Elizabethan textile industry.

The fraternity of ballad men that Deloney joined was not highly thought of. A French critic has described him as half workman,

10. Quoted in F. O. Mann, *The Works of Thomas Deloney* (Oxford, 1912), p. viii. See also the Introduction generally for Deloney's life and work.

11. *Pierce's Supererogation* (1593). Quoted in Mann, op. cit., p. ix.

12. Quoted in Mann, op. cit., p. ix.

13. John Stow, *Survey of London*, ed. Strype (1720), p. 333.

half minstrel, going from this to this, reciting stories and singing his own compositions.[14] The precarious life led by such men and the fact that they were never settled in one place for long called forth outspoken criticism from more staid Elizabethans, and the preoccupation of the Government with legislating for vagabonds is well known. Henry Chettle, a contemporary, spoke for respectable opinion: 'A company of idle youths, loathing honest labour and dispising lawful trades, betake themselves to a vagrant and vicious life in every corner of Cities and market Townes of the Realme, singing and selling of ballads and pamphlets full of ribaudrie, and all scurrilous vanity . . .'[15] Likewise Philip Stubbes, whose *Anatomy of Abuses* was published in 1583. He asked rhetorically: 'Who be more bawdie than they? Who uncleaner than they? Who more licentious and loose-minded?'[16]

In the end, of course, Deloney's personality eludes us. He is rather the focusing glass through which we can discern, with varying degrees of clarity, the sub-world of crowded, compact Elizabethan London, far from the Queen's court and the corridors of power. This picture can be extended a little into provincial England, into the 'Cities and market Townes of the Realm'. We can make out something more than the criminal underworld – we catch a glimpse of petty tradesmen, workmen, apprentices, housewives and other ordinary folk going about their business. For such insights we must be grateful.

Another staple element in early popular literature, the jestbook, cannot always offer such insights. On the other hand it does throw considerable light upon the attitudes and values – even prejudices – of ordinary men and women. Collections of jokes have been popular in England from the fifteenth century, when Caxton published in his 1484 edition of Aesop eleven supplementary 'fables' by 'Poge the Florentyn'. This referred to Poggio Bracciolini (1380–1459), a scholar, said to be the inventor of the early italic

14. Michel Ragon, *Histoire de la littérature ouvrière* (Paris, 1953).
15. Quoted in Mann, op. cit., p. x.
16. Stubbes, *Anatomy of Abuses* (1583), p. 171.

handwriting known as humanist script. He travelled in Europe and served as secretary to a number of popes. In about 1420, when he was living in Florence, he wrote, amongst other works, a book of humorous tales called *Liber facetiarum*, which he introduced with a slightly self-conscious note of self-justification – despite the fact that the Church was much more disposed to tolerate ribaldry than heresy.

The ribald quality of many of these tales does not need to be stressed. Adulterous friars, cuckolded husbands, faithless wives were all stock characters treated with rough and ready humour which covered a wryly cynical view of many churchmen. This kind of satire did not possess too sharp a cutting edge; it established stock figures to poke fun at, and there was no reason why priests should be exempt from the process.

What is more interesting about Poggio is that he represented one element of a European tradition from which both the known and the unknown compilers of English jestbooks drew their material. It is not necessary here to trace the genesis of specific jokes, nor to follow their transmigrations across frontiers and in time; but we can in passing note such examples as the Faust legend from Germany, Valentine and Orson from France, Poggio Bracciolini from Italy. The near-universality of these themes seems to suggest that the culture of Europe possessed a much greater unity in the sixteenth century than it does today.

Certainly a number of European countries provided subject matter for jestbooks. In every case the form of such a book was the same: a collection of jokes and facetious tales, which might be random or might be grouped round a character who could be fictional or real – Howleglas (Till Eulenspiegel) and Scoggin were fictional; John Skelton and George Peele, on the other hand, were not. The jests themselves, in either case, showed little change in subject or presentation. There were jokes, quips, witty replies, sometimes with a moral tag-line, boiled down to the dimensions of an anecdote. Stories of this kind had been in circulation since the Middle Ages – even earlier – and jestbooks remained extremely popular throughout the sixteenth and seventeenth centuries.

Amongst the earliest were the following: *A C. Mery Tales*, an *ad hoc* collection of one hundred jests, printed in 1526 by John Rastell, Sir Thomas More's brother-in-law; *Howleglas* (?1528), the London version of a book which had first appeared about nine years before, printed in English at Antwerp (it was probably based upon a Netherlands original); *Tales and Quick Answers* (?1535); *Merrie Tales Newly Imprinted and Made by Master Skelton* (1567); *The Mirrour of Mirth* (1583); *Merrie Conceited Jests of George Peele* (earliest known edition 1607); *Scoggins Jests* (1626 – but it was probably first published in 1565 or 1566 by Thomas Colwell, who paid fourpence to the Stationers' Company for a licence to print it). According to Holinshed, Scoggin was a learned gentleman and an Oxford graduate; but there is some confusion here, as there was a Henry Scogan, a poet, who lived in the reign of Henry IV, and with the somewhat erratic spelling of the times the problem of identity is difficult to unravel. These titles, and many more, were printed and reprinted. Such was their popularity, however, that only a handful of copies have survived. The survivals we have are, for the most part, available in reprinted editions – for example, W. C. Hazlitt's three volumes containing the texts of fifteen jestbooks is readily available,[17] and more recently P. M. Zall and John Wardroper have both made forays into this field.[18]

These two anecdotes from *A C. Mery Tales* are typical of the contents:

It fortuned divers to be in communication, among whom there was a curate, or a parish priest, and one John Daw, a parishioner of his – which two had communication more busy than others, in this manner. This priest thought that one might not by feeling know one from another in the dark. John Daw, his parishioner, of contrary opinion, laid with his curate for a wager 40 pence.

17. See Bibliography, p. 269.
18. See Bibliography, p. 269.

Whereupon, the parish priest, willing to prove his wager, went to this John Daw's house in the evening and suddenly got him to bed with his wife – where, when he began to be somewhat busy, she feeling his crown said shortly with a loud voice: 'By God, thou art not John Daw!'

That hearing, her husband answered: 'Thou sayest truth, wife – I am here, John Daw. Therefore, Master Parson, give me the money for ye have lost your 40 pence.'

By this tale ye may learn to perceive that it is no wisdom for a man, for the covetous of winning of any wager, to put in jeopardy a thing that may turn him to greater displeasure.

A wife there was which had appointed her 'prentice to come to her bed in the night – which servant had long wooed her to have his pleasure – which according to the appointment came to her bedside in the night, her husband lying by her. And when she perceived him there, she caught him by the hand and held him fast, and incontinent wakened her husband and said: 'Sir, it is so ye have a false and an untrue servant to you which is William your 'prentice, and hath long wooed me to have his pleasure, and because I could not avoid his importunate request, I have appointed him this night to meet me in the garden in the arbor. And if ye will array yourself in mine array and go thither, ye shall see the proof thereof, and then ye may rebuke him as ye think best by your discretion.'

This husband thus advertised by his wife put upon him his wife's raiment and went to the arbor. And when he was gone thither, the 'prentice came into bed to his mistress where for a season they were both content and pleased each other by the space of an hour or two. But when she thought time convenient, she said to the 'prentice: 'Now go thy way into the arbor and meet him, and take a good waster in thy hand, and say thou didst it but to prove whether I would be a good woman or no, and reward him as thou thinkest best.'

This 'prentice, doing after his mistress' counsel, went to the arbor where he found his master in his mistress' apparel and said: 'A, thou harlot! Art thou come hither? Now I see well – if I would be false to my master, thou wouldst be a strong whore. But I had lever thou were hanged than I would do him so traitorous a deed. Therefore I shall give thee some punishment as thou, like an whore, hast deserved.' And therewith he lapped him well about the shoulders and back and gave him a dozen or two good stripes.

The master, feeling himself somewhat to smart, said: 'Peace, William, mine own true good servant – for God's sake, hold thy hands, for I am thy master and not thy mistress!'

'Nay, whore,' quod he, 'thou liest – thou art but an harlot, and I did but to prove thee –' and smote him again.

'Alas, man,' quod the master, 'I beseech thee – no more – for I am not she – for I am thy master – feel, for I have a beard!' And therewith he spared his hand and felt his beard.

'Alas, master,' quod the 'prentice, 'I cry you mercy.' And then the master went unto his wife and she asked him how he had sped and he answered: 'I wis, wife, I have been shrewdly beaten. Howbeit, I have cause to be glad, for I thank God I have as true a wife and as true a servant as any man hath in England.'

By this tale ye may see that it is not wisdom for a man to be ruled always after his wife's counsel.

Most jestbooks were anonymous, and in only one or two cases is anything known of the authors. Andrew Borde (c. 1500–1549), a Sussex itinerant doctor, is reputed to have been the original 'Merry Andrew', and is said to have collected Scoggin's jests together. Thomas Hearne, the eighteenth-century antiquary, said of Borde that he 'frequented markets and fairs where a conflux of people used to get together to whom he prescribed, and to induce them to flock more readily, he would make humorous speeches'.[19]

Richard Johnson (1573–?1659) was another popular author. He speaks of himself as an apprentice, and later as a Freeman of the City of London, but few details of his life are known. He was the author of the *Famous Historie of the Seaven Champions of Christendom*, entered at Stationers' Hall in 1596, a romance which was being reprinted in a very truncated form as a chapbook well into the eighteenth century. In 1607 his jestbook, *The Pleasant Conceites of Old Hobson the Merry Londoner*, appeared. Hobson, a haberdasher, had died in 1581, and these tales have some interest

19. Quoted in S. A. Allibone, *A Critical Dictionary of English Literature* (Philadelphia, 1882), I, p. 220.

as pictures of the time, although since a number of them had been adapted from *Merry Tales and Quick Answers*, they can hardly be taken as authentic biography.

The following two anecdotes are characteristic of the contents of the book, besides providing further examples of jestbooks in general:

HOW MAISTER HOBSON FOUND OUT THE PYE STEALER

In Christmas holy-dayes, when Ma. Hobsons wife had many pyes in the oven, one of his servants had stole one of them out, and at the taverne had merrilie eaten it. It fortund that same day some of his friends dined with him, and one of the best pyes were missing, the stealer whereof at after dinner he found out in this maner. He caled all his servants in friendly sort together into the hall, and caused each of them to drinke one to another both wine, ale and beare, till they were al drunke; then caused hee a table to be furnished with very good cheare, whereat hee likewise pleased them. Being set all together, he said: why sit you not downe, fellowes? We be set all redy, quoth they. Nay, quoth Maister Hobson, he that stole the pye is not set yet. Yes, that I doe (quoth he that stole it); by which meanes he knew what was become of the pye: for the poore fellow being drunke could not keepe his owne secretts.

HOW MAISTER HOBSON MADE A LIGHT BANQUET FOR HIS COMPANY

Upon a time, Maister Hobson invited very solemnly the whol livery of his company to a light banquet, and for the same provided the greatest taverne in all London in a redines. The appoynted houre being come, the cittizens repaired thether richly atired, the better to grace Maister Hobsons banquet; but expecting great cheare and good intertainement, they were all utterly disapoynted: for what found they there, thinke you? Nothing, on my word, but each one a cup of wine and a manchet of bread on his trencher, and some five hundred candles lighted about the roome, which in my mind was a very light banquet, both for the belly and for the eye. By this merry jest, hee gained such love of his companie, that hee borrowed gratis out of the hall a hundred and fiftie pound for two yeares.

The tendency to gather groups of anecdotes round a central character, real or imaginary, and to relate them to a background familiar to the reader, is apparent. In looking at this from the standpoint of the twentieth century, we can surely understand the appeal of the familiar character when we recall, for example, Billy Bunter of the Greyfriars stories, popular in a continuing series for some half a century. This tale from Howleglas (?1528) might equally have been told of Skelton, Tarlton, Peele or Scoggin:

HOW HOWLEGLAS SET HIS HOSTESS UPON THE HOT ASHES WITH HER BARE ARSE

As Howleglas was come from Rome, he came to an inn where his host was not at home. And when he was within, he asked his hostess if that she knew not Howleglas, and the hostess said: 'Nay, but I hear say that he is a false deceiver and beguiler.' Then said Howleglas: 'Wherefore say ye so? Ye know him not.' Then said the hostess: 'That is truth. But I have heard speak much of his unhappiness.'

Then said Howleglas: 'Good woman, he hath done to you never no harm. Wherefore slander ye him for the words of other people?' The hostess said: 'I say no other of him than the people do. For I have heard him be spoken of, of many of my guests that have lodged here.' Then held Howleglas his peace, and spake no more till in the morning.

And then spied he abroad the hot ashes on the hearth, and then took he the hostess out of her sleep and set her thereon on her bare arse. And so was his hostess well burned. Then said he to her: 'Now may ye say boldly that ye have seen the false deceiver and beguiler Howleglas.'

Then cried the hostess for help and lowered upon him. Then went he out of her doors and said to her: 'Should not men correct and reprove slanderers and backbiters that say it of men and never saw them – nor never had done harm to them? Yes, it is a charitable thing to do.' And then took he his horse and departed from thence.

Howleglas (or Till Eulenspiegel as he was known in Europe) is an interesting character, whose literary origins are to be found in Marcolfus, the mythical jester at King Solomon's court. In the

rye Jeſt of a man that was called Howleglas, and
of many maruelous thinges and Jeſtes that
he dyd in his lyfe, in Eaſtlande and in many
other places.

2. The earliest known edition in English of a popular story book which first
appeared in Antwerp in about 1510

jestbooks bearing his name Howleglas is presented as a real person who lived in the fourteenth century and had a Latin epitaph on his grave. In the character of a Saxon peasant he delights in playing the fool by following instructions absolutely literally, or by making some witty reply. Although episodes connected with him can be readily duplicated in other jestbooks, it is of some significance that his victims are usually craftsmen, employers of labour, members of the clergy, innkeepers, and only rarely his fellow villagers. Sometimes the satire is ambiguous – he causes a number of priests to fall downstairs in one story, simply to make them appear foolish. When directed against masters the satire is more pointed, and Howleglas sides with apprentices against those who employ them. In one story a niggardly baker refuses him a candle to work by, saying that he can sift flour by moonlight; in mock obedience he then throws the flour out of the window. Howleglas, then, was a genuine folk hero who has passed into popular tradition – both Simple Simon and Norman Wisdom are equally part of it.

Such was the stuff of popular Elizabethan fiction at its lowest level with, for many, the broadside and the jestbook the commonest fare; but this was not all, as a contemporary writer pointed out. Robert Laneham was a London mercer and protégé of the Earl of Leicester, and because of this association he was present at the visit of Queen Elizabeth to Warwick Castle in 1575. He wrote a letter to his friend, Humfrey Martin, in London, describing the pageants and festivities which took place, and this letter, which was published in the same year,[20] mentions a Captain Cox, Coventry stone-mason, of whom Laneham says 'great oversight hath he in matters of storie'.

Whether or not the Captain was a figment of Laneham's imagination is not known, but there is certainly no reason to suppose that he was. The list which Laneham gives of books in Cox's

20. See Bibliography, p. 270, for F. J. Furnivall's edition of the *Letter*, which contains a long Introduction on Elizabethan popular literature and its origins.

possession consists of more than fifty items, and is an illuminating contemporary survey of what was available to the Elizabethan common reader. The titles mentioned fall into seven categories:[21]

(1) romances of chivalry which had survived from the Middle Ages, of which *Huon of Bordeaux*, *Bevys of Hampton* and *Syr Gawyn* are examples;

(2) Renaissance fiction, its vogue foreshadowed here by *Lucres and Eurialus*, an interesting tale showing Boccaccio's influence and written in Latin during the fifteenth century by a son of the Church who later became Pope Pius II (an Italian version appeared in 1554, and was followed by at least three English editions);

(3) jestbooks; as one would expect, a number of these, including *Howleglas*, *Skogan*, *A C. Mery Tales*;

(4) a small group of plays;

(5) almanacs and prognostications;

(6) ballads;

(7) finally, a forerunner of the books about rogues which were much enjoyed in Queen Elizabeth's reign, Robert Copland's *Hye Way to the Spyttel House*, which described the beggars and imposters who came to the hospital of St Bartholomew.

Clearly the notion of popular literature is interpreted widely in Captain Cox's collection, and a study of the titles in it – and indeed its lacunae – prompts both question and comment. Who could afford to buy books? Who could read them? We know, regrettably, little enough about Elizabethan bookbuyers, but we can be certain that books were not cheap. A slim quarto play costing 6d. could represent an outlay well beyond the means of a labourer, or even a skilled workman, and it is obvious that books were priced out of the reach of many who may have been able to read them. One significant fact about Captain Cox's list is the very small number of broadside ballads contained in it. Since the collector was presumably a substantial tradesman who could afford to buy

21. I am indebted to Mr Graham Gilmour for this analysis.

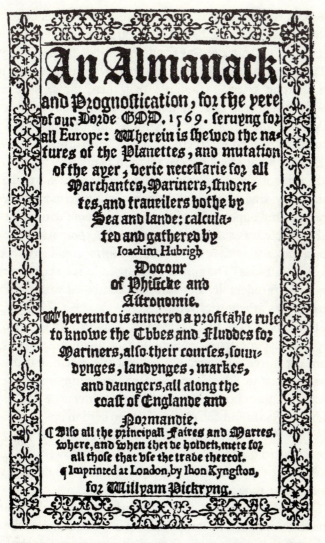

An Almanack

and Prognostication, for the yere
of our Lorde GOD. 1569. seruyng for
all Europe: Wherein is shewed the natures of the Planettes, and mutation
of the ayer, verie necessarie for all
Marchantes, Mariners, studen-
tes, and traueilers bothe by
Sea and lande: calcula-
ted and gathered by
Ioachim Hubrigh.
Doctour
of Phisicke and
Astronomie.
Whereunto is annexed a profitable rule
to knowe the Ebbes and Fluddes for
Mariners, also their courses, sound-
dynges, landynges, markes,
and daungers, all along the
coast of Englande and
Normandie.
¶ Also all the principall Faires and Martes,
where, and when they be holden, mete for
all those that vse the trade thereof.
¶ Imprinted at London, by Ihon Kyngston,
for Willyam Pickryng.

XV (B lxix).   Joachim Hubright.   Almanack and
Prognostication for 1569.   W. Pickering.
(British Museum copy.)

3.   An early almanac

books, it is possible that he regarded broadsides as beneath his notice. Only seven are listed; all are traditional, none is topical. Laneham, it is true, does say that Cox possessed 'a hundred more' ballads, but the fact that few of them are considered worthy of enumeration seems to indicate that these flimsy sheets were readily available in large numbers. It seems safe to assume from this sheet volume that the broadside ballad formed the largest element in printed Elizabethan popular literature.

Equally within the financial reach of many who would demur at the price of a book, or be totally unable to afford it, was the most elementary kind of almanac, which might give merely the conjunctions and oppositions of the sun and moon, dates of eclipses and movable feasts. Such sheets were the poor man's practical astronomy, and in their least elaborate form would have been, in effect, broadsides. The appeal of the pseudo-science of astrology was very considerable, and almanacs combined with prophecies were sold as prognostications.

It is here, where the single-sheet almanac, while in no whit displaced in popularity, develops into the prognostication – rather more expensive and certainly beyond the reach of many purchasers – that we are able to approach the shifting and ill-defined frontier that lies between printed popular literature and the oral tradition. Songs and ballads, it is not too hard to imagine, quickly took on a life of their own and circulated by word of mouth. So too, I suspect, did many of the jests which were printed in book form, together with the more bizarre prophecies which appeared in prognostications.

The oral circulation of such material was stimulated and in some cases initiated by its appearance in print. Much of the story and song that was current formed an important element in the assumptions, attitudes, modes of reasoning – the 'mental baggage' – of the unlettered. Fundamental ideas about work, mortality and life are implicit in the small change of conversation, and if the inner world of the inarticulate can be understood in even the most superficial manner, then one method of doing so is to look at the region where a printed and an oral culture meet and react upon each other. The relationship between the two, and the ways in which the contents of a book or ballad sheet passed into the consciousness of those who could not read, are not easy to follow. It may be that familiarity with the spoken version of a jest, a ballad, or even a name may in some measure have made printed versions easier to cope with; but the relationship is one of subtlety and complexity.

Two examples may serve to illustrate this: Robin Hood, and riddles. The famous outlaw, despite the fact that many of the extant ballads which tell of his exploits date from the sixteenth and seventeenth centuries,[22] came from a world already almost forgotten. The forest laws had fallen into disuse, archery was no longer a pastime practised throughout the country and, above all, the abbeys and great religious houses which the outlaws had robbed and whose monks and abbots they continually outwitted had been dissolved. Precisely because it was so far away in time, this world was one in which anything could happen, and it is beyond doubt that it laid a firm hold upon men's imaginations and has done so ever since. The earliest printed version of Robin Hood was issued by Caxton's successor, Wynkyn de Worde; in recent years he has appeared on both cinema and television screens, to say nothing of books and comics. This adds up to a pretty impressive run of popularity.

It is, moreover, a popularity which has over the last few years given rise to cogent academic arguments that the Robin Hood legends and ballads were a 'by-product of the agrarian social struggle' which went on for about 150 years and culminated in the rising of 1381.[23] The whole discussion is an important footnote to the wider and certainly less sophisticated vogue for the outlaw

22. M. Keen, *The Outlaws of Medieval Legend* (1961), p. 99.
23. See R. H. Hilton, 'The Origins of Robin Hood', in *Past and Present*, 14 (November 1958), pp. 30–44; and J. C. Holt, 'The Origins and Audience of the Ballads of Robin Hood', *Past and Present*, 18 (November 1960), pp. 89–110. See also on this theme E. J. Hobsbawm, *Bandits* (1969; Penguin, 1972).

which was described over one hundred years ago by Samuel Bamford, writing of his childhood:

The old women would tell me strange stories of ghosts and hob-goblins; the old men narrated shipwrecks and battles, or they would chant the song of the famous outlaw, how

> 'He blew so loud and shrill;
> Till a hundred and ten
> Of Robin Hood's men
> Came tripping over the hill.'

And I was quite delighted with the idea of a free life in 'the merrie green-wood'.[24]

Elsewhere in his autobiography[25] Bamford mentions visiting the shop run by G. Swindells, a Manchester printer of chapbooks and ballad sheets. Amongst his purchases was *Robin Hood's Songs*. Too much should not be made of this, but it does suggest strongly that the Robin Hood tradition owed its continuing popularity to both oral and printed versions.

Riddles illustrate the same kind of thing equally well. *The Demaundes Joyous*[26] was a book of eight pages published by Wynkyn de Worde in 1511. Only one copy is known to survive of this work, the earliest collection of riddles derived from a some-what larger French collection, *Demandes joyeyses en maniere de quolibets*. A number of ribald and scatological riddles do not appear in the English version, but it goes almost without saying that the contents were so familiar as to be part of the stock-in-trade of conversation. The printed versions, in fact, gave a permanence to traditional material. There is always an interplay between oral culture and popular literature – although in the end the printed popular literature becomes predominant. How much of the former has been lost in this process we can never know. Thomas

24. Samuel Bamford, *Early Days* (1849), p. 70.
25. ibid., p. 90.
26. See John Wardroper's edition (1971). It contains a facsimile reprint, transcription of the blackletter (with notes), an introduction and a bibliography.

Hardy made the point that the old ballads were being sung in Dorset until the railway was extended to Dorchester in the mid nineteenth century, with '. . . the orally transmitted ditties of centuries being slain at a stroke by the London comic songs that were introduced'.[27]

If this statement is true of Dorset, to what extent does it hold good for other parts of England? The fascination and the wide-ranging nature of this question should not, however, be allowed to obscure another which must be asked at this point: to what extent was popular literature read and, following from this, what sort of people read it?

The problem of readership is not easy, for this early period is not one to which one can apply a procedure – whether valid or not – of counting the signatures of those who signed their names in parish registers, a practice which seems to have become fairly standard for the centuries when such records existed. More than forty years ago J. W. Adamson read a paper before the Biblio-graphical Society entitled 'Literacy in England in the Fifteenth and Sixteenth Centuries',[28] in which he concluded, cautiously perhaps, that England in the fifteenth and, especially, the six-teenth centuries was by no means an illiterate society, 'and that facilities for rudimentary instruction at least were so distributed as to reach even small towns and villages'. Adamson takes the term 'literacy' to mean simply the ability to read an English book, and he draws a clear distinction between being able to read and being able to write, pointing out that in the past the two abilities were by no means so inseparably linked as they are today, and that in former times the number of readers was very much greater than the total of those who could write – 'writing being,' he goes on, 'treated as a stage so far in advance of reading that only a few pupils would learn it.'[29]

27. Florence Emily Hardy, *The Life of Thomas Hardy* (1962), p. 20.
28. Printed in the *Library* (September 1929). Reprinted in J. W. Adamson, *The Illiterate Anglo-Saxon* (Cambridge, 1946).
29. *The Illiterate Anglo-Saxon*, p. 38.

Amongst the evidence which Adamson puts forward is the point that in 1489 a change was made in the rules as to benefit of clergy. From 1351 laymen who were able to read had enjoyed the privilege which, as Lawrence Stone has pointed out, meant that 'to a petty thief the capacity to read a sentence of the Bible made all the difference between death by slow strangulation at the end of a rope and life with a scarred thumb'.[30] In nearly 150 years, however, the number of men who could read but had not the least pretence of being clergymen had so increased that the law had to be altered.

Puritanism gave a great stimulus to literacy, with its stress upon the necessity for individual reading of the Holy Scriptures. There is a reference to 'dyveres poore men' in Chelmsford, Essex, who read the Bible – but also a scandalized comment by Stokesley, Bishop of London (1530–39), who declined thus to share in a translation initiated by Cranmer: 'I marvel what my lord of Canterbury meaneth that thus abuseth the people in giving them liberty to read the Scriptures, which doth nothing else but infect them with heresy.'[31]

Such a comment – though perhaps too much should not be made of it – lends substance to Sir Thomas More's assumption that just over half the population could read.[32] The total evidence marshalled by Adamson points unmistakably to the existence of a wide range of readers in Tudor England. Of course it cannot be expressed statistically, but the argument is too strong to be resisted.

What about the social class of readers? The phrase 'poore men' has already been used, and it is too vague to provide a starting point for discussion; but it does seem reasonable to suppose that the ability to read – with whatever degree of proficiency – was not

30. Lawrence Stone, 'The Educational Revolution in England, 1560–1640', in *Past and Present*, 28 (July 1964), pp. 42–3.

31. *The Illiterate Anglo-Saxon*, p. 45.

32. *The Works of Sir Thomas More* (1557), p. 850; quoted in J. W. Adamson, *The Illiterate Anglo-Saxon*, p. 45.

confined to those who had attended a grammar school. Generalization beyond this would be precarious. What is more interesting
is the somewhat oblique light shed upon the nature of the reading
public by those who criticized popular literature in print. Attacks
upon such material grew more frequent at the turn of the sixteenth
century, some of them written by Puritan moralists such as
Edward Dering, who wrote off romances as 'childish follye'.[33]
More will be said about the development of the reading public, as
deduced from contemporary assumptions about it, in the chapters
devoted to the following centuries; but, as we have seen, there is
some evidence to suggest that the audience for the ephemeral
literature of earlier times was wide enough to make the broadside,
jestbook, riddle and so on fairly universally popular. If such
publications lacked variety, they did at least have a liveliness
which reflected the life of the times.

33. Preface to *A bryefe and necessary catechisme or instruction, very needful
to be known by all Householders* (fourth edition, 1606).

TWO

1600–1700

We have choice of songs, and merry books too,
All pleasant and witty, delightful and new,
Which every young swain may whistle at plough,
And every fair milk-maid sing at her cow.
Then maidens and men, come see what you lack,
And buy the fine toys that I have in my pack!

'The Pedlar's Lamentation',
A Book of Roxburghe Ballads, ed. J. P. Collier (1847)

*The arraignement and burning of Margaret Ferne-seede, for the Murder of
her late Husband Anthony Ferne-seede, found dead in Packham Field neere
Lambeth, having once before attempted to poyson him with broth, being
executed in S. Georges-fields the last of Februarie . . .*

Title of a pamphlet published 1608/9
(Copy in the British Museum)

I now intend a Voyage here to write,
From London unto York, help to indite,
Great Neptune lend thy aid to me who past
Through thy tempestuous waves with many a blast,
And then I'll true describe the towns, and men,
And manners, as I went and came agen.

John Taylor, Prologue to *A Verry Merry
Wherry-ferry Voyage: or Yorke for My
Money* (1622)

A Wench coming to be Confessed, confessed abundance of her sins, but the
chief was lying with men. 'Well,' said the Friar, 'Whoredom is a thing which
doth much displease God.' 'Faith,' says she, 'I am sorry for that, for I am
sure it pleased me.'

William Hicks, *Oxford Jests* (1671)

Seventeenth-century popular literature presents a splendid
hotch-potch of broadsides and paper-covered books which were

sold on the bookstalls around St Paul's Cathedral, in Pye Corner, on London Bridge and elsewhere in the capital, besides being retailed by hawkers and pedlars who carried them to the four corners of the kingdom.

The subject-matter covered romance, crime, traditional songs, strange happenings; marvels and portents were widely enjoyed in a credulous age: it was a mirror to the times, with well-tried themes finding a ready market, and few innovations. What was new was the emergence of the first best-selling popular author who depended for his fame not merely upon what he wrote but equally upon his reputation amongst his contemporaries as a 'character'. This was John Taylor, the 'Water Poet', and some aspects of his life and work will be considered later in this chapter.

Continuities with the previous century are emphasized by a consideration of ballad-mongers. Both Deloney and Elderton were probably dead by 1600, but their tradition was carried on by Martin Parker (died 1656?). Little is known about his life, but he was probably a Londoner. A contemporary described him as one 'who made many base ballads against the Scots',[1] but his best-known work was a song written to support the cause of Charles I. 'When the King Enjoys His Own Again' achieved an instant success when it appeared in 1643. According to one critic[2] it was 'the most famous and popular air ever heard in this country'. Its vogue outlasted the period of conflict and it remained a favourite long after the Restoration, being taken up by the Jacobites. For some two hundred years altogether this was heard about the streets of London:

> What Booker doth prognosticate
> Concerning King or kingdom's 'fate',
> I think myself to be as wise
> As 'he' that gazeth on the skyes:

1. See *Dictionary of National Biography* XV, pp. 252-4, for details of Parker's career.

2. Joseph Ritson, *Ancient Songs and Ballads* (1790), third edition (1877), p. 367.

My skill goes beyond
The depth of a Pond
Or Rivers in the greatest rain:
Whereby I can tell
All things will be well,
When the King enjoys his own again.

There's neither Swallow, Dove, nor Dade,
Can sore more high or deeper wade;
Nor 'show' a reason, from the stars,
What causeth peace or civil wars.
The man in the moon
May wear out his shoo'n
By running after Charles his wain:
But all's to no end,
For the times will not mend
Till the King enjoys his own again.

Full forty years this royal crown
Hath been his father's and his own;
And is there anyone but he
That in the name should sharer be?
For who better may
The scepter sway
Than he that hath such a right to reign?
Then let's hope for peace,
For the wars will not cease
Till the King enjoys his own again.

Though for a time we see White-hall
With cobweb-hangings on the wall,
Instead of gold, and silver brave
Which, formerly, 'twas wont to have.
With rich perfume
In every room,
Delightful to that princely train;
Which again shall be,
When the time you see
That the King enjoys his own again.

Did Walker no predictions lack,
In Hammond's bloody Almanack?
Foretelling things that would ensue,
That all proves right, if lies be true;
>> But why should not he
>> The pillory foresee
Where in poor Toby once was ta'en?
>> And also foreknow
>> To th' gallows he must go,
When the King enjoys his own again.

Then (fears) avaunt! upon 'the' hill
My Hope shall cast 'her' anchor still,
Untill I see some peaceful Dove
Bring home the Branch I dearly love;
>> Then will I wait
>> Till the waters abate
Which 'now disturb' my troubled brain,
>> Else never rejoyce
>> Till I hear the voice
That the King enjoys his own again.[3]

The tune to which this was sung was both traditional and popular. Small wonder that it caught the public fancy – the Parliamentary side, despite its strength in military matters, could not match this. Neither John Milton nor Andrew Marvell stooped to the street ballad: the former wrote his propaganda in prose, while the latter did not turn to political poetry until some years later. It is not necessary to be familiar with all the allusions to realize the appeal of such a ballad.

This was only one of many ballads written by Parker who, like Deloney before him, also turned his hand to prose. He was the author of *A True Tale of Robin Hood*, published in 1632, and a jestbook, *Harry White His Humour*, together with other fugitive pieces of this kind. Parker was a scribbler with a talent for writing words to well-tried tunes – a ballad-monger in the tradition of the

3. Ritson, op. cit., pp. 368–70.

earlier century – besides being able to turn out a tale in prose when it was wanted.

There were other continuities. One was the reprinting in 1584 of Clement Robinson's *A Handefull of Pleasant Delites*. No copy seems to have survived of the 1566 edition, but the later one gives a very good idea of the favourite songs and ballads of the period; many of them, including for instance 'Greensleeves', would have been whistled and sung around the streets well into the seventeenth century.

The character of ballad literature, then, showed no discernible change after 1600; but there was much more of it. The great collections of broadsides from this period offer a wealth of song and narrative in verse, and what has survived is, of course, nothing like the total of what was published. However much we may deplore what was lost through being read to pieces, or pasted onto walls, enough remains to be enjoyed. Scholars have taken these ephemeral sheets and their passing songs very seriously indeed. Initially at least the reason seems to have been a Shakespearian interest, and it is certainly true that no other branch of popular literature has been so intensively studied from a literary, social or bibliographical point of view. Today the view is increasingly that of a seventeenth-century collector of broadsides, John Selden, who remarked that 'More solid Things do not show the Complexion of the Times so well as Ballads . . .'[4]

It is to collectors like Selden that we are indebted for the preservation of broadsides which would otherwise have perished. His collection formed the basis of the five volumes of Pepys ballads now in Magdalene College, Cambridge. Since Pepys was collecting in 1702, the year before his death, and he had taken some pains to acquire specimens from the late sixteenth century, the entire collection is fairly representative of the seventeenth century as a whole. There is a gap between 1640 and 1675; on the other hand, for the reigns of James II and William and Mary the

4. Quoted in L. Goldstein, 'The Pepys Ballads', in the *Library*, Fifth Series, Vol. XXI, No. 4 (December 1966), p. 290.

collection is without rival. Pepys's ballads are arranged under ten headings:

1. Devotion and morality
2. History – True and Fabulous
3. Tragedy – vizt Murd.^{rs} Execut.^{ns} Judgm.^{ts} of God
4. State and Times
5. Love – Pleasant
6. do – Unfortunate
7. Marriage, Cuckoldry, etc.
8. Sea – Love, Gallantry & Actions
9. Drinking & Good Fellowshipp
10. Humour, Frollicks, etc. mixt.

The manuscript title page of Volume 1, embellished with a portrait of Pepys, reads as follows:

My Collection of Ballads Vol. 1. Begun by Dr Selden; improved by ye addition of many Pieces elder thereto in Time; and the whole continued to the year 1700. When the Form, till then peculiar thereto, vizt of the Black Letter with Pictures, seems (for cheapness sake) wholly laid aside, for that of White Letter without Pictures.

By 'Black Letter' Pepys meant the Gothic type used by early printers in Europe as opposed to the Roman or italic ('White Letter') which superseded it and is still in general use.

Pepys's classification of ballads under these ten headings indicates the scope of the seventeenth-century broadside. Pepys was not, however, the only collector: Robert Harley, First Earl of Oxford (1661–1724), was another. His collection, plus a few additions made by a subsequent owner, is now in the British Museum where it is known as the 'Roxburghe Ballads', after the duke who acquired it in 1788. In the same library are the three volumes of broadsides collected by John Bagford (1650–1716), shoemaker and bibliophile, who had an abiding passion for ephemeral printed sheets. In the Bodleian Library are the remains of Anthony à Wood's collection – 279 ballads. Wood, who lived from 1623 to 1695, was an ardent collector with an eye for the grotesque and the unusual. There is some evidence to suggest that he in fact collected a much larger number of ballads, and that in Harley's time about two or three times the number of those now in Wood's collection found their way into the Roxburghe collection. Also in the Bodleian is the Rawlinson collection of 218 ballads which may also have come from Anthony à Wood. In the Library of the University of Glasgow there is the Euing collection, consisting of 408 ballads.

Incomplete as this list of collections is, it does give some idea of the mass of material which has survived both the ravages of time and the handling of contemporary readers, who were as likely to throw broadsides aside like yesterday's newspaper when their novelty was exhausted as they were to use them for wrapping paper. Hyder Rollins lists over 3,000 titles issued between 1557 and 1709 by licensed printers; and how many more came from printers who did not bother to register with the Stationers' Company? 'There could,' says Leslie Shepard, 'have been more than 15,000 different ballads in circulation during the period.'[5] For the survival of a substantial fragment of these fugitive sheets we owe a great debt to the collectors of the past, without whose bibliophily the study of popular literature would scarcely be possible.

So far, then, from there being a problem of insufficient examples from which to generalize, it is rather a matter of making sense of a scattered abundance of sheets which on the one hand enshrine the traditional songs of England and on the other, with themes of monsters, unnatural happenings, scandal and murder, look forward perhaps to the popular press of the twentieth century.

Imagination suggests that traditional and popular songs and their tunes were sung or whistled about the streets of London, up and down the country, in taverns – wherever, in fact, men and women worked or took their leisure. To say this is not to take an over-romanticized view of the past: the current popularity of the transistor radio, or during the War of broadcast programmes like

5. Leslie Shepard, *The History of Street Literature* (1973), p. 34.

'Music While You Work', hint at a long-standing tradition. There is, it is true, little hard evidence to go on, but there are frail threads which suggest the living tradition of song in seventeenth-century England. In 1688, for example, the song 'Lillibullero' took the public fancy. 'The whole army, and at last the people, both in city and country, were singing it perpetually,' wrote Gilbert Burnet.[6] This may have been exceptional; but there are also indications of song at a more local level. The barber's shop has, writes John Harley, 'always been a place where the idle could pass the time, where gossip could be exchanged, and a masculine refuge from domesticity, and for a long period it was an established practice to have handy there an instrument (usually a cittern) for the use of waiting customers or the barber.'[7] Philip Stubbes in his *Anatomy of Abuses*, first published in 1583, had referred to the connection between barbers and music: 'You shall have also your orient perfumes for your nose, your fragrant waters for your face, wherewith you shall bee all to besprinkled; your musicke againe and pleasant harmonie shall sound in your eares, and all to tickle the same with vaine delight.'[8] Thomas Dekker in *The Honest Whore* (Second Part, 1630) alludes to the same thing: '. . . a barber's cittern for every serving-man to play upon'.[9] Then, too, there was Golding the Greenwich barber, mentioned by Pepys, who played the violin.[10]

Those who sold broadsides in the streets came in for criticism. Then, as now, the itinerant street vendor was the object of suspicion, and sometimes hostility. The ballad singer or seller – often they were one and the same – was bedevilled by a host of regulations, the tone of which was set by an old bye-law referring to 'Hawkers, Vendors, Pedlars, petty Chapmen, and unruly people'.

6. Quoted in Thomas Percy, *Reliques of Ancient English Poetry*, ed. H. B. Wheatley (1886), Vol. II, p. 339.

7. John Harley, *Music in Purcell's London* (1968), pp. 42–3.

8. Quoted in J. O. Halliwell, *A Catalogue of Chap-books, Garlands, and Popular Histories* (1849), pp. 24–5.

9. Quoted in Halliwell, op. cit., p. 24.

10. See Harley, op. cit., p. 43.

4. A seventeenth-century ballad-seller

There is no reason to think that Henry Chettle's phrase, 'that idle, upstart generation of ballad singers', did not sum up the attitude of many in the seventeenth century, although it dates from 1593. Chettle, in fact, throws an interesting light upon the trade:

> There is many a tradesman, of a worshipful trade, yet no stationer, who, after a little, bringing up apprentices to singing brokery, takes into his shop some fresh men, and trusts his old servants of a two months' standing with a dozen groats-worth of ballads. In which, if they prove thrifty, he makes them petty chapmen. able to spread more pamphlets by the State forbidden than all the booksellers in London.[11]

The catch-as-catch-can approach implied by Chettle does indeed seem to have been a characteristic of the ballad trade, although we shall see later that as the century progressed there were developments in the organization of printing and printers.

What of the product itself? Despite the profusion of titles and themes there was, it must be admitted, a sameness about the

11. For both references from Chettle see his *Kinde Harts Dreame* (1593); see also E. Duncan, *The Story of Minstrelsy* (1907), p. 277.

writing of ballads. As with so much of the popular fiction of the nineteenth century and so many of the eighteenth-century chap-books, innovation was generally frowned upon in seventeenth-century ballads. While sensation was welcomed, the method of presenting it was nearly always the same. Almost always the tune to which the words were sung was traditional, but occasionally 'an excellent new tune' was specified – which might, after the Restoration, have derived from a popular stage hit, or perhaps had taken the public fancy in some other way.

The two ballads which follow are quoted entire, and catch the flavour of seventeenth-century popular sheets. The first deals with a problem conspicuously with us in the twentieth century, that of traffic in London. As early as 1601 hackney coaches had become a nuisance, and there was legislation 'to restrain the excessive use of them'. The streets of London in the early 1600s were said to be crowded by some 6,000 coaches, and in about 1630 the sedan chair was introduced, adding to the confusion in narrow streets. Blackfriars, with the coming and going of theatre audiences, suffered especially and in 1631 the inhabitants petitioned the Privy Council against the number of coaches. This ballad, dating from about 1636, was one of several pieces to seize upon the subject.

THE COACH'S OVERTHROW

To the Tune of 'Old King Harry'

As I pass'd by the other day,
  where sacke and claret spring,
I heard a mad crew by the way,
  that lowd did laugh and sing
High downe, dery, dery downe,
  with the hackney coaches downe!
    Tis cry'd aloud,
    They make such a crowd,
Men cannot passe the towne.

The boyes that brew strong ale, and care
   not how the world doth swing,
So bonny, blith, and joviall are,
   their lives are drinke and sing;
Hey downe, dery, dery downe,
   with the hackney coaches downe!
     To make them roome
     They may freely come,
And liquor the thirsty towne.

The Collier he's a sack of mirth,
   and though as black as soote,
Yet still he tunes and whistles forth,
   and this is all the note:
Heigh downe, dery, dery downe,
   with the hackney coaches downe!
     They long made fooles
     Of poore Carry-coales,
But now must leave the towne.

The Carriers of every shire
   are, as from cares immune,
So joviall in this packe horse quire,
   and this is all their tune,
Hey downe, dery, dery downe,
   with the hackney coaches downe!
     Farewell, adew
     To the jumping crew,
For they must leave the towne.

Although a Carman had a cold,
   he straind his March-bird voice,
And with the best a part did hold,
   to sing and to rejoyce.
Heigh downe, dery, dery downe,
   with the hackney coaches downe!
     The Carmen's cars,
     And the merchants wares,
May passe along the towne.

The very slugs did pipe for joy
   that coachmen hence should hye,
And that the coaches must away,
   a mellowing up to lye.
Hey downe, dery, dery downe,
   with the hackney coachmen downe!
     Passe they their scope,
     As round as a rope,
Wee'l jogge them forth of the towne.

Promoters and the informers,
   that oft offences hatch,
In all our times the money-wormes,
   and they are for to catch,
Heigh downe, dery, dery downe,
   with the hackney coaches downe!
     For these restraints
     Will with complaints
Fill all [the noisy towne].

The world no more shall run on wheels
   with coach-men, as't has done,
But they must take them to their heeles,
   and try how they can run.
Heigh downe, dery, dery downe,
   With the hackney coaches downe!
     Wee thought they'd burst
     Their pride, since first
Swell'd so within the towne.

The Sedan does (like Atlas) hope
   to carry heaven pick-pack,
And likewise, since he has such scope,
   to beare the towne at's back.
Heigh downe, dery, dery downe,
   With the hackney coachmen downe!
     Arise, Sedan,
     Thou shalt be the man
To beare us about the towne.

I love Sedans, cause they doe plod
   and amble every where,
Which prancers are with leather shod,
   and neere disturbe the eare.
Heigh downe, dery, dery downe,
   With the hackney coaches downe!
     Their jumpings make
     The pavement shake,
Their noyse doth mad the towne.

The elder brother shall take place,
   the youngest brother rise;
The middle brother's out of grace,
   and every tradesman cryes,
Heigh downe, dery, dery downe,
   with the hackney coaches downe!
     Twould save much hurt,
     Spare dust and durt,
Were they cleane out of towne.

The sick, the weake, the lame also,
   a coach for ease might beg,
When they on foot might lightly goe,
   that are as right's leg.
Heigh downe, dery, dery downe,
   With the hackney coaches downe!
     Lets foot it out,
     Ere the yeare comes about,
Twill save us many a crowne.

What though we trip ore boots and shoes,
   twill ease the price of leather:
We shall get twice what once we loose,
   when they doe fall together.
Heigh downe, dery, dery downe,
   with the hackney coaches downe!
     Though one trade fall,
     Yet in generall
Tis a good to all the towne.

Tis an undoing unto none
    that a profession use:
Tis good for all, not hurt to one,
    considering the abuse.
Then heigh downe, dery, dery downe,
    with the hackney coaches downe!
      Tis so decreed
      By a royall deed,
To make it a happy towne.

Coach-makers may use many trades
    and get enough of meanes;
And coach-men may turne off their jades,
    and helpe to draine the fens.
Heigh downe, dery, dery downe,
    With the hackney coaches downe!
      The sythe and flayle,
      Cart and plow-tayle,
Doe want them out of towne.

But to conclude, tis true, I heare,
    they'l soone be out of fashion;
Tis thought they very likely are
    to have a long vacation.
Heigh downe, dery, dery downe,
    With the hackney coaches downe!
      Their terme's neere done,
      And shall be begun
No more in London towne.[12]

The second ballad exemplifies another facet of seventeenth-century popular taste. The fate of Mr Thompson, a waterman, must have had a peculiar fascination for the superstitious reader. 'Drinking healths to the Devil,' remarks Professor Hyder E. Rollins in his introduction to the ballad, 'has always been a ticklish business.' He goes on to mention the case of Andrew Stonesby, a Cavalier who drank a health to the devil in an ale-house at Listelleth in Cornwall. No sooner had he done so than the

12. Quoted in J. P. Collier, *A Book of Roxburghe Ballads* (1847), pp. 291–7.

devil appeared, and poor Stonesby died raving blasphemously. An equally unpleasant fate overtook a soldier who drank to the devil in a Salisbury tavern. Divine intervention is a notion which had some force in the seventeenth century, and it is worth recalling a headline in the *New York Times* for 24 November 1923: 'May God Punish Me With Death If Guilty Says Man, Then Dies'.

TERRIBLE NEWS FROM BRAINFORD

A perfect and true Relation of one Thompson *a Waterman, and two more of that Function, being drinking in excess at* Brainford, *at the House of one Mrs* Phillpots, *Thursday night*, September 12. *began a Health to the Devil, and another to his Dam; at which falling dead against the Table: With the Devils appearing in the Room visible, the Burial of the sinful Wretch; his Corps seeming heavy at first, but the Coffin afterward as light, as if there had been nothing in it.*

To the Tune of, Chievy Chase

All you which sober minded are,
   come listen and Ile tell,
The saddest story Ile declare,
   which in our dayes befell:
Therefore 'tis for example sake,
   the business written is,
That others may a warning take
   by such lewd lives as these.

My matter now I have in hand,
   doth very doleful run;
In *Brainford* you shall understand
   this horrid act was done:
Three Watermen a drinking were,
   some say in *Phillpots* house,
Who very desperately did swear,
   they would have one Carouse.

To every friend as they could think,
   abroad the world so wide,

A Glass unto his Health would drink,
    whatever did betide?
So many Healths about did pass,
    which is a shame to tell;
They knew not who to drink unto,
    except the Devil of Hell.

Quoth one and swore the Pot shall pass,
    be it to good or evil;
And if thou wilt but pledge a Glass,
    Ile drink unto the Devil:
The other said I willing am,
    call in for Sack about us;
Ile drink another to his Dam,
    it shall not go without us.

With that he bowed down his head,
    and suddenly did fall;
He sunk against the Table dead,
    in presence of them all:
His vitals then with death was stung,
    throughout eternally,
His Nose upon the Table hung,
    a ghostly sight to see.

The second Part, to the same Tune

The others then with fearfulness,
    their legs were smitten so
With horrour and with feebleness,
    they knew not what to do:
But staring in the dead mans face,
    they dolefully did cry,
Good people help us in this place,
    help, help, or else we dye.

Which horrid doleful voices then
    put all the house in fear,
Who nimbly up the stairs ran,
    to see what news was there:

And being come, good Lord how then
   they trembled in the place;
And questioned then the living men,
   like wretches void of Grace.

How came this horrid dismal fate,
   declare it good or evil;
For we did hear you once relate
   A Health unto the Devil:
Tis very true, quoth they, by stealth
   that act we once began;
And I my self did pledge the Health,
   and drank unto his Dam.

At which they all were trembling than,
   though faint and yet unable;
They did endeavour with the man,
   to lay him on the Table:
Which time one knocked at the door,
   but going for to see,
An ill-shap't Devil in did bore
   amongst their company.

And being come unto the light,
   their hearts were very cold;
The Devil did appear in sight,
   more wonderous to behold:
But when they on their knees did fall,
   and to the Lord did pray;
The Devil vanisht from them all,
   and quickly went his way.

But when the morrow did begin,
   a Coffin then was brought;
And placed then the Corps therein,
   which all this mischief wrought.

The four Bearers did complain,
   and to the people say,
It seem'd the heaviest Corps that e're
   they carried on the way:

But yet the case did alter quite,
    e're to the Church they came,
The Coffin it did seem so light,
    as if nothing had been in.

Now let all men a warning take,
    by *Thomsons* dreadful fall,
And drunken company forsake,
    so God preserve us all,
And keep us still from great excess
    of drinking which is evil;
And never in such drunkenness
    drink healths unto the Devil.

FINIS

Printed for F. Coles, M. Wright, T. Vere, and W. Gilbertson,
1661.[13]

Love and romance were always popular, of course. There was
one ballad entitled: 'The Ruined Lovers. Being a rare Narrative
of a young Man that dyed for his cruel Mistress, in June last, who
not long after his death, upon a consideration of his intire Affec-
tion, and her own coyness, could not be comforted, but lingered
out her dayes in Melancholly, fell desperate sick, and so dyed.'
The final verse pointed the moral:

Let all fair Maids that are in love,
    by this poor Soul take warning,
Lest that like her, you sadly prove
    the purchase of her scorning;
Lest all by this, mend what's a miss,
    before grief over-run (ye);
Lest you be forc'd to die, and cry,
    thy death hath quite undone me.[14]

There was, too, the sailor's plea to his love:

13. Quoted in Hyder E. Rollins, *The Pack of Autolycus* (1927), 1969
edition, pp. 76–80.
14. *The Euing Collection of English Broadside Ballads* (1971), p. 516.

> Remember me on shore,
>   as I thee on the main,
> So keep my love in store
>   till I return againe.[15]

In some ballads what is almost a populist note can be discerned. 'A Looking Glass for Corn-hoarders' tells the story of 'John Russell a Farmer dwelling at St Peters Chassant in Buckinghamshire, whose horses sunke into the ground the 4 of March 1631'. In the first three verses the scene is set – a strange happening, divine intervention in Buckinghamshire; then, in the fourth, the sympathies of the writer are made plain:

> The poore being abus'd
>   by the rich, by the rich
> And by them cruelly us'd
>   in every Towne:
> But God that heares their moane,
>   for their sakes hath this showne,
> That's already noysed and blowne
>   over the Land.

Having agreed to sell corn to a poor man the farmer, Russell, raises the price when he is due to deliver it. The extra money is found and paid without complaint:

> He quietly indured
>   and gave it him:

At this point God intervened: the ground in front of a plough-team opened up and two horses sank into it – 'They did so strangely vanish'. The rest of the team followed, but they were later rescued. Clearly this was a warning to the avaricious farmer, as the final verse makes plain:

> Let them take heed how they
>   doe oppresse, doe oppresse
> The poore that God obey,
>   and are beloved.

15. ibid., p. 519.

74

God will not let these long
   alone, that doe his wrong,
Though ne'r so rich and strong
   that are oppressors.[16]

A more fatalistic sentiment is expressed in 'A Warning-piece for Ingrossers of Corne; being A true Relation how the Divell met with one Goodman Inglebred of Bowton, within six miles of Holgay in Norfolk . . .':

So to Conclude and make an end
   for Peace and Plenty, let us pray
That God may stand y[e] poor-man's freind
   for y[e] Poore are now the rich-man's pray.[17]

Street ballad commentary upon the times was often at a very low level. Visually, the leaden quality of the verses was very often relieved by the crude but lively woodcuts with which so many of these sheets were embellished. As for the contents, in their dual function of amusing, and sometimes informing, contemporary readers they have in fact bequeathed a commentary from below on life as it was more than three centuries ago.

How many copies of a broadside would be printed and sold? There is no way of estimating this with any certainty. Unlike publishers of a later century who were very much less reticent about sales figures, or keener upon promotion of their products ('Fourteenth Edition, making 77,000', said one on the cover of a shilling book), the seventeenth-century printer-cum-publisher turned out sheets for just so long as there was a market for them. There were broadside-ballad titles on offer in their thousands. It was, said Louis B. Wright, 'a form that unlearned men could soon acquire the trick of writing'.[18] And many of them did so; but save for the few, their names are unknown. We have seen

16. Hyder E. Rollins, *A Pepysian Garland* (1922), 1971 edition, pp. 370–75.
17. Hyder E. Rollins, *The Pack of Autolycus* (1927), 1969 edition, pp. 31–5.
18. Louis B. Wright, *Middle-class Culture in Elizabethan England* (1935), 1964 edition, p. 420.

that the standard of their writing was not high, but it was probably no worse than that of much subsequent popular journalism. John Earle, author of *Micro-cosmographie* (1628), described a ballad writer:

A POT-POET

Is the dregs of wit; yet mingled with good drink may have some relish. His inspirations are more real than others'; for they do but feign a God, but he has his by him. His verses run like the tap, and his invention as the barrel ebbs and flows at the mercy of the spigot. In thin drink he aspires not above a ballad, but a cup of sack inflames him and sets his muse and nose afire together. The Press is his Mint, and stamps him now and then a sixpence or two in reward of the baser coin his pamphlet. His works would scarce sell for three half-pence, though they are given oft for three shillings, but for the pretty title that allures the country Gentleman: and for which the printer maintains him in ale a fortnight. His verses are like his clothes, miserable centos and patches, yet their pace is not altogether so hobbling as an Almanac's. The death of a great man or the burning of a house furnish him with an argument, and the Nine Muses are out straight in mourning gown, and Melpomene cries 'Fire, Fire'. His other poems are but briefs in rhyme, and like the poor Greeks' collection to redeem from captivity. He is a man now much employed in commendations of our Navy, and a bitter inveigher against the Spaniard. His frequentest works go out in single sheets, and are chanted from market to market, to a vile tune and a worse throat; whilst the poor country wench melts like her butter to hear them. And these are the stories of some men of Tyburne, or a strange monster out of Germany; or sitting in a bawdy-house, he writes God's judgements. He ends at last in some obscure painted cloth, to which himself made the verses, and his life like a can too full spills upon the bench. He leaves twenty shillings on the score, which my Hostess loses.[19]

If little is known about the authors, it is possible to trace a little more clearly the history of the printers who supplied the ballad market. From about the middle of the seventeenth century it

19. John Earle, *Micro-cosmographie* (1628); undated later edition, ed. H. Osborne.

became increasingly dominated by two separate groups of printers and one or two individuals. The composition of these two groups changed through death and marriage, but their continuing existence and increasing involvement in broadside printing, together with the fact that copyrights were jealously guarded – although usually, it must be added, to little effect – suggest strongly the profitability of the ballad trade. The increasing formalization of ballad-printing seems an indication of continuing demand rather than of rationalization carried out to recoup losses in a dwindling market.[20]

Inevitably, perhaps, traditional black-letter ballads lost favour with the public towards the close of the seventeenth century, and those printers like J. Blare or P. Brooksby who were forward-looking went into chapbooks, and perhaps topical ballads, while those who did nothing to bring their lists up to date gradually went out of business. Many of them were substantial members of the London printing fraternity – Thomas Vere, for instance, a traditionalist, was at one time Master of the Stationers' Company – but it is possible that less well-established printers may have suffered financial hardship.

It is not easy to give a clear reason for the decline of black letter. The innate conservatism of the common reader had been, perhaps, the sole reason for its survival long after pretty well everything else was being printed in 'white letter', or Roman type. By about 1700, for whatever reason, popular literature was no longer being printed in so archaic a style; but this fact reflects not so much a change in the kind of thing offered to the public as a realization that black letter was outdated and, indeed, not so easy to read – particularly when printed on the comparatively small page of the chapbook, which had by this time to a very great extent taken the place of the broadside in public favour. Chapbooks will be considered in more detail in the following chapter, but essen-

20. For this argument I am indebted to the late Cyprian Blagden's 'Notes on the Ballad Market in the Second Half of the Seventeenth Century', published in *Studies in Bibliography*, Vol. 6 (1953-4).

tially they were small books or pamphlets, easier for vendors to handle and transport than a pile of ballad sheets, and probably offering better value for money in that, unlike broadsides, they were printed on both sides of the paper.

Pamphlets were, of course, not unknown to seventeenth-century readers, who were deluged at one time or another with religious and political controversy in this form. Orthodox believer, antinomian, parliamentarian, royalist, all thundered at each other in pamphlets, each convinced of the justice of his cause. Polemic of this kind apart, any sensational or scurrilous affair which might catch the public fancy could be written up as a pamphlet and produced for sale very speedily. In the case of a particularly nasty murder or a case of witchcraft, both pamphlet *and* broadside could be exploited to bring the story to sensation-hungry readers. The writer of such pamphlets often banked upon the fact that his reader would in all probability be extremely credulous; moreover, with centres of production based almost entirely in London, a writer could be fairly confident that the facts of any event taking place in a country district would not be known to his readers. Thus a mixture of fact, hearsay, rumour, legend and half-truth could be concocted into a narrative which would certainly find readers who would believe a good deal of what they found in the pamphlet. Pre-industrial man lived in a world of magic, wonders and marvels – a world which had not yet reached what Lucien Febvre has called 'an awareness of the impossible'.[21] An enjoyment of sensation is probably very natural, and persists – in, for example, the popular press – to this day; but credulity has become considerably tempered with scepticism. The Loch Ness Monster crops up now and again, but on the whole it battles in vain for our serious attention.

Typical, when it was published in 1614, was an account of a Sussex dragon. The title ran as follows:

True and Wonderfull. A Discourse relating a strange and monstrous

21. Lucien Febvre, *A New Kind of History* (1973), p. 192.

Serpent (or Dragon) lately discovered, and yet living, to the great Annoyance and divers Slaughters both of Men and Cattell, by his strong and violent Poyson: In Sussex, two Miles from Horsam, in a Woode called St Leonards Forrest, and thirtie Miles from London, this present Month of August, 1614. With the true Generation of Serpents.[22]

The monster is described thus:

This Serpent, or Dragon, as some call it, is reputed to be nine Feete, or rather more, in Length, and shaped almost in the Forme of an Axel-tree of a Cart, a Quantitie of Thickness in the Middest, and somewhat smaller at both Endes. The former Part, which he shootes forth as a Necke, is supposed to be an Elle long, with a white Ring, as it were, of Scales about it. The Scales along his Backe seem to be blackish, and so much as is discovered under his Bellie appeareth to be red; for I speak no nearer Description than of a reasonable ocular Distance. For coming too neare it hath already beene too dearely payd for, as you shall heare hereafter.

It is likewise discovered to have large Feete, but the Eye may be there deceived; for some suppose that Serpents have no Feete, but glide upon certain Ribbes and Scales, which both defend them from the upper Part of their Throat unto the lower part of their Bellie, and also cause them to move so much the faster.

In order to kill, the monster emits a venom. A man and a woman were found dead, 'being poysoned and very much swelled, but not prayed upon'. One man went to hunt it:

... as he imagined, to destroy it with two Massive Dogs, as yet not knowing the great Danger of it, his Dogs were both killed, and he himselfe glad to returne with hast to preserve his own Life. Yet this is to be noted, that the Dogs were not prayed upon, but slaine and left whole; for his Food is thought to be, for the most Part, in a Conie-Warren, which he much frequents, and it is found much scanted and impaired in the Encrease it had woont to afford.

Finally, the truth of this account is attested by three people,

22. See *The Harleian Miscellany*, Vol. 3 (1745), pp. 106–9.

two who append their names, together with a third who is rather vague:

John Steele
Christopher Holder
And a Widow Woman dwelling nere Faygate.

No price is shown on the title page, but it cannot have cost more than a copper or two. The same sort of 'marvel' was readily available more than sixty years later in an eight-page pamphlet called:

Wonderful News from Wales: Or, a True Narrative of an old Woman living near Lanselin in Denbighshire, whose Memory serves her truly and perfectly to relate what she hath seen and done one-hundred and thirty years ago. Having now the full Number of her Teeth; the most of them were lost, when she was Three-score Years and Ten. She is also remembered, by some of ninety years old, to be taller than she is by seventeen or eighteen Inches; with several other Circumstances of her Life, which shew her to be the Wonder of her Age.[23]

The pamphlet was published in 1677, and the final paragraph is addressed to the reader who may be sceptical: 'If any Person question the Truth of this Narrative, or desire to satisfy their Curiosity, let them repair to West-Smithfield, where she is daily expected to convince the World of the Truth thereof.'

Sensation of a rather different kind, and much nearer home for London readers, was provided in an eight-page pamphlet which was published in 1684.[24] As usual the long title provides a summary of its contents:

The She-Wedding: Or, a Mad Marriage, between Mary, a Seaman's Mistress, and Margaret, a Carpenter's Wife, at Deptford. Being a full Relation of a cunning Intrigue, carried on and managed by two Women, to hide the Discovery of a great Belly, and make the Parents of her Sweet-heart provide for the same; for which Fact the said Parties were both committed; and one of them now remains in the Round-House at Greenwich, the other being bailed out.

23. *The Harleian Miscellany*, Vol. VI (1745), pp. 65–8.
24. Reprinted in *The Harleian Miscellany*, Vol. VI, pp. 370–73.

The story begins in a usual enough way. Mary, a serving-maid at the King's Head in Deptford, was keeping company with a sailor called Charles Parsons, 'insomuch,' says the anonymous author, 'that the Neighbours looked upon her as either married to him, or at least as free of her Favours as if she had; and in a little Time her squeamish Stomach gave her Mistress Cause to regard her more narrowly, and she began to suspect that her Sweet-heart had given her a Belly full of Love, as afterwards it proved but too true . . .'

This was not perhaps too novel a situation in Deptford, where seamen were constantly coming and going. Mary went to see Parsons's mother with a view to getting some help, but the old woman was suspicious and said she would assist with the expenses attendant on the birth only if the girl was genuinely her daughter-in-law. To this end she insisted upon seeing the marriage certificate.

If Mary had not been resourceful this might have proved an insuperable problem, but she hit upon an original solution. She would go through a form of marriage with her friend Margaret, the wife of a local carpenter. Even so, there were difficulties, for although the 'groom' might – and in the event did – pass muster dressed as a man, there would be the matter of the date upon the certificate.

The marriage took place at St George's Church, Southwark, the ceremony slightly marred by the fact that the 'groom' referred to 'I Margaret . . .', but this was smoothed over by an explanation that this was the name of a sister who had recently married a sailor. When the ceremony was over, the 'husband' drew the Parish Clerk aside:

. . . telling him, that true it was, dabbling with his said Wife before Marriage, he had got her with Child, and that she was very forward, being near six Months gone of her Time; and fearing that his Wife's Relations, and his own, might take Notice of the Date of the Certificate to his Disadvantage, desired that the same might be antedated, promising the Clark to reward him for so doing.

After what were called 'many Importunities' the Clerk was persuaded, money changed hands, the certificate was dated six months previous to the 'marriage', and the two girls took it back with them to Deptford. Old Mrs Parsons was taken in. Delighted with her daughter-in-law, she began 'rummaging her old Chests for Linnen to provide for Clouts and other Necessaries'.

All might have been well had the two girls not aroused the suspicions of neighbours with their chatter. Not only did Mary and Margaret refer to themselves, banteringly, 'by the Name of Husband and Wife', but they also put about a tale which brought forth ribald and indignant comment: 'they knew a Couple that had been for six Weeks wedded, and both as likely as any two in England, and yet neither of them had one Bout since they were married.' Despite the laughter suspicions grew, and Mrs Parsons made it her business 'to go and inquire at the Church where the Certificate had mentioned her Son and supposed Daughter-in-Law to have been married'.

Of course the truth came out, and the 'she marriage' became the talk of Deptford. Both girls were arrested and a magistrate committed them to Greenwich Roundhouse where, concludes the chronicler, 'Margaret hath been since bailed out, and Mary yet continues there.'

True or false – and there is nothing inherently improbable in the narrative – this was a good story, and not dissimilar from the kind of thing found in some newspapers today. The glimpses we get of ordinary people's gossip, and of their attitudes to sex and to bribery, are illuminating.

So much for the lighter side of seventeenth-century pamphlet literature. About the more lurid themes of witchcraft and murder Professor J. H. Marshburn has written splendidly, and if I draw largely upon the rich harvest of contemporary material that he has gathered,[25] it is a tribute to his thoroughness.

Murder and witchcraft were the perennial themes which caught

25. J. H. Marshburn, *Murder and Witchcraft in England 1550-1640* (Norman, Oklahoma, 1971).

the imagination of readers in earlier ages – much as they do today. Homicide, sex and public executions, together with witchcraft (however broadly defined), were topics which had formed an element in popular literature from about 1550. Details of violent death, sometimes linked with adultery, and the fascination of the occult world were the mainsprings of a taste for violence and the bizarre which printers were able to exploit in several ways: broadside, pamphlet and play. So ephemeral was a good deal of this literature that it seems safe to assume that many items have perished, while others, like the Roxburghe collection's broadside ballad on the 'Arden of Faversham' murder, survive only in single copies.

The Arden case was a *cause célèbre* of 1550. A detailed account of the events is to be found in the Holinshed *Chronicles*, and John Stow also recounts this murder story. The culmination of several attempts on the life of Thomas Arden, a wealthy man, arranged by his wife Alice and her lover Mosbie, was a pretty revolting story, and provided just the kind of subject which a ballad-writer could be expected to exploit. Thus the execution of the culprits gave rise to *The Complaint and Lamentation of Mistresse Arden*, a ballad of forty-eight stanzas of four lines each. Although undated, this probably preceded a play on the same theme, *Arden of Feversham*, of which three editions are extant, the first published in 1592 and the last in 1633; and in many ways the ballad version agrees both with that of the chroniclers and with the play.

According to Holinshed, Thomas Arden was battered with a fourteen-pound pressing-iron administered by one Black Will, hired for this purpose by Alice following several unsuccessful attempts at the murder – including the poisoning of Arden's breakfast porridge. The dying man's face was then torn open, and Alice rounded off the killing by giving her husband 'seven or eight pricks on the brest'. Evidently she had a strong stomach, for the room in which the murder had taken place was straightened up and she played hostess to two London grocers, Prune and Cole, who had been invited for supper. She wondered 'where maister

Arden is; we will not tarie for him'; so they had a pleasant evening, dancing after the meal to the music of the virginals played by Alice's daughter.

The body had been dragged into the churchyard, and soon there was a hue and cry after Arden, whose corpse was discovered and identified by Prune. Murder will out, and it was not long before Alice was crying, 'Oh the bloud of God helpe, for this bloud have I shed.' Mosbie was subsequently found in bed at a local inn, the Fleur de Luce, and he and Alice, with several accomplices, were brought to justice. Alice was burned at Canterbury; Mosbie and his sister, also involved, were hanged at Smithfield. Other participants came to equally bad ends.

The ballad, in the form of Alice Arden's confession, presents her as, at the end, a penitent woman. She states that she and her husband had lived in 'great tranquillity' until, it is implied, she fell victim to Mosbie's seductive charms:

> Until I came in Mosbie's company
> Whose sugred tongue, good shape, and lovely looke,
> Soon won my heart and Arden's love forsooke.

Her husband was jealous, and she and Mosbie decided to take his life. At this point the plot becomes more involved – although certainly no more so than appears to have been the case as we have it from the *Chronicles*. Arden is setting out for 'London faire', and Alice persuades his servant Michael to murder him before his return. She had already promised the hand of her lover's sister to a painter on condition that he should supply poison, although whether or not Michael was to make use of this is not clear. In any case, doubtful about Michael's determination to kill his master, she approaches Green, a neighbour 'which to my husband bore no great good will', and asks for his help:

> You must be circumspect to doe this feat;
> To act the deed your selfe there is no need,
> But hire some villaines, they will do the deed.

Green starts out for London, and on the way meets Shakebag and Black Will:

> ... that did use in Kent
> To rob and murder upon Shooter's-hill.

They find Arden in London, but 'by strange chance' lose their intended victim in the vicinity of 'Paul's church':

> For where these villaines stood and made their stop,
> A prentice he was shutting up his shop,
> The window falling light on Black Will's head,
> And broke it soundly, that apace it bled.

Next, the would-be murderers prevail upon Michael to leave open the door of his master's lodging during the night. This plan is frustrated because Arden, 'having strange dreames and visions', himself secures the door. The following day an ambush is planned during the return of Arden and Michael to Faversham. Black Will and Shakebag lie in wait at Rainham Down, but because of the number of people in Arden's party 'they were crost againe'.

While her husband was in London, Alice and Mosbie 'did revel night and day', not expecting that Arden would return. When he does so, he tells his wife that he has to visit Lord Cheyney on the following day. Another opportunity for an ambush; but the weather was foggy, so once more Arden 'scap'd these villaines where they lay'.

More drastic measures are called for, and it is decided to kill Arden in his home that night. At a given signal, while he and Mosbie are playing a game at the table, Shakebag and Black Will burst into the room and stab their victim 'with swordes and knives to the heart'.

Justice, of course, caught up with the criminals, and Alice's remarks just before her death were, in the convention of murder ballads where pious resignation is almost *de rigueur*, predictable enough:

And thus my story I conclude and end,
Praying the Lord that he his grave will send
Upon us all, and keep us from ill,
Amen say all, if't be thy blessed will.

As poetry, *The Complaint and Lamentation of Mistresse Arden*[25] is quite unremarkable: as the product of some unknown hack writer it is entirely typical. The themes of subterfuge, violent death and adultery can still be found, in rather different forms, commanding a substantial readership in the second half of the twentieth century. Nevertheless, Tudor sensibilities must have been rather more blunted than ours, and if the horrors of this case seem, to the modern mind, to be overdone, this would not have seemed so to contemporary readers. The melodrama of the broadside ballad dealing with crime, so far from offering a new and vicarious experience of violence, sudden death and sexual irregularities, was all too often a pale reflection of life as many Elizabethans knew it.

The play already alluded to was probably founded upon an earlier piece, *Murderous Michael*, of which no copy is known to have survived – but it is recorded that it was played at court before Queen Elizabeth in 1578/9. The stage versions must have given an extra dimension to the lurid details. *Arden of Feversham* is, in fact, an extremely good murder play, and it is not difficult to see its appeal to theatre audiences accustomed not only to the hurly-burly of Elizabethan London but also to sports like bear-baiting and to the institutionalized cruelty of public floggings, together with the burning, hanging, drawing and quartering of prisoners. Art, in ballad or stage play, was clearly imitating life, and there is no reason to doubt the popularity of murder and witchcraft as absorbing topics in popular literature. The former was nourished by a robust view of the precariousness of life and the frailty of human flesh in the face of temptation, the latter by a deep sense of credulity which flourished in a world where hearsay could not

26. J. H. Marshburn, *Murder and Witchcraft in England 1550–1640* (Norman, Oklahoma, 1971), pp. 3–22.

always be disentangled from truth, and even educated men believed in fairies.

The Arden case set a pattern which was to be worked and re-worked, at least until the outbreak of the Civil War. There was Margaret Ferne-seede, who lived a life of 'beastiall lasciviousness', running a brothel in her house near the Tower of London. The body of her husband was discovered in Peckham Field near London with the throat cut. He was a very respectable tradesman, apparently unaware of his wife's calling, and the investigation of his death led to Margaret, who was duly tried and burned. At the place of execution, St George's Field, she was asked to confess but refused to do so, and 'the reeds were planted aboute, unto which fier being given she was presently dead.' The quotation here is from a pamphlet, the title of which is given at the head of this chapter. A broadside entitled 'The woman that was Lately burnt in Saint Georges feildes' was entered in the Stationers' Register on 7 March 1608/9, but no copy seems to have survived. From about the 1580s pamphlets had begun to appear as an alternative – or indeed an addition – to the ballad sheet. They could be lengthier and were more expensive, but they were not subject to the same kind of wear and tear and, copy for copy, they probably lasted longer amongst contemporaries than the ephemeral ballad sheets. In either case we can picture them becoming progressively more tattered as they passed from hand to hand or were read aloud to unlettered audiences agog for lurid details, while many of the broadsides were pasted up on the walls of ale houses and cottages.

Not only murder, however, pulled in the pennies of the reading public, for reference has already been made to the vein of credulity and superstition which ran through the seventeenth-century mind at all levels of society. The case of the witches in Lancashire which gained notoriety in 1612, and again in 1634, illustrates the preoccupation with the dark side of things – a preoccupation which could erupt into the brutal violence which attended the investigations of the repulsive self-styled 'Witch Finder Generall',

The wonderfull dif-

couerie of ELIZABETH SAVVYER
a Witch, late of Edmonton, her
conuiction and condemnation
and Death.

Together with the relation of the Diuels
accefe to her, and their conference together.

Written by HENRY GOODCOLE Minifter of the
Word of God, and her continuall Vifiter in the
Gaole of Newgate.
Publifhed by Authority.

London, Printed for *VVilliam Butler*, and are to be fold at his Shop in Saint
Dunftons Church-yard, Fleetftreet, 1621,

5. A seventeenth-century witchcraft pamphlet

Matthew Hopkins, who was active in the middle years of the century. The fact that he was able to flourish as he did, trafficking in ignorance and superstition, is an indication that belief in witchcraft and prophecy represented something far more fundamental in people's minds than merely a vicarious enjoyment of other folks' crime or misdemeanour. It is, however, not part of my purpose to discuss the social setting of witchcraft, still less to evaluate what it meant in people's lives. This has already been done by scholars like Keith Thomas, whose book, *Religion and the Decline of Magic* (1971), is both profound and immensely readable.

Dealings with the devil were always grist to the mill of pamphleteer, ballad-writer and printer. In 1612 it was alleged that witches were meeting in a ravine near Pendle Hill, Lancashire.[27] Arrests were made, and in the following year appeared a pamphlet entitled *The Wonderfull Discoverie of Witches in the Countie of Lancaster*. The author was Thomas Potts, who had been a court clerk during the trial, and he included in his pamphlet the confessions of several witches. One of them, who died in jail before she could be brought to trial, was a widow, Elizabeth Sowthernes, alias Dembike. She was said to be the devil's 'general agent', and she admitted to a pact with him. According to her, the simplest way to kill a person was to make a 'clay picture' in the shape of the victim, dry it thoroughly and then prick it with a pin.

Elizabeth Sowthernes seems to have been a pretty formidable influence upon others. Anne Whittle, alias Chattox, another of the group, claimed that Elizabeth had persuaded her to become a witch and to murder three people by means of witchcraft. Alison Device, Elizabeth's granddaughter, accused her grandmother of murdering a small girl by the same means.

Charge and counter-charge followed. Two women and one man were found guilty; but the witches were to reappear in Lancashire. Some twenty-two years later another frenzy erupted,

27. J. H. Marshburn, *Murder and Witchcraft in England 1550-1640* (Norman, Oklahoma, 1971), pp. 145-50.

and reports coming out of the county suggested that sixty people had been taken into custody. It was said that 'a huge pack of witches' had been discovered, and that more and more names were being revealed daily. The King's life had been put at risk when they raised a storm off the coast of Scotland. In the flurry and heated atmosphere rumours were rife, and one had it that nineteen 'weird sisters' had been condemned. A more sober witness, Bishop Bridgman of Chester, wrote to say that he had been ordered to examine seven condemned witches in Lancashire. By the time he arrived three of them, one man and two women, had died in jail, and one woman, Jannet Hargreaves, 'laid sick past hope of recovery'. The three remaining women – one of them, Margaret Johnson, described as a 'penitent witch' – were taken by the Sheriff of Lancaster to London. They were held at the Ship Tavern in Greenwich, where they were to be examined by mid-wives who had received their instructions from William Harvey, the King's physician.

The results of the examination seem to have been negative, but the atmosphere was such that a ten-year-old boy from Whalley, Edmund Robinson, could testify that he had seen his two dogs turn into human beings and be believed by some – although he later retracted his evidence.

All of this, of course, made splendid copy. Potts's pamphlet, a copy of which survives in the British Museum, caught the interest of Sir Walter Scott, who edited and reprinted it. The tradition of Lancashire witches found its way into two chapbooks, *The Famous History of the Lancashire Witches* ... and *The Lancashire Witches* ... There was also a play which was entered in the Stationers' Register on 28 October 1634, *The Witches of Lancashire, etc.*, and this must surely have played to packed houses.

There were witches in Northampton, too. The year 1612 seems to have been a good one for amateurs of the black art, for Agnes Browne, Joane Vaughan, Arthur Bill, Helen Jenkinson and Mary Barber were all executed at Northampton on 22 July. Their exploits are recounted in a pamphlet called *The Witches of Northamptonshire*, printed in 1612.[28]

Lincoln also had a minor witch-frenzy. In a pamphlet entitled *The Wonderful Discoverie of the Witchcrafts of Margaret and Phillip Flower, etc.* (1619) there are very full accounts of the examinations of those charged with witchcraft. Of Margaret it was said:

> Shee confesseth, that shee hath two familiar Spirits sucking on her, the one white, the other black spotted; the white sucked under her left breast, and the black spotted within the inward parts of her secrets. When shee first entertained them shee promised them her soule, and they covenanted to doe all things which shee commanded them, etc.[29]

The credulous reader fed eagerly upon this kind of thing.

Jestbooks continued to find favour with many readers. Besides offering light relief, they possessed for the most part a comfortable familiarity for readers who saw them as essentially traditional fare. Jocular literature had been enjoyed by generations of readers. Elizabethan titles gave way to fresh ones in Stuart times, but the subject matter remained essentially the same. 'The large increase in number,' writes Professor P. M. Zall, 'reflects the fact that the making of jestbooks became an industry in the seventeenth century, expanding with the development of a larger reading public. Jestbooks flourished throughout the land, feeding upon one another in a happy self-sustaining cycle. Badly printed, crudely written, they were welcome alike in parlour and pulpit, playhouse and pub.'[30]

If these little books performed a social function it was to provide an instant culture. Anecdotes and witticisms could be quoted

28. See *Witchcraft in Northamptonshire*: facsimile reproductions of six rare and curious tracts dating from 1612 (Gerald Coe Ltd, Wilbarston, Northants., 1967).

29. I quote from p. 23 of the facsimile of a Victorian reprint (Stephen Austin & Sons, Hertford, 1970; 500 copies printed).

30. P. M. Zall (ed.), *A Nest of Ninnies* (Lincoln, Nebraska, 1970), p. ix.

from them, and their contents plundered to make conversation – and probably even sermons – sparkle with borrowed wit. In the previous century jestbooks had been put together by anonymous hack writers, and this practice was largely continued in the ensuing one, but some recognizable popular authors did begin to appear.

One was Anthony Copley, secret agent for the King of Spain and distant relative of Queen Elizabeth. His biography is understandably obscure; but he travelled abroad a good deal, and his *Wits, Fits and Fancies* (1614) was a little unusual. He was not content, as so many similar authors were, merely to rework old jests; he looked further afield and gathered material from Spain and elsewhere which he put to good use in his jestbook. The following brief jest is typical:

> One advised a great Drunkard still to mingle water with his wine. He answered, 'If that were good, God would have done it in the Grape.'[31]

Robert Armin (1568–1614) was a goldsmith, pamphleteer and actor. He joined Shakespeare's company in about 1600 and had some reputation as a comedian. A jestbook by him, *A Nest of Ninnies*, was published in 1608. The jests and anecdotes in the book tend to be longer than usual and are sometimes interspersed with verses. A few titles indicate the flavour of the entire book: 'How Jack Oates played at Cards all alone'; 'How Jack hit a Nobleman a box on the ear'; 'How Jack Oates eat up a Quince Pie, being of choice provided for Sir William'; 'How this fat Fool Jemy Camber ran with the King's best Footman for a wager and won it'; 'How Lean Leonard eat up his Master's Hawk and was almost choked with the Feathers'. The book is in fact a view of several jesters or fools employed in noble households – Jack Oates, for example, was the fool of Sir William Hollis, and Will Sommers, who figures in several episodes of Armin's book, had been court fool to Henry VIII.[32] Armin was making capital – and

31. ibid., p. 12.

32. *A Pleasant History of the Life and Death of Will Sommers* was published in 1676. It probably embodies some genuine tradition, but there are anecdotes and stock jokes which are quite untrue.

doing it fairly skilfully – out of the reputations of men around whom traditions had gathered, and who were entertainers in their own right.

Conceits, Clinches, Flashes, and Whimzies (1639) by Robert Chamberlain was a collection of short punning jokes. Chamberlain (c. 1607–60) specialized in puns, and his book was sufficiently popular to be reprinted the year after its original appearance in an expanded version, *Jocabella or a Cabinet of Conceits*. Little is known about the author. He was at Oxford around 1637, but did not take a degree.

Equal obscurity surrounds the career of Captain William Hickes, whose *Oxford Jests* came out in 1671, and for the most part the compilers of these books were nameless.

These very brief notes are merely suggestive of the light reading of three hundred and more years ago. Just how did this kind of literature strike contemporaries? Not a rhetorical question this, for one articulate man, a lexicographer besides being the author of a jestbook, did say something on the subject. Abel Boyer (1667–1729) was a Huguenot refugee living in London from 1689. When he was French tutor to the young Duke of Gloucester he wrote a simple French textbook, *The Complete French Master* (1694). Reading matter was printed with the English and French equivalents on facing pages, and amongst the passages deemed suitable were twenty-five jests ancient and modern. Eventually these were expanded into 191 ancient and 151 modern jests which were published separately as *The Wise and Ingenious Companion* in 1700.

The jests are very much what one might expect, with no startling originality, but the 'Prefatory Introduction' does make some interesting points. First of all, Boyer stresses the antiquity of jokes: the 'Ancient Greeks and Romans', he points out, thought it worth-while to collect them. He defines the different types of joke, and finally he justifies their study and collection in the following words:

We may draw a double advantage from true Jests, for besides they serve to make us merry and revive now and then a fainting conversation, several of them are full of good and wholesome Instructions, applicable to the different Exigencies of Life, both in a public and private Fortune.

As for Stories, they differ from Jests in that they express their Subject in its full Latitude and generally leave nothing to be guessed at, as Jests do. They are sometimes divertingly Instructive, but their chief aim is to make the Heavens merry by relating sometimes a concurrence of Comical Accidents, sometimes a piece of Simplicity or Ignorance, and sometimes Malicious Tricks that have been put upon anyone to make sport for others. In all these we must use the same Caution as we have mentioned about Jests; that is, we must take care not to confound good Stories with many pieces of low Buffoonery which tickle mean and vulgar ears by their smuttiness, daubed over with paltry Equivocations.[33]

Wise words! Standing as he does at the close of one century and the outset of another, Boyer represents a civilized and articulate reaction to the boisterous humour of the jestbook. Despite his caveat, the element of 'low Buffoonery' persisted in the collections of jokes which continued to be printed. 'I published this book to make men merry,' said Andrew Borde in his prologue to *The Jests of Scogin*, and this remained the rationale of the jestbook. It has had a long run, and continues in one form or another to the present day.

If I have emphasized in this chapter continuing themes and traditions in popular literature, it is because I believe such continuities to have existed and to be an important factor in the view we form of the period. But because we are considering *popular* literature, we must consider also the range of its appeal and readership, and any changes therein. From about the middle of the seventeenth century we can discern an assumption on the part of some writers that the character of the reading public has somehow changed. Traditional tales, which formed a substantial element in popular literature, had found favour right across the social spectrum; but it is here that this change can be found, and

33. Quoted in P. M. Zall (ed.), *A Nest of Ninnies*, p. 253.

perhaps the best documented account of it is 'The Vogue of Guy of Warwick' by R. S. Crane.[34] Although more than fifty years old this study has not been superseded, nor indeed has its argument been developed or modified in any significant way.

Whereas in the early days of printing editions dealing with the adventures of this old English hero had been produced to appeal to sophisticated readers, besides the ballad versions for the street trade, from about 1650 we find the former disappearing. Guy of Warwick no longer attracted readers from the cultivated public, the gentlemen or nobles, but became rather the property – with a whole lot more traditional material – of the unlettered, unsophisticated reader.

The evidence supporting this generalization offers three main points. First, publications for men of letters no longer showed any leaning towards medieval romances. Second, it was the ballad printers and those catering for the popular market who issued broadside versions and abridged story-book editions. Finally, writers of the time were themselves suggesting that a taste for the old literature of romance was characteristic of servants, children and old women.

A study some years later of the development of *Valentine and Orson*,[35] a late medieval romance, gives further support to this argument. A bibliography of English editions from about 1510 to 1919[36] shows that a change in the *kind* of edition published had taken place in the second half of the seventeenth century. Such a change could very easily be attributed to the Civil War, which marked the ending of an era. As so often, war and its resulting social turbulence brought about far-reaching changes in the tastes of society.

If the audience at this time was becoming narrower, I shall hope in the following chapter to demonstrate that it became very

34. PMLA, Vol. XXX, 2 (1915), pp. 125ff. I am greatly indebted to this article for my argument.

35. Arthur Dixon, *Valentine and Orson* (New York, 1929).

36. ibid., pp. 284–98.

much deeper, so that it proved worth-while for printers and publishers to specialize in the popular market.

Reference was made at the opening of this chapter to a new element in the seventeenth-century popular-literature scene – the emergence of a writer who is also a 'character'; a man whose undoubted charisma leads one to feel that in a later age he would have been a television personality besides being the author of several best-selling works. John Taylor, one such, was known as the 'Water Poet', because at one time he was a waterman on the river Thames.

Of the few writers for the popular market known by name little enough is known.[37] Amongst them were Samuel Rowlands and John Shirley, and it is perhaps of interest to record that both produced versions of *Guy of Warwick*. In fact, they published a good deal, cobbling up tales in prose and verse to amuse their readers. Taylor, however, was rather different. He did not rely upon traditional tales and revamp them for printers and booksellers, but produced original works written in a vigorous, highly individual style; moreover, he hit upon an ingenious scheme for selling them which ensured that he was known to the public.

Taylor was born in Gloucester in 1580,[38] attended the local grammar school, and was subsequently apprenticed to a London waterman. As a pressed man in the Navy he was present at the siege of Cadiz in 1596, and according to his own account in *The Pennyless Pilgrimage* (1618) made sixteen voyages before leaving the service with a 'lame leg'. He earned his living as a Thames waterman for a number of years after his discharge, and earned something of a reputation for independence, wit and conviviality. Towards the middle of the reign of James I, however, life on the river became more difficult, and he complained in various pamphlets of 'hired hackney-hell carts' taking away business from the

37. Entries in the *Dictionary of National Biography* confirm this. For Samuel Rowlands see Edmund Gosse, *Seventeenth Century Studies* (1883).

38. See *Dictionary of National Biography* XIX; and Wallace Notestein, *Four Worthies* (1956).

THE
PENNYLES
PILGRIMAGE,
OR
The Money-leſſe perambulation,
of I O H N T A Y L O R, *Alias*
the Kings Majeſties
Water-Poet.

HOW HE TRAVAILED ON FOOT
from *London* to *Edenborough* in *Scotland*, not carrying
any Money to orfro, neither Bégging, Borrow-
ing, or Asking Meate, drinke or
Lodging.

With his Deſcription of his Entertainment
in all places of his Iourney, and a true Report
of the vnmatchable Hunting in the *Brea*
of *Marre* and *Badenoch* in
Scotland.

With other Obſeruations, ſome ſerious and
worthy of Memory, and ſome merry
and not hurtfull to be Remembred.

Laſtly that (which is Rare in a Trauailer)
all is true.

L'ONDON
Printed by *Edw: All-de*, at the charges of the
Author. 1 6 1 8.

6.   A Taylor pamphlet

waterman who plied for hire at the Thames side. Another factor which made for a decline in the trade of these men was the removal of theatres from the Surrey side of the river. All in all, Taylor – like all who picked up their living ferrying passengers – was having an increasingly thin time.

He was quick to turn a talent for doggerel to account, and for a modest fee he would celebrate in headlong verse birthdays, weddings and deaths. In 1612 he published a pamphlet, *The Sculler's Travels*, in which he addressed some uncomplimentary lines to Thomas Coryate, a traveller who at the climax of his career walked to India. Coryate replied in kind, and London – or that part of it which followed such things – was enlivened by a literary brawl.[39] Taylor wrote:

> A pamphlet there was *The sculler* nam'd
> Wherein Sir Thomas much my writing blam'd;
> Because an Epigram therein was written,
> In which he said he was nipt gald and bitten.
> He frets, he fumes, he rages, and exclaimes,
> And vows to rouze me from the River Thames.
> Well I to make him some amends for that
> Did write a book was cald *Laugh and be fat*.[40]

The skirmish went on, and Taylor got the best of it. But then he extended his activities, and for sums of money wagered by sponsors he undertook a number of journeys. Before setting out he issued prospectuses – 'Taylor's bills' he called them – in which details of the proposed trip were outlined and people were invited to lay money upon his success. Amongst those who did so were several prominent men of letters, including Ben Jonson, Thomas Dekker and Nicholas Breton. One cannot resist the thought that John Taylor may well have been the originator of our present-day 'sponsored walks' – although I suspect that it would be difficult

39. See M. Strachan, *The Life and Adventures of Thomas Coryate* (1962), pp. 149–57.

40. Quoted in Strachan, op. cit., p. 150.

to find evidence that Taylor devoted the proceeds to any causes other than his own!

Upon his return from these journeys, accounts were written and published under unusual titles. In *The Pennyless Pilgrimage* he undertook to walk to Edinburgh and back 'not carrying any Money to or fro, neither Begging, Borrowing, or Asking Meate, drinke or Lodging'. The pamphlet was dedicated to the Marquis of Buckingham, and the narrative is written in prose and verse. This is how he blended the two:

> That Thursday morn, my weary course I framed,
> Unto a town that is Newcastle named.
> (Not that Newcastle standing upon Tyne)
> But this town situation doth confine
> Near Cheshire, in the famous county Stafford,
> And for their love, I owe them not a straw for 't;
> > But now my versing muse craves some report,
> > And whilst she sleeps I'll spout a little prose.

In this town of Newcastle, I overtook a hostler, and I asked him what the next town was called, that was in my way toward Lancaster, he holding the end of a riding rod in his mouth, as if it had been a flute, piped me this answer, and said Talk-on-the-Hill; I asked him again what he said Talk-on-the-Hill: I demanded a third time, and the third time he answered me as he did before, Talk-on-the-Hill. I began to grow choleric, and asked him why he could not talk, or tell me the way as well there as on the hill; at last I was resolved, that the next town was four miles off me, and that the name of it was Talk-on-the-Hill: I had not travelled above two miles farther: but my last night's supper (which was as much as nothing) my mind being informed of it by my stomach . . .

After breakfast at the Sun, and some comments upon the bill:

> And now with sleep my muse hath eased her brain
> I'll turn my style from prose to verse again.

And so on . . . Before setting out upon this journey Taylor had collected some sixteen hundred signatures; but on his return to

99

London he found that roughly half the signatories refused to pay up on the grounds that he had not observed the conditions laid down. Nevertheless, some four and a half thousand copies of the pamphlet were printed. The defection of his sponsors provoked him to write *A Kicksey Winsey: or a Lerry Come-twang*, which came out in 1619. 'I have published this Pamphlet,' wrote Taylor, 'to let my rich debtors understand, that as often as I meet them, I do look that they should pay me: and although I am shamefaced in not asking my due, yet I would not have them shameless in detaining it from me, because the sums are but small, and very easy for them (in general) to pay, and would do me a particular good to receive.'

The debtors were divided into seven groups, the last of which – 'Those roarers that can pay, and will not' – aroused his greatest ire:

> ... a worthy worthless crew
> Such as heaven hates and hell on earth doth spew.

Whether or not Taylor ever received the money due to him we do not know. He continued to write voluminously, and the collected edition of his works which appeared in 1630 is far from complete. Five further volumes of his work were issued by the Spencer Society between 1870 and 1878.

The best of Taylor's work is characterized by liveliness and wit, together with a talent for narrative. He had a shrewd eye for the English scene and was sensitive to the upheavals of the Civil War: 'Eight yeares a frenzy did this land molest . . .' he wrote.[41]

His last years, when he was an innkeeper, were clouded by legal troubles and the suspicion on the part of the authorities that he was a 'malignant'. He died at his inn in 1653 and was buried in the near-by churchyard of St Martin's in the Fields.

More than any other popular writer of the seventeenth century, Taylor epitomized the author who was as well known for his flamboyant life-style as for what he wrote. The same could not be

41. John Taylor, *Wanderings to See the Wonders of the West* (1649).

said of any comparable writer in the eighteenth century, and his like in popular literature – and even then in a somewhat different form – was not to be seen again until Pierce Egan was writing in the days of the Regency.

THREE

1700–1800

Sunday 10 July (1763)
And here I must mention that some days ago I went to the old printing-office in Bow Church-yard kept by Dicey, whose family have kept it fourscore years. There are ushered into the world of literature *Jack and the Giants*, *The Seven Wise Masters of Gotham*, and other story-books which in my dawning years amused me as much as *Rasselas* does now.

James Boswell, *London Journal 1762–1763* (1950), p. 289

When the Empire of the Fairies was governed by the Empress Trussio, there reigned a King and Queen, who had two sons and one daughter; the daughter was every way lovely, and as she grew up became the mother's darling. This made them consult the Fairies concerning her fortune. They all agreed, that she should pass many difficulties, and at length arrive to lasting happiness; and that her two brothers should be condemned to death on her account.

Fairy Stories (Aldermary Church-Yard, Bow Lane, London, undated)

Rejoice you good Writers; your pens are set free;
Your thoughts and the Press are at full Liberty;
For your King and your Country you safely may write;
You may say Black is Black, and prove White is White;
　　Let no Pamphleteers
　　Be concerned for their Ears;
　　For every Man now shall be try'd by his Peers
Twelve good honest Men shall decide in each Cause
And be Judges of Fact, tho' not Judges of Laws.

Eighteenth-century political broadside ballad, *The Honest Jury*, by William Pultney. Quoted in Milton Percival (ed.), *Political Ballads Illustrating the Administration of Sir Robert Walpole* (Oxford, 1916), p. 27.

When Guy, Earl of Warwick, and Parismus and Parismenus, and Valentine and Orson, and the Seven Champions of England, were handed round at school – were they not all purchased with my pocket-money?

Uncle Toby in *Tristram Shandy*, Book VI, chapter 32

BY the end of the seventeenth century, as we have seen, the popularity of the black-letter broadside ballad was waning. 'There was, of course,' said Cyprian Blagden, 'no nice clean ending; it guttered out in the stronger light of the eighteenth-century chapbook.'[1]

In outlining developments in popular literature during this century, we must therefore look first at the characteristics and contents of chapbooks and suggest why they thrived, largely at the expense of the traditional ballad sheets.

Part of a typical example of an eighteenth-century chapbook is reproduced on p. 104. It was a small paper-covered book or pamphlet, usually measuring some three and a half inches by six inches, containing 4, 8, 12, 16 or 24 pages, and almost always enlivened by the inclusion of crude woodcut illustrations. These latter were not always even appropriate to the subject matter, but they undoubtedly added a degree of visual charm. In content chapbooks did not differ to any marked extent from the non-topical ballad sheets which had preceded them, offering stories, riddles, jokes – in fact, all kinds of traditional material – together with manuals of prophecy and fortune telling. Collections of ballads in chapbook form were known as garlands.

In seeking to account for the very considerable growth of this type of product for the unsophisticated reader at this period we meet, in Cyprian Blagden's terms, 'no nice clean explanation'. Shifts in public taste often defy analysis; but there was, first, a likely practical reason. Chapbooks were offered for sale by pedlars, hawkers and other itinerant merchants, who were known collectively as chapmen. Distribution thus became increasingly widespread, and ease of transport may well have become a consideration. Topical ballad sheets could, of course, sell like hot

1. Cyprian Blagden, *Studies in Bibliography* VI, p. 179.

THE
WORLD
TURNED
UPSIDE DOWN,
OR, THE
FOLLY of MAN;
EXEMPLEFIED
In Twelve comical Relations.
UPON
Uncommon SUBJECTS.

Illustrated with Twelve curious CUTS, truly adapted
to each Story

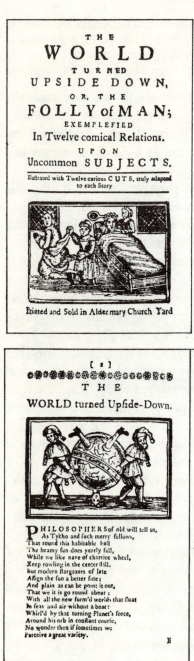

Printed and Sold in Aldermary Church Yard

7. An eighteenth-century chapbook

---

[2]

THE
WORLD turned Upside-Down.

PHILOSOPHERS of old will tell us,
As Tycho and such merry fellows,
That round this habitable ball
The beamy sun does yearly fall,
While we like nave of charriot wheel,
Keep rowling in the center still,
But modern stargazers of late
Assign the sun a better fate;
And plain as can be point it out,
That we it is go round about:
With all the new form'd worlds that float
In seas and air without a boat:
Whirl'd by that turning Planet's force,
Around his orb in constant course,
No wonder then if sometimes we
Perceive a great variety.

II

[3]

Sometimes this huge ball is found,
By chance of place Turn'd Upside-down,
Revolutions strange appear
Within the compass of the sphere;
Men and things succession know,
Hence by confession of the learned,
Who have the same by art discerned,
Is allow'd the world we live in
Always round the sun a-sailing;
Since it is we see a thousand things
Experience to our knowledge brings:
And art than nature wiser grown,
Turns every object upside-down
Crimes epidemic take their rise,
And constancy becomes a vice.
He that to-day is fortunate,
The darling minion of his fate,
To-morrow feels his fate's displeasure,
Who'd his hoarded Idol treasure,
Would like this man this emblem shews,
Sudden revolution knows.
His fortune grows profoundly scurvy,
Turns the poor earth-worms topsy-turvy,
Becomes the tennis ball of fools,
Beings form'd quite out of nature's rules,
As you see like Atlass bear
On their backs this mighty sphere.
The young, the old, the middle aged,
All in this great task engaged,
And strive with wond'rous eagerness,
Each shall the greatest part possess.
Usefully then has got the ascendant,
A most a fool that han't a hand in't,
As the mad brim'd world runs round
Keeps towards the rising ground.

The

cakes while they remained matters of the moment; then demand would fade as other subjects took the field. Chapbooks, on the other hand, lacking this topicality, could be expected to sell steadily and widely over a much longer period; and a bundle of small books would be easier to store and keep clean, and no doubt to transport, than a pile of broadsides. Perhaps, too, the polemical religio-political pamphlets of the Civil War period and afterwards had awakened people's minds to the ease of handling a small book rather than a larger, unwieldy sheet. I suspect that this factor of convenience was an important one.

Further influences in this shift in public taste arose from the increasing extent to which ordinary men and women were exposed to the printed word, and from the increasing opportunities to acquire a basic measure of education – education to the extent, at least, of achieving an ability to read. It is difficult to escape the conclusion that from these developments would stem a feeling that reading, at all levels of society, was becoming a more private experience; and the chapbook would be very much more personal to the reader than the broadside, which was often pasted up in a public place, or on the wall inside a house.

The period between 1700 and 1800 was one in which there was a considerable increase in the extent to which the printed word became part of the background of men and women who had not previously been exposed to it. The use of flysheets and tradesmen's handbills became more prevalent, as did the use of printed wrapping paper; and in 1762 the shopkeepers' signs which had for so long been a feature of London's streets were abolished, and their place taken by printed notices and announcements above the windows or doors of shops. Too much should not be made of this, for it is true that the eighteenth century did not suffer from the extreme profusion of ephemeral printed material, often of a commercial nature, which characterized the Victorian age as it does our own. But this period did see the beginning of modern methods in producing popular literature, and the emergence – to be detailed later in this chapter – of an outstanding entrepreneur whose family made a considerable fortune over several generations from specializing in this market.

The other influence upon the market for popular literature during this century was, it is suggested, the movement towards the spread of literacy, in so far as this is interpreted as the ability to read a printed page. For the children of the poor who could pay a trifling weekly fee, some sort of education could be acquired at the random, private-venture establishments set up by, perhaps, a 'dame' or an old soldier – almost anyone, in fact, who was unsuccessful or incapable in any other sphere of activity. The eighteenth century, however, also saw the rise of charity schools. These were indeed charitable undertakings; but their objective was not at all proved in their result, and certainly it was not in the minds of the promoters of the charity-school movement that those who acquired the ability to read should use it for the enjoyment of the entertainment offered by chapbooks – or that by the end of the century the skill would be directed into rather different channels.

The concept of providing elementary education for poor children was quite hotly debated, but it is interesting that on both sides of the argument the ultimate aim was the same: the maintenance of the social order. The hope of the advocates of these provisions was that children who were equipped to read the Church of England catechism, the Bible and perhaps a few other publications of a moral and improving nature would be brought to habits of diligence, industry, thrift and respect for their betters. They would, it was argued, thus see for themselves that it was part of God's plan that they should remain hardworking and virtuous.

Amongst such advocates were people like Isaac Watts and, later, Hannah More. Watts held that the ability to read the Bible was essential to an understanding of religion, and that poor children should receive instruction in reading for two or three hours each day. One of Hannah More's characters in a tract entitled *The Sunday School*, published towards the end of the eighteenth century, replies in ringing tones to a farmer who regards teaching the poor to read as the worst of 'foolish inventions and new-fangled devices to ruin the country': '. . . And I, farmer, think that to teach good principles to the lower classes is the most likely way to save the country. Now in order to do this, we must teach them to read.'

Outright opponents of the idea of charity schools included Bernard de Mandeville, arguing that the good of the nation depended upon the continued ignorance of those who were needed for the drudgery, and George Hadley, a forgotten historian of Kingston-upon-Hull, who asked whether any ploughman who was freed from subordination to the extent of being able to read would ever be content with his lot.

It is one of the ironies of history that the advocates of charity schools and their teaching of reading were in the end proved wrong, and their opponents shown to be right. The pious hope that those who laboriously learned to read would be content with the Bible and religious tracts was illusory, for with their new-found skill they turned to chapbooks. The traditional material which formed the mainstay of chapbooks nourished and extended the ability and taste for reading, and by the end of the century a mass reading public had grown and was becoming more sophisticated, so that it became more receptive to the written word in a political vein. In 1792 Thomas Paine[2] referred, somewhat obliquely, to this mass reading public and to the fact that cheap editions of his *Rights of Man* were in demand. The ability of poor people to read at the close of the eighteenth century played an important part in the making of working-class politics at the beginning of the next.

In tracing the way in which all this came about we have already seen that as the seventeenth century progressed the public for popular literature came increasingly from the unsophisticated levels of society. We find the development of this literature in the

2. 'A Letter Addressed to the Addressers of the Late Proclamation', re-printed by E. Truelove in *The Complete Works of Thomas Paine*, I (undated), p. 437.

more convenient and more personal form of the chapbook, but we find it embodying a great deal of the traditional lore, beliefs and customs of England's peasantry. The prototypes of Tom Thumb, Simple Simon and Robin Hood are of very great antiquity, and eighteenth-century chapbooks were tangible expressions of a deeply rooted folk culture which had laid hold upon men's imaginations long before the invention of printing. There were, too, unauthorized adaptations and abridgements of books by John Bunyan, Daniel Defoe and others; and characters like Long Meg of Westminster and Guy of Warwick, who had delighted the readers of a black-letter jestbook, turned up in chapbooks with their adventures somewhat shortened. Besides fiction of this kind, there were manuals of prophecy and fortune-telling and collections of ballads and jokes, all of which now appeared in chapbook form.

It was to the publication of this kind of material that a number of leading men in the ballad trade had turned towards the end of the seventeenth century, so that by the 1690s chapbooks had begun to appear in quite considerable numbers. In 1693 restrictions upon printers were lifted, and from that time the production of popular literature took place to an increasing extent in provincial towns, although London remained the centre of the book trade. Thus William Dicey, founder of a quite outstandingly successful family business,[3] moved to the capital early in the eighteenth century after starting his career as a printer in St Ives, Huntingdonshire and in Northampton.

It is probable that he was in London in 1713, although he was still concerned at that time and for several subsequent years in printing ventures in the provinces. His printing office in Northampton was well known; he was concerned in the establishment of the *Northampton Mercury* in 1720, and indeed the name Dicey appeared upon every issue of the paper up until 2 May 1885. By 1725, however, he had severed a partnership with Robert Raikes

3. For an account of William Dicey and his successors, see Victor E. Neuburg, 'The Diceys and the Chapbook Trade', in the Transactions of The Bibliographical Society, the *Library* (September 1969), pp. 219-31.

(whose son of the same name was to be well known as a founder of Sunday-schools) in St Ives, where the two men had started the *St Ives Post Boy*. In that same year he published in Northampton *The Life of Jonathan Wilde*, price 4d. This, of course, was comparatively expensive; but he followed it up with the host of chapbooks with which his name is today chiefly associated and it is these which have survived in surprisingly large numbers, while the more ephemeral day-to-day printing which he also undertook has largely disappeared.

Dicey advertised that he would engage in '. . . all the Common Business that may fall our way as Books, Bonds, Bills, Tickets, Receipts, etc., which will be carefully and exactly printed'. A trade card issued by William and his son Cluer,[4] who joined him in the business in the 1720s, shows pictures of a 'letter' press and a 'rolling' press at work in the printing office. William also made an arrangement with the makers of a famous patent medicine, 'Dr Bateman's Pectoral Drops', that supplies should be sold by the newspaper-sellers. At his death William left a one-third share in the rights of this remedy to his eldest son, Cluer – an indication that this was a worth-while sideline. The patent-medicine connection was extended to an interest in Daffy's Cordial, a mixture which was recommended once to Mary, the sister of Charles Lamb. Dicey's interest was celebrated in what must have been one of the earliest of advertising jingles:

> Daffy's Cordial, warm and spicy,
> Sold in Bow-Church-Yard by Dicey.

I stress this part of Dicey's activities because it does indicate his enterprise and ambition. It was not unknown for publishers to combine books with quack remedies – John Newbery, who published *Goody Two Shoes*, made a great deal of money in this way, and he too was an ambitious and energetic businessman.

Cluer Dicey took over the business, in which he had been participating for many years, upon his father's death in 1756.

4. See P. M. Handover, *Printing in London* (1960), Plate XIII.

Cluer himself died in 1775, and his will shows him to have been not only a man of shrewd business sense like his father but also a man of substance owning property in Little Claybrooke, Leicestershire, and in Stoke Newington, London. Reference is also made in the will to his 'share in the Business carried on in Bow Church Yard London and in the town of Northampton'. Thomas Dicey took his father's place and was still in business in 1800, although it seems doubtful whether he was still printing chapbooks at that time.

From their beginnings as jobbing printers this family clearly became one of fortune and one attracting respect. As indications of their rise in the world, Cluer Dicey's epitaph was written by Hannah More, the bluestocking friend of Dr Johnson and certainly no democrat, and the great-grandson of the founder went to Cambridge, where he became a Senior Wrangler. An important element in this success was the Diceys' pre-eminence in the sphere of popular literature.

In addition to the printing offices in London and Northampton there were various partnerships with other printers which contributed to the continuing expansion of the business. William Dicey was a shrewd and hard-headed businessman. He was not the first printer or publisher to cater for the rising popular market, but unlike so many of his rivals he did not regard chapbooks and ballad sheets as merely a sideline to more orthodox kinds of book production: he specialized in ephemera of this kind, and for something over seventy-five years three generations of the family went on turning it out.

We can gain an impression of the range of the Diceys' profitable productions from one of their catalogues, which was published in 1764. At that time Cluer Dicey was in partnership with Richard Marshall. The 104-page catalogue gives us a great deal of information about the tastes of the unsophisticated customer in the eighteenth century.

Only a fraction of this huge production has survived but, so far as prints are concerned, a selection of those issued by another eighteenth-century firm, some years after the Dicey catalogue,

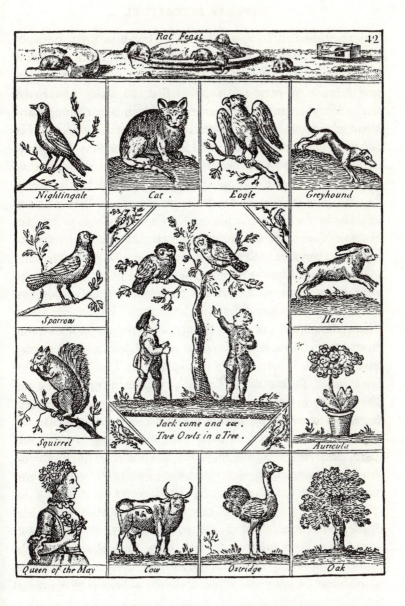

Rat Feast

42

Nightingale   Cat.   Eagle   Greyhound

Sparrow   Hare

Squirrel

Jack come and see.
Tvo Owls in a Tree.

Auricula

Queen of the May   Cow   Ostridge   Oak

8.   An eighteenth-century popular print

was published in facsimile in 1970.[5] These pictures could be
purchased cheaply and were to be found pinned up on the wall of
a cottage or an alehouse. An example is shown on p. 111,
and there is no reason to suppose that the Dicey prints were
very different. In the catalogue with which we are concerned,
those advertised covered a wide range of subjects, including 'The
ten commandments, with a fine Head of Moses' and 'A prospect
of Sheerness' (on one sheet of Elephant paper) at a wholesale
price of thirteen to the dozen, 4s. per dozen. Smaller sheets could
be had wholesale very much more cheaply, while the price
charged by the retailer would have varied with demand. Some of
the sheets were offered coloured, at twice the price of plain ones,
and these were undoubtedly used for decorative purposes.

There were drawing-books, elementary primers for use in
school and table games printed on sheets of paper known as
'copper royals'. One of these, 'The Game of Goose', for which
Dicey charged 2s. per quire, twenty-six to the quire, was offered
in an American bookseller's catalogue in 1965 for $350.00 – a very
rare survival. What are we to make of titles like 'The landlord
well paid by the handsome Tenant', or 'The intriguing wife and
the Sharping Gallant'? Altogether there are more than four
hundred prints or broadsides listed as 'copper royals' in the
catalogue. Then there are more than sixty county maps advertised, and various sheets of prints and views, some in colour,
covering a wide range – one series was 'Twelve Views of Chinese
Cities', suggesting a surprisingly outward-looking approach!

Four pages are devoted to chapbooks, described thus: 'A catalogue of histories. Printed in a neater manner, and with better
cuts, more truly adapted to each story than elsewhere.' The
wholesale cost of these was 2s. 6d. for 104. Many old ballads were
available at 8s. per ream, while more topical ballads were printed
on 'slips' and sold at 4s. per ream, although the catalogue does
not attempt to list these: 'There are near Three Thousand different Sorts of S L I P S: of which new Sorts coming out almost daily

5. *Catchpenny Prints* (Dover Publications, New York, 1970).

render it impossible to make a Complete Catalogue.' Finally, there is a selection of 'patters' (small books of 8, 12 or 16 pages which seem to have been similar to chapbooks), 32-page children's books and 8-page collections of ballads.

The range of the catalogue is considerable and covers, I imagine, all that was available to the common reader in the days before there were newspapers, magazines, sensational serial fiction and cheap editions of the classics.

The extent to which the Diceys and other printers thought it profitable, from quite early in the eighteenth century, to exploit the popular market, together with the fact that the century saw an immense growth in the establishment of printing offices in provincial towns, where ballad sheets and chapbooks were produced alongside the usual jobbing tasks, argues strongly that this market was an expanding one, and that at this level the spread of literacy was moving at a faster rate than is generally realized.[6] From the somewhat scanty autobiographical evidence which is available we are able to see this development taking place.

Not all of those few working men of the eighteenth century who wrote the stories of their lives were as categorical as William Hutton, who declared: 'I hated all books but those of pictures.' He outgrew his dislike and went on to become a successful bookseller in Birmingham. Others were rather more specific about the books they read in childhood. Thomas Holcroft, the playwright, born in 1745, speaks of reading chapbooks when he was young. So too does William Gifford, born in 1756, who was to become first editor of the *Quarterly Review*, and Samuel Bamford, Radical leader, whose visit to a bookshop full of ballads and chapbooks is described in his autobiography:

At the corner of Hanging Bridge, near the Old Church yard, was a book-shop kept by one Swindells, a printer. In the spacious windows of this shop, which is now 'The Wedding-Ring Coffee House', were exhibited numerous songs, ballads, tales and other publications, with

6. See the present writer's *Popular Education in Eighteenth Century England* (1971), *passim*.

horrid and awful-looking woodcuts at their head; which publications with their cuts had a strong command on my attention. Every farthing I could scrape together, was now spent in purchasing 'Histories of Jack the Giant Killer', 'Saint George and the Dragon', 'Tom Hickathrift', 'Jack and the Bean Stalk', 'History of the Seven Champions', tale of 'Fair Rosamond', 'History of Friar Bacon', 'Account of the Lancashire Witches', 'The Witches of the Woodlands', and such like romances.[7]

Thomas Carter, the asthmatic tailor whose autobiography, *Memoirs of a Working Man*, was published in 1845, talks of the little books he read as a child at the close of the eighteenth century: 'I had even then a taste for reading which was here gratified by my being permitted to read all the little stories which she kept on sale. They were, in truth, childish trifles; but I still think of them with pleasure because they were associated in my case with many pleasant recollections.' The reference here was to his visits to the shop of a sweetmeat-seller who was obviously generous in allowing him access to her other wares.

A story was told by Francis Douce – whose splendid chapbook collection is now in the Bodleian Library – about Sir Joseph Banks's sister, who was herself a collector of chapbooks. She went into a shop in Shoe Lane, selected a dozen penny books and paid one shilling for them. To her surprise she was given threepence change and told to take two more. The bookseller was under the impression that she was a trade customer, and was offering her the usual discount on penny histories, or chapbooks – thirteen or fourteen to the dozen for ninepence.

The poetry and autobiographical sketches of John Clare also provide references to the chapbooks which formed part of the background of those who had acquired a bare literacy. He describes a 'heap of pamphlets among which was the "History of Jane Shore", "The King and the Cobler"', and other chapbooks in a farmhouse.[8]

7. Samuel Bamford, *Early Days* (1840), p. 90.
8. E. Robinson and G. Summerfield (eds.), *Selected Poems and Prose of John Clare* (1967), p. 29.

A CHAPMAN.

From "The Cries and Habits of the City of London," by M. Lauron, 1709.

9. Penny histories – later known as chapbooks – would have formed an important part of the stock-in-trade of eighteenth-century pedlars like this one

The question of distribution, accounting for the fact that these books were to be found not only in the towns but also in farmhouses such as that mentioned by Clare, was an important one. The pedlar or hawker – otherwise known as the chapman – purchased his stocks at the kind of prices which have already been indicated and proceeded then to ply his wares in the streets, at fairs and public executions, in market places, taverns, coffee houses or wherever else people gathered in large numbers. But many of his kind spent their working lives much further afield, tramping up and down the country, visiting villages and remote farmhouses with a pack containing the small necessities which could otherwise have been obtained only with great difficulty by those living outside the towns. Chapbooks formed a valuable part of the chapman's stock-in-trade, and the importance of this wandering fraternity cannot be overstressed. They provided the essential link between the printer/publisher (the distinction between the two is difficult to maintain with regard to the fragile sheets and pamphlets of the eighteenth century) and his public.

There are few contemporary references to chapmen, but one anonymous seller left a scrap of autobiographical verse which was published in the *Weekly Register* on 9 January 1731. He goes to the printing office for his songs:

> Thence I receive them, and then sally
> Strait to some market place or alley,
> And sitting down judiciously
> Begin to sing. The people soon
> Gather about, to hear the tune.
> One stretches out his hand, and cries
> Come, let me have it, what's the price?
> But one poor halfpenny, says I,
> And sure you cannot that deny.
> Here, take it then says he, and throws
> The money. Then away he goes,
> Humming it as he walks along,
> Endeavouring to learn the song.

Not all the sellers were so law-abiding. An item in *Fog's Weekly Journal* of 22 July 1732 reports: 'an Irish ballad seller, who used to entertain the good people of England with a song, while his companions were picking their pockets, was taken up and committed to Bridewell.' Then there was 'light footed Phillis' who, according to the *Grub Street Journal* of 26 August 1731, daily visited the coffee houses round Temple Bar, commenting wittily upon the ballad sheets she offered for sale, to such good effect that she was able to sell where others failed.

This picture of those concerned in the distribution of popular literature of course makes it plain that the chapbook was not the only reading matter available. Both topical and non-topical ballads were always saleable. Usually the older ballads were issued in collections called garlands, while the topical ones were printed on single sheets, or 'slips'. Such political ballads were a feature of the ceremonies held around political bonfires, at election meetings and at political clubs.

To a great extent the political slip ballad was an urban phenomenon. The sheer topicality of its subject, together with the fact that London was essentially the seat of government and the centre of political controversy, indicates that this type of ballad would have been enjoyed by an urban audience in the capital. This is not to argue that there were not local issues in politics, nor that ballads on purely regional or town issues were not produced by printers in some of the larger provincial centres; but it was emphatically national politics which provided the subject-matter for the vast majority of slips which were published in London.

Ballads were much less a political instrument, however, than they had been in the preceding century: their place was increasingly being taken by the newspaper and the pamphlet. The former was a fairly new medium, but the latter had multiplied and been influential in the seventeenth century. By the beginning of the eighteenth this was already being commented upon: 'Les feuilles volantes ont plus d'efficace en Angleterre qu'en tout autre pays...,' wrote Leibnitz.[9] A Tory commentator remarked in 1792 that pamphlets were 'of late much made use of for propagating what is thought most material to instil into the mob'.[10] Misson, a Frenchman, observed that 'England is a country abounding in printed papers which they call pamphlets', and was shocked by their outspoken criticism of the Government.[11] Nearer home Ned Ward, shrewdest observer of street life in early eighteenth-century London, spoke of strolling there:

> Where Pamphlets lay in Shops and Stalls
> Pil'd up as thick as Stones in Paul's.[12]

Elsewhere he describes the sellers:

> Hawkers like Wild-geese flew along
> In Trains and cackl'd to the Throng;
> Stretch'd wide their Throats, and strained their Vitals,
> To tempt both Parties with their Titles.[13]

Political controversy spilled over onto the streets. Government and Opposition fought it out with the aid of ephemeral printed matter which was readily available. To a public accustomed to the ballad, those which dealt with political matters were just an extension of something which had been around in the streets almost from the time when printing began. In the *Craftsman* for 12 August 1727 there is a report that 'some persons were seized and carried before Lord Townshend for uttering scandalous and seditious ballads, one of which is said to be entitled *The Honest Voters, or Robin's Downfall*.'[14] On 29 May 1731 the same journal reports: 'On Wednesday two hawkers were seized by the two Willis's informers, for crying about a paper called *First Oars to*

9. Quoted in Lecky, *History of England in the Eighteenth Century* (Cabinet Edition), Vol. I, p. 76 (note).

10. Quoted in M. Percival, *Political Ballads Illustrating the Administration of Sir Robert Walpole* (Oxford, 1916), p. xii.

11. ibid., p. xii.

12. *Hudibras Redivivus* (1705), Part 1, Canto ii.

13. *Vulgus Britannicus* (1710), Part 4, Canto xi.

14. Percival, op. cit., p. 15.

Lambeth, etc. and were sent to Tothill Fields, Bridewell.'[15]
The sheets on which topical songs were printed strike the present-day reader as dull. Nothing is more dead than past controversy, and the issues about which eighteenth-century men and women felt so strongly can mean little to us now. In nearly every case the tune to which the words were sung was traditional, and it is clear from some verses that the ballads were written to be sung in chorus at political meetings, in taverns and mug-houses:

> My Westminster Friends,
> Now we've gained our Ends,
> Here's a Health and I'm sure 'twont repent ye;
> With Gratitude think,
> To the Health let us drink
> Of the glorious Two Hundred and Twenty.[16]

Another verse from a ballad entitled 'The True-Blue' also indicates this:

> I hope there's no Soul
> Met over this Bowl,
> But means honest Ends to pursue;
> With the Voice to the Heart,
> And let's never depart
> From the Faith of an honest True-Blue,
> From the Faith of an honest True-Blue.[17]

Political ballads like this were undoubtedly 'popular', but in rather a different sense from chapbooks and more traditional ballads. Songs which were sung at political meetings and hawked round the streets at election time would have appealed to a more broadly based audience – certainly not, given the fact that political sheets were for the most part an urban phenomenon, a larger one, but an audience which was drawn from wider sections of society.

15. ibid., p. 53.
16. ibid., p. xxxi.
17. ibid., p. 107.

The membership of political clubs in the eighteenth century would not have included the inarticulate and precariously literate public to whom chapbook literature made its appeal. Nevertheless, political ballads were of concern to this public when issues seized the popular fancy, and were not restricted to the fairly narrowly defined electorate – party feeling was not the prerogative of voters! In London the election of a Lord Mayor could, and often did, provoke strong emotions, as did the conflict between Court and City: 'The City in Glory or Downing-street in the dumps' exemplifies both issues.

'The strained political situation of 1739,' wrote Milton Percival,[18] 'brought on a struggle between Court and City which resulted in disturbances in two successive elections for Lord Mayor. The trouble began with the election of 1739. According to the customary principle of rotation, Sir George Champion would have been chosen to that office; but he had incurred unpopularity by voting, in his capacity as Member of Parliament, for Aylesbury . . .' With his candidacy opposed, a lively controversy ensued and formed the subject of newspaper articles, pamphlets and ballads.

In this case, of course, the interest would have been mainly confined to London. Similarly, the 'Admiral Hosier affair' would have centred upon the capital, although perhaps in this case interest might have flickered in Portsmouth and other naval towns. The admiral had died of fever in the West Indies in 1727 and, as a result of some controversial decisions which had preceded his death, his demise sparked off angry discussion. A ballad, 'Admiral Hosier's Ghost', was essentially a party song. Its tune, 'Come and listen to my Ditty', was popular – as Horace Walpole wrote: 'The Patriots cry it up, and the courtiers cry it down, and the hawkers cry it up and down.'[19]

Chapbooks could not boast sensational successes like this: there was no seven-days wonder about their traditional material,

18. op. cit., p. 148.
19. ibid., p. 144.

which had often been part of an oral heritage over several centuries, finally becoming petrified in print. Yet, in the long run, bearing in mind the evidence both of those who spoke and wrote at the time about chapbooks and of the expansion in those sections of the printing trade which specialized in this type of popular literature, I believe such publications to have been more important in the formation of the mass reading public than anything else that was available to the poor in the eighteenth century. A study of the printing trade does seem to provide strong corroboration of the claim that a 'mass reading public' was coming into being during this period. Those members of the trade who chose to produce popular literature in its various forms on a large scale were, after all, hard-headed businessmen who must have seen that there was a considerable profit to be made from an expanding market. To say this is in no way to denigrate their achievement; clearly they saw a need in society, and fulfilled it.

However, just as traditional tales and medieval romances had begun during the previous century to lose their appeal for the upper levels of the social spectrum, so now the widening mass reading public tended to grow a little more sophisticated. By the end of the eighteenth century the mass market for chapbooks showed some signs of decline. Their unsophisticated contents had laid hold upon the popular imagination for a long time; they provided the means by which unlettered members of a pre-industrial society could move into an urban industrial society increasingly dominated by print. The tales, jests and lore of a rural past became of less interest to those who found themselves willy-nilly members of the working class rather than just 'the poor' or 'the meaner sort'.

It is true that chapbooks did linger long into the nineteenth century as reading matter for children, although they were then better produced and often somewhat smaller in size;[20] but, this function apart, they had perhaps served their purpose in providing readily available material upon which the dawning ability to read could be exercised. Once literacy amongst the poor was a

20. See the present writer's *The Penny Histories* (1968), *passim*.

fact it was to prove a force whose potency could not have been foreseen by the pious eighteenth-century reformers who had speeded its growth in the belief – mistaken as it turned out – that this bare literacy would encourage men and women to accept uncomplainingly their established place in the social order. Society was to be very seriously upset by the fact that once the unlettered had learned to read they could turn readily to political and free-thinking publications.

It was, of course, the Industrial Revolution – however we define it – which had changed beyond recognition the public which for so long had been content with chapbook tales and simple ballads. In the crowded, rapidly growing towns of the industrial north there existed an entirely new public, different indeed from the rustic villagers who had awaited the arrival of the chapman or pedlar with his gossip, his wares and his bundle of books priced at no more than one penny each. Moreover, since industrialism was gathering momentum and spreading over large regions, many village communities were no longer so isolated. Perhaps the most radical effect of this change in the structure and feeling of society is that to which I have already referred – the creation of a working class. Inevitably social unrest accompanied the changes, and the failure of crops which led to a food crisis and the mass unemployment caused by the cessation of the French wars aggravated the transition. Small wonder, then, that the factory operative who could read might turn more eagerly to a paper-covered copy of Thomas Paine's *Rights of Man* than to a tract which counselled acceptance of an existence which was all too often bleak and defined by poverty and deprivation.

The choice between the two kinds of literature was not, however, entirely clear-cut. Although the chapbook in its eighteenth-century form was dead, the tradition did in fact cling on vigorously in the street ballad of the nineteenth century. To some extent I have anticipated the early years of that century, and it is to the residual chapbook tradition, which can be termed 'street literature', that we now turn.

FOUR

1800–1897

Three yards a penny!

Cry of the long song seller.

At the present time books are plentiful, and books are cheap. Formerly books were written for the privileged few; now they are printed for the million. Books of every description, and at almost any price, are to be met with. All tastes are catered for; all opinions find their peculiar expository organ.

Everything for a penny. Penny Pulpit – Penny Magazine – Penny Shakespeare – Penny Novelist – Penny Medical Adviser – Penny Educator – Penny Cyclopaedia.

John Parker, Meliora (second series, 1853)

Sandwiches, oranges, and penny novelettes are the three great requisites for English travelling – for third class travelling, at least . . .

Agnes Repplier, Points of View (1895)

STREET BALLADS[1]

BALLAD literature maintained a vigorous life in nineteenth-century streets. Printed in 'broadside' form, on one side only of flimsy paper, with no consistency as to size, these sheets were essentially simple to produce. Sometimes they carried woodcut illustrations which, with the *ad hoc* typography used, gave many of them a lively, if somewhat crude, visual appeal. The cries of the sellers – 'Three yards a penny!' or 'Two under fifty for a fardy!' – as the sheets were hawked around the streets and in public houses were one kind of sales promotion; there were other sellers

1. This section contains the substance of the present author's article 'The Literature of the Streets', first published in *The Victorian City*, ed. H. J. Dyos and Michael Wolff (1973), Vol. I.

10.   A Victorian ballad-seller

who sang the words of the ballads they offered; and there were the 'pinners up' who attached samples of their wares to a convenient wall or hoarding, or who exhibited their stock by affixing it to a pole.

Henry Mayhew moved amongst this fraternity, and what little we know of them is due to his investigations.[2] 'Do I yarn a pound a week?' asked one street-seller of ballads rhetorically, in response to Mayhew's query. 'Lor' bless you no. Nor 15s., nor 12s. I don't yarn one week with another, not 10s. sometimes not 5s. . . I am at my stall at nine in the morning, and sometimes I have walked five or six miles to buy my "pubs" before that. I stop till ten at night oft enough. The wet days is the ruin of us; and I think wet days increases.' This man sold his sheets at a halfpenny a time, a penny if he could get it; and this seems to have been the usual price, although it must be said that the economics of the street trade are obscure. Depending upon the quality of the paper, songs

2. *London Labour and the London Poor* (4 vols., 1861–2), I, pp. 213–51, 272–85.

were bought usually at twopence or even twopence-halfpenny a dozen. Manifestly weather was a crucial factor – on summer days trade was likely to be a great deal brisker than in winter, and clearly the seller of street literature depended upon the kindness of the weather for his livelihood quite as much as the medieval peasant had done centuries earlier.

From Mayhew's pages we can learn something at least of the life of these itinerant vendors. It was precarious and, except upon the few occasions when a sensational murder took the public fancy, little money was to be made out of it. There are one or two other books which suggest the shifting, insecure background of wandering sellers and showmen, and there are autobiographies from at least two of them;[3] but in general our picture remains uncertain.

When, however, we come to ask what the nature of the stock-in-trade of the street-sellers was, we are upon very much firmer ground, for much of it has survived. In the British Museum there are the Baring-Gould and the Crampton collections, and in a number of the larger provincial libraries locally printed sheets are preserved. Not only, indeed, is there no shortage of original material, but also the rambling, untidy books – compilations, perhaps, is a better word – by Charles Hindley offer examples of street literature which but for him would have disappeared.[4] Nevertheless, this mention of the debt we owe to Charles Hindley does highlight the fact that there has been no real attempt to classify or quantify the output of broadsides. The two collections in the British Museum offer no classification, presenting only selections of these sheets mounted in guard books; and it must be borne in mind that, because of the very nature of this literature,

3. Charles Hindley (ed.), *The Life and Adventures of a Cheap Jack* (1881); 'Lord' George Sanger, *Seventy Years a Showman* (1910); *The Life, Adventures and Experiences of David Love, Written by Himself* (third edition, 1823); William Cameron, *Hawkie: The Autobiography of a Gangrel*, ed. John Strathesk (1888).

4. C. Hindley, *The Catnach Press* (1869); (as ed.), *Curiosities of Street Literature* (1871); *The Life and Times of James Catnach, Late of Seven Dials, Ballad Monger* (1878); *The History of the Catnach Press* (1886).

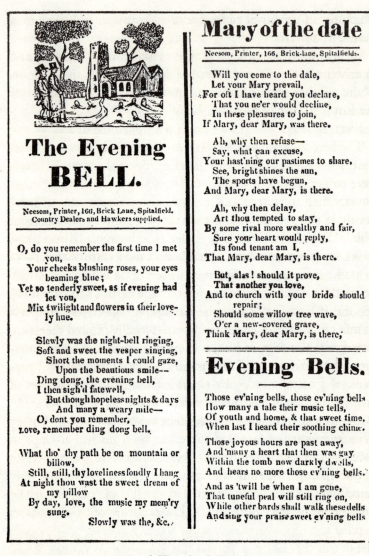

11. A Victorian ballad sheet

its survival poses an immediate problem. It may be that the most popular of its items were those most readily available for preservation; or is it in fact more likely that the less popular items, of which copies remained unread and undiscarded, had the better chance of survival?

In any event, the material which we have is certainly sufficient to enable us to make some generalizations about street ballads. There were four broad categories: street drolleries; ballads about the Royal Family or politics; 'ballads on a subject'; and ballads concerning crime.

The first of these, which could be in verse or in prose, covered general themes and included 'cocks' or 'catchpennies', which were in fact fictitious narratives offered to a gullible public as though they were true and topical. The sales patter, shouted noisily in the streets, would make much of such words as 'Horrible', 'Dreadful', 'Murder', 'Love', 'Seduction', 'Blood', and so on. Imaginary murders, usually with a lurid love interest, seem to have been the most popular, and could by a practised patterer be made to sound extremely plausible. A broadside entitled 'Shocking Rape and Murder of Two Lovers' was typical of these. It was an account in both prose and verse, embellished with a horrifying woodcut, of how one John Hodges, a farmer's son, raped Jane Williams and afterwards murdered her and her lover, William Edwards, in a field near Paxton. 'This,' declares the anonymous author, 'is a most revolting murder. It appears Jane Williams was keeping company, and was shortly to be married to William Edwards, who was in the employment of Farmer Hodges.' John, his son, made approaches to the young lady, 'who although of poor parents was strictly virtuous'. After the rape, Edwards came upon Hodges, who immediately turned on him with a bill-hook, which he afterwards used to kill the girl. He was then apprehended and 'committed to take his trial at the next Assizes'. The last two of the 'Copy of Verses' which follows the prose account run thus:

> Now in one grave they both do lie,
> These lovers firm and true,
> Who by a cruel man were slain,
> Who'll soon receive his due.

In prison now he is confined,
To answer for the crime.
Two lovers that he murdered,
Cut off when in their prime.

This 'cock' or 'catchpenny' is entirely representative of its type of street literature. There was another large, and rather more attractive, sub-class of 'street drolleries' proper, from which it is much more difficult to select typical examples. Titles such as 'The Full Particulars of "Taking Off" Prince Albert's Inexpressibles', 'The Perpetual Almanack', 'How to Cook a Wife', 'The Dunmow Flitch' and 'Secrets, for Ladies During Courtship' are found, and some of these are illustrated with woodcuts not necessarily relevant to the text – the producers of street literature appeared to use woodblocks with inconsequential abandon! 'How to Cook a Wife', for example, has a dramatic woodcut showing a soldier with a knife, menacingly approaching two distressed females – one swooning – in a sylvan glade.

One of the most interesting titles is: 'Railroad to Hell, from dissipation to poverty, and from poverty to desperation. This line begins in the brewery, and runs through all public-houses, dram-shops, and jerry-shops, in a zigzag direction, until it lands in the Kingdom of Hell.' Although undated, the imprint 'T. Such, Union street, Boro'' suggests that this broadside was issued, almost certainly not for the first time, in the 1870s. Such was a commercial printer who carried a large stock of sheets, and the fact that he thought it worth-while to exploit a temperance theme throws an interesting light upon the saleability of street ballads which took a strong line over the demon drink. Not many did, but the subject was not entirely unusual. More immediately striking, perhaps, is the railway imagery which is used in these leaden-footed verses:

Such Taverns as these are Railroads to Hell,
Their barrels are engines which make men rebel;
Their jugs and their glasses which furnish their Trains,
Will empty their pockets and muddle their brains.

And thus drunkards ride to Hell in their pride,
With nothing but steam from the barrels inside.

A companion piece from the same printer is: 'The Railway to
Heaven. This line runs from Calvary through this vain world and
the Valley of the Shadow of Death, until it lands in the Kingdom
of Heaven.'

> The Railway mania does extend,
> From John o' Groats to the Land's End;
> Where'er you ride, where'er you walk
> The Railway is the general talk.
>
> Allow me, as an old divine,
> To point to you another line,
> Which does from earth to heaven extend,
> Where real pleasures never end.
>
> Of truth Divine the rails are made,
> And on the Rock of Ages laid;
> The rails are fixed in chains of love,
> Firm as the throne of God above.

The final couplet, too, is worth quoting:

> 'My son', says God, 'give me thy heart,
> Make haste, or else the train will start.'

This railway symbolism had its origins in what Americans
knew as the 'Great Awakening' – a shrill evangelical revival which
found expression in the camp meetings held mostly in upper New
York State during the 1830s. The evangelists later brought their
message to England, where 'The Railway to Heaven' became
popular at revival meetings in the North. In fact, Americans
absorbed machinery into the imagery of their popular literature
much more rapidly than did the English.

The tone in these ballads is broadly evangelical, and mention is
made – always with approval – of the Church of England, the
Quakers, the Baptists, the Independents and the Methodists 'both
old and new'. Such an approach to religious matters is characteris-

tic of street literature, which rarely if ever reflects the religious conflicts of the nineteenth century, and a simple explanation of this is the desire to achieve the widest possible sales. The fact that religion formed the subject matter of broadsides at all appears interesting, for recent research has indicated that the working classes had little or no interest in formal religious practices. Why then should commercial printers have concerned themselves with the subject? The answer is probably that such sheets in most cases had a seasonal sale. A number of Christmas ballad sheets have survived, and it is possible that at this time of the year, and perhaps at Easter, ballads could be sold which appealed to a residual religious emotion which had nothing to do with church-going.

Many street ballads took as their subject the Royal Family, while others had political themes. The former often exhibited an adulatory, unsophisticated attitude to royalty such as we find in much journalism today. Fairly typical of this group is 'A New Song on the Birth of the Prince of Wales', with its chorus:

> So let us be contented and sing with mirth and joy
> Some things must be got ready for the pretty little boy.

Should a measure of criticism be found, it would fall far short of anything approaching full-blooded republicanism.

Political ballads are in every way more interesting, and the striking feature of most of them is their moderation. There is seldom a strident note, and little rabble-rousing. 'The temper of the ballads on such questions as strikes and lock-outs,' wrote a contemporary, 'has struck us as singularly fair and moderate . . . In the middle of the bitter struggle of the last three years in the building trades, we find nothing really violent or objectionable.' A verse, quoted in the *National Review* of October 1861 from 'The Glorious Strike of the Builders' catches the mood of many political broadsides:

> They locked us out without a cause –
> Our rights was our desires, –

> We'll work for Trollope, Peto, Lucas,
> For all the world, and Myers.
>
> If we can only have our rights,
> We will go to work much stronger:
> Nine hours a day, that's what we say,
> And not a moment longer.

Strikes apart, there were other issues which provided material for the political broadside. Reform was one, political personalities another. Then there were political litanies of various kinds, similar in form to those for which William Hone had been tried in 1817. Crimean ballads, too, fall into this category.

The political tone of street literature, then, was muted. 'The Great Battle for Freedom and Reform' is clearly reformist, but by no stretch of imagination extremist:

> With Gladstone, Russell, Beales and Bright
> We shall weather through the storm,
> To give the working man his rights,
> And gain the Bill – Reform.
>
> We want no Tory government
> The poor man to oppress,
> They never try to do you good,
> The truth you will confess.
>
> The liberals are the poor man's friend,
> To forward all they try,
> They'll beat their foes you may depend,
> And never will say, die.

A sense of bitterness with one's lot – and this is very different from revolutionary fervour – is to be found in those ballads which deal with wages and the cost of living. 'Fifteen Shillings a Week' provides a complete budget for a working man who was in receipt of this wage. Husband, wife and seven children! Rent cost one shilling and ninepence, tobacco eightpence, tea eightpence, fuel one shilling and tenpence halfpenny. Clothes were bought second-hand – a jacket for sixpence, threepence for socks. This

particular ballad is of considerable interest, purporting as it does
to outline working-class expenditure in the 1870s (a date which
can be inferred from Such's imprint, although earlier versions
may exist).

Similarly, 'How Five and Twenty Shillings Were Expended in
a Week' gives in detail the weekly spending of a tradesman and
his wife. This sheet is probably earlier than 1870. In this case no
children are mentioned. Rent costs three shillings and twopence,
meat four shillings, tobacco sixpence, and so on. The incidental
comments illuminate the picture:

> Last Monday night you got so drunk, amongst your dirty crew,
> It cost twopence next morning for a basin of hot stew.

Breakages:

> There's a penny goes for this thing, and twopence that and t'other,
> Last week you broke a water jug, and I had to buy another.

Hygiene:

> A three farthing rushlight every night, to catch the bugs and fleas.

So far, then, as the cost of living is a political issue, these ballads
were in essence political. More obviously so was 'Dizzy's
Lament':

> O dear! Oh dear! What shall I do
> They call me Saucy Ben the Jew
> The leader of the Tory crew
> > Poor old Benjamin Dizzy.
> I'd a great big house in Buckinghamshire
> My wages was Five Thousand a Year;
> But now they have turned me out of place,
> With a ticket for soup, in great disgrace.
> I had a challenge last Monday night
> Billy Gladstone wanted me to fight;
> The challenge was brought by Jackey Bright
> To poor old Benjamin Dizzy.

Disraeli, Gladstone, Bright – clearly these were names which entered the consciousness of the humblest reader. It would of course be possible to offer further extracts from ballads of this kind. Almost always they were anti-Tory, but their keynote was reform rather than revolution. Ernest Jones's 'The Song of the Lower Classes' was circulated as a broadside round about 1848, and was later reprinted – once, together with an English translation of 'The Marseillaise', as a Socialist League broadside. There were titles like 'The Chartists Are Coming' and a number of Corn Law ballads were produced; but certainly in all the street ballads I have examined it remains true that anything more than a fairly mild reformism, and occasional support for Chartism, is entirely absent.

Those pieces which fall under the heading of 'ballads on a subject' show the kind of themes which could take the fancy of the public, and illustrate too the ingenuity of the unknown hack writers who produced these effusions. Here we find them seizing upon every event which the contemporary scene provided. As we might expect, the Tichbourne claimant, 'Bloomers', 'Wonderful Mr Spurgeon', the Volunteer forces and the opening of Holborn Viaduct were all celebrated in street literature, and a splendid opportunity for this kind of enterprise was provided by the death of the Duke of Wellington. As victor of Waterloo he had been a popular hero: as a Conservative prime minister this was clearly not the case. His death on 14 September 1852 was followed by a lying-in-state at Chelsea Hospital from 10 to 17 November, and he was buried at St Paul's on 18 November. The demise of a man so widely known, and the splendour of his funeral, presented street printers with an occasion when unusually large sales could be counted on. Wellington is presented only as a popular hero, with no mention of his political activities.

DEATH OF WELLINGTON

On the 14th of September, near to the town of Deal,
As you may well remember, who have a heart to feel,

Died Wellington, a general bold, of glorious renown,
Who beat the great Napoleon, near unto Brussels town.

Chorus

So don't forget brave Wellington, who won at Waterloo,
He beat the great Napoleon, and all his generals, too.

He led the British Army on through Portugal and Spain,
And every battle there he won, the Frenchman to restrain,
He ever was victorious in every battle field,
He gained a fame most glorious because he'd never yield.

He drove Napoleon from home, in exile for to dwell,
Far o'er the sea, and from his home, and all he lov'd so well,
He stripped him quite of all his power, and banish'd him away,
To St Helena's rocks and towers, the rest of his life to stay.

Then on the throne of France he placed Louis, the King, by right,
In after years he was displaced all by the people's might;
But should the young Napoleon threaten our land and laws,
We'll find another Wellington should ever we have cause.

He's dead, our hero's gone to rest, and o'er his corpse we'll mourn,
With sadness and with grief oppress'd, for he will not return,
But we his deeds will not forget, and should we, e'er again,
Follow th' example that he set, his glory, we'll not stain.[5]

The language is simple, and the emphasis is upon Wellington's martial glory. It requires no great leap of the imagination to picture this sheet selling in its thousands to the crowds who watched the funeral procession or who filed past the catafalque. Not all its purchasers would have been working-class readers, but in both style and form it is a typical product of street literature. One of the surviving copies of this ballad, together with a similar one entitled 'Lamentation on the Death of Wellington', was printed by John Harkness of Preston, Lancashire, and this illustrates the way in which topical themes, usually originating in the metropolis, were pirated immediately by provincial printers. The converse is less true, and examples of ballads on anything like national themes

5. Quoted in John Ashton, *Modern Street Ballads* (1888), pp. 311–12.

originating in provincial towns and being subsequently printed in London are virtually non-existent.

Another ballad for which there would have been a ready public deals with the Great Exhibition of 1851, and is called 'Crystal Palace'.[6]

CRYSTAL PALACE

Britannia's sons an attentive ear
One moment lend to me,
Whether tillers of our fruitful soil,
Or lords of high degree.
Mechanic too, and artizan,
Old England's pride and boast,
Whose wondrous skill has spread around,
Far, far from Britain's coast.

Chorus

For the World's great Exhibition,
Let's shout with loud huzza,
All nations never can forget,
The glorious first of May.

From every quarter of the Globe,
They come across the sea,
And to the Chrystal Palace
The wonders for to see;
Raised by the handiwork of men
Born on British ground,
A challenge to the Universe
It's equal to be found.

Each friendly nation in the world,
Have their assistance lent,
And to this Exhibition
Have their productions sent.
And with honest zeal and ardour,
With pleasure do repair,
With hands outstretch'd, and gait erect,
To the World's Great National Fair.

6. ibid., pp. 284ff.

The Sons of England and France
And America likewise,
With other nations to contend,
To bear away the prize.
With pride depicted in their eyes,
View the offspring of their hand,
O, surely England's greatest wealth,
Is an honest working man.

It is a glorious sight to see
So many thousands meet,
Not heeding creed or country,
Each other friendly greet.
Like children of one mighty sire,
May that sacred tie ne'er cease,
May the blood stain'd sword of War give way
To the Olive branch of Peace.

But hark! the trumpets flourish,
Victoria does approach,
That she may long be spared to us
Shall be our reigning toast.
I trust each heart, it will respond,
To what I now propose –
Good will and plenty to her friends,
And confusion to her foes.

Great praise is due to Albert,
For the good that he has done,
May others follow in his steps
The work he has begun;
Then let us all, with one accord,
His name give with three cheers,
Shout huzza for the Chrystal Palace,
And the World's great National Fair!!

The tone here is unmistakably one of triumph and self-congratulation. Chauvinism and fervour for the Royal Family are the keynotes. This fact in itself is hardly remarkable, and the lines

'O surely England's greatest wealth/Is an honest working man' are entirely consistent with the tone of the ballad. There is, however, some evidence to suggest that working men did not necessarily see the matter in this light. In 1851 G. J. Holyoake produced a pamphlet entitled 'The Workmen and the International Exhibition'. Its aim was to show the conditions in which many working men lived and the misery which existed in workshops and houses where many of the striking exhibits had been prepared. The cost in human terms was thus stressed by Holyoake. The pamphlet, however, was not in any sense street literature, and the comparison does seem to show that the tendency of the latter was to romanticize reality – to offer a kind of cultural jingoism – in order to achieve as wide a sale as possible.

Street ballads such as the two quoted above include verse which is often slipshod and exhibit a superficiality which provides heroes whose less attractive qualities are conveniently ignored. There is little evidence in the sheets of anything more than a vaguely sketched class-consciousness – class and economic antagonisms are, indeed, played down.

We come now to the most popular group of ballads – those concerned with crime. Sheets relating the execution of a criminal were the most numerous of all and were bought with 'singular eagerness'. Almost all of them were illustrated, and it was usual to see the criminal or criminals dangling from the gallows, with an account of the execution in prose followed by a 'copy of verses' often alleged to have been written by the condemned felon in his cell on the eve of execution.

Occasionally such a broadsheet was memorable. The 'Confession of the Murderess', which was published on a sheet entitled 'The Esher Tragedy. Six children murdered by their mother', has a quality of horror which is both credible and moving:

On Friday last I was bad all day; I wanted to see Mr Izod, and waited all day. I wanted him to give me some medicine. In the evening I walked about, and afterwards put the children to bed, and wanted to go to sleep in a chair. – About nine o'clock, Georgy (meaning Georgi-

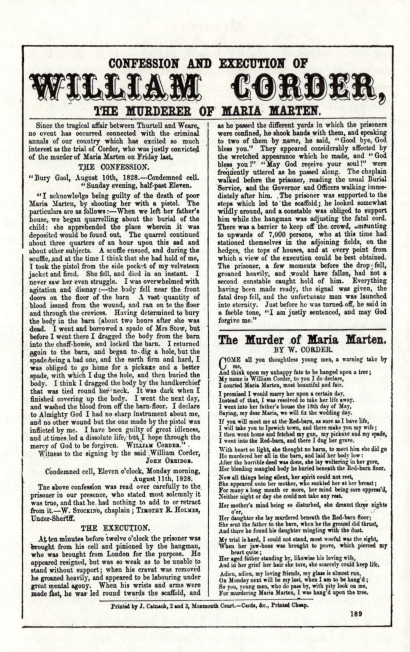

CONFESSION AND EXECUTION OF
WILLIAM CORDER,
THE MURDERER OF MARIA MARTEN.

Since the tragical affair between Thurtell and Weare, no event has occurred connected with the criminal annals of our country which has excited so much interest as the trial of Corder, who was justly convicted of the murder of Maria Marten on Friday last.

THE CONFESSION.

"Bury Gaol, August 10th, 1828.—Condemned cell.
"Sunday evening, half-past Eleven.

"I acknowledge being guilty of the death of poor Maria Marten, by shooting her with a pistol. The particulars are as follows:—When we left her father's house, we began quarrelling about the burial of the child: she apprehended the place wherein it was deposited would be found out. The quarrel continued about three quarters of an hour upon this sad and about other subjects. A scuffle ensued, and during the scuffle, and at the time I think that she had hold of me, I took the pistol from the side pocket of my velveteen jacket and fired. She fell, and died in an instant. I never saw her even struggle. I was overwhelmed with agitation and dismay:—the body fell near the front doors on the floor of the barn A vast quantity of blood issued from the wound, and ran on to the floor and through the crevices. Having determined to bury the body in the barn (about two hours after she was dead. I went and borrowed a spade of Mrs Stow, but before I went there I dragged the body from the barn into the chaff-house, and locked the barn. I returned again to the barn, and began to dig a hole, but the spade being a bad one, and the earth firm and hard, I was obliged to go home for a pickaxe and a better spade, with which I dug the hole, and then buried the body. I think I dragged the body by the handkerchief that was tied round her neck. It was dark when I finished covering up the body. I went the next day, and washed the blood from off the barn-floor. I declare to Almighty God I had no sharp instrument about me, and no other wound but the one made by the pistol was inflicted by me. I have been guilty of great idleness, and at times led a dissolute life, but I hope through the mercy of God to be forgiven. WILLIAM CORDER."

Witness to the signing by the said William Corder, JOHN ORRIDGE.

Condemned cell, Eleven o'clock, Monday morning, August 11th, 1828.

The above confession was read over carefully to the prisoner in our presence, who stated most solemnly it was true, and that he had nothing to add to or retract from it.—W. STOCKING, chaplain; TIMOTHY R. HOLMES, Under-Sheriff.

THE EXECUTION.

At ten minutes before twelve o'clock the prisoner was brought from his cell and pinioned by the hangman, who was brought from London for the purpose. He appeared resigned, but was so weak as to be unable to stand without support; when his cravat was removed he groaned heavily, and appeared to be labouring under great mental agony. When his wrists and arms were made fast, he was led round twards the scaffold, and as he passed the different yards in which the prisoners were confined, he shook hands with them, and speaking to two of them by name, he said, "Good bye, God bless you." They appeared considerably affected by the wretched appearance which he made, and "God bless you!" "May God receive your soul!" were frequently uttered as he passed along. The chaplain walked before the prisoner, reading the usual Burial Service, and the Governor and Officers walking immediately after him. The prisoner was supported to the steps which led to the scaffold; he looked somewhat wildly around, and a constable was obliged to support him while the hangman was adjusting the fatal cord. There was a barrier to keep off the crowd, amounting to upwards of 7,000 persons, who at this time had stationed themselves in the adjoining fields, on the hedges, the tops of houses, and at every point from which a view of the execution could be best obtained. The prisoner, a few moments before the drop fell, groaned heavily, and would have fallen, had not a second constable caught hold of him. Everything having been made ready, the signal was given, the fatal drop fell, and the unfortunate man was launched into eternity. Just before he was turned off, he said in a feeble tone, "I am justly sentenced, and may God forgive me."

The Murder of Maria Marten.
BY W. CORDER.

COME all you thoughtless young men, a warning take by me,
And think upon my unhappy fate to be hanged upon a tree;
My name is William Corder, to you I do declare,
I courted Maria Marten, most beautiful and fair.

I promised I would marry her upon a certain day,
Instead of that, I was resolved to take her life away.
I went into her father's house the 18th day of May,
Saying, my dear Maria, we will fix the wedding day.

If you will meet me at the Red-barn, as sure as I have life,
I will take you to Ipswich town, and there make you my wife;
I then went home and fetched my gun, my pickaxe and my spade,
I went into the Red-barn, and there I dug her grave.

With heart so light, she thought no harm, to meet him she did go
He murdered her all in the barn, and laid her body low:
After the horrible deed was done, she lay weltering in her gore,
Her bleeding mangled body he buried beneath the Red-barn floor.

Now all things being silent, her spirit could not rest,
She appeared unto her mother, who suckled her at her breast;
For many a long month or more, her mind being sore oppress'd,
Neither night or day she could not take any rest.

Her mother's mind being so disturbed, she dreamt three nights o'er,
Her daughter she lay murdered beneath the Red-barn floor;
She sent the father to the barn, when he the ground did thrust,
And there he found his daughter mingling with the dust.

My trial is hard, I could not stand, most woeful was the sight,
When her jaw-bone was brought to prove, which pierced my heart quite;
Her aged father standing by, likewise his loving wife,
And in her grief her hair she tore, she scarcely could keep life.

Adieu, adieu, my loving friends, my glass is almost run,
On Monday next will be my last, when I am to be hang'd;
So you, young men, who do pass by, with pity look on me,
For murdering Maria Marten, I was hang'd upon the tree.

Printed by J. Catnach, 2 and 3, Monmouth Court.—Cards, &c., Printed Cheap.

189

12. Murder in the Red Barn – a Catnach sheet that sold over one and a half million copies

anna) kept calling me to bed. I came up to bed, and they kept calling me to bring them some barley water, and they kept calling me till nearly 12 o'clock. I had one candle lit on the chair – I went and got another, but could not see, there was something like a cloud, and I thought I would go down and get a knife and cut my throat, but could not see. I groped about in master's room for a razor. I went up to Georgy, and cut her first; I did not look at her. I then came to Carry, and cut her. Then to Harry – he said 'don't mother'. I said, 'I must' and did cut him. Then I went to Bill. He was fast asleep. I turned him over. He never woke, and I served him the same. I nearly tumbled into this room. The two children here, Harriet and George, were awake. They made no resistance at all. I then lay down myself.

This statement was signed by the miserable woman.

Few other broadsides rival this in style. The mounting tension and understatement give one the sense of being present at a nightmare. For the most part these murder sheets possess for us all the dullness of sensational news that has passed into obscurity. The prose and verse are largely stereotyped, while the illustrations are scarcely credible. This, however, is what the nineteenth-century public wanted, as the continuing popularity of broadsides dealing with crime bears out. As a street-seller said to Henry Mayhew, 'There's nothing beats a stunning good murder after all.'

The producers of street literature were printers in London and in the larger provincial towns and cities.[7] The Worrall family in Liverpool, Bebbington in Manchester and Harkness in Preston were amongst the leading provincial printers in this field, and the list could be considerably extended. A great deal of plagiarism went on – successful items were shamelessly copied – and local themes were of course exploited by local printers. Production of street ballads could be readily and easily undertaken by any printer when there was material about to catch the public fancy, and it was easy to combine this kind of work with the usual jobbing

7. V. E. Neuburg, *Chapbook Bibliography* (second edition, 1972), pp. 55–64; this lists, with dates, a number of provincial printers.

tasks – labels, notices, letterheads, catalogues, and so on – which formed the greater part of his work.[8]

The most noted specialist in producing street literature was James Catnach,[9] who supplied many hawkers in London and elsewhere with the wares which they cried in the street, sold at fairs and races or offered for sale by 'pinning up'. His business was founded in London in the second decade of the nineteenth century and was flourishing in the hands of his successors for well over fifty years. Catnach himself died in 1841 and was buried in Highgate Cemetery, having made a great deal of money out of street literature – and also out of publishing cheap books for children. It is said that his sheets were sold to their sellers for coppers, his employees were paid in pennies and halfpennies, and he would hire a hackney coach each week to convey the coins to the Bank of England. Even so, he was the recipient of many bad pence, and legend has it that these were embedded in plaster of Paris in the kitchen behind his printing office. Catnach was the doyen of street printers and a specialist in this kind of publication, besides being sufficiently astute a businessman to pick up job lots of printers' old stock, including blocks a century and more old which he used to excellent effect.

It is almost entirely due to the industry of Charles Hindley, Catnach's biographer, that we know something of the life and work of this printer. Catnach's neighbour and rival printer, John Pitts, has been the subject of a book in which, rescued from the limbo of the nineteenth-century periodical press, there is a vivid account of Pitts's manager, Bat Corcoran, selling ballad sheets to hawkers and others:[10]

8. For a valuable account of such a local printer see C. R. Cheney *et al.*, *John Cheney and His Descendants, Printers in Banbury since 1767* (1936).

9. Little or no recent research has been done upon Catnach. Various magazine articles have appeared, and in 1955 the Book Club of California published in a limited edition *Catnachery*, by P. H. Muir.

10. Leslie Shepard, *John Pitts: Ballad Printer of Seven Dials, London, 1765–1844* (Private Libraries Association, 1969), p. 71.

But let us see Bat amidst his customers – see him riding the whirl-wind – let us take him in the shock, the crisis of the night when he is despatching the claims of a series of applicants. 'I say, Blind Maggie, you're down for a dozen "Jolly Waterman", thirteen to the dozen. – Pay up your score, Tom with the wooden leg. I see you are booked for a lot of "Arethusas". – Master Flowers, do you think that "Cans of Grog" can be got for nothing, that you leave a stiff account behind you. – Sally Sallop, you must either give back "The Gentle-men of England" or tip for them at once. – Friday my man, there are ever so many "Black-eyed Susans" against you. – Jimmy, get rid of the "Tars of Old England" if you can; I think "Crazy Janes" are more in vogue. What say you to an exchange for "Hosier's Ghost"?'

Although this account dates from 1825, the method of selling ballads wholesale cannot have changed significantly throughout the century. It is, moreover, the only description of this aspect of the trade which appears to have been written, or at any rate to have survived.

Little was said anywhere about the writers of street literature. Who were they? Unknown hacks in the truest sense. Henry May-hew tracked one of them down; so too did Charles Hindley in 1870. This was John Morgan, who had worked for Catnach and recalled rather bitterly how difficult it had been to secure adequate payment from him. The printer, of course, was in a difficult position, for if a ballad sheet was successful it was immediately pirated, and much of the profit was dissipated. How then could he afford to pay more than one shilling, or more rarely half a crown, for a work which would cease to be his as soon as it was published? A persistent legend has it that Catnach was himself the author of many of his broadsheets, and this may have been true. What is more certain is that of the approximate sum of £12,000 which Henry Mayhew estimated was spent upon broadside ballads and the like in the late 1840s and early 1850s only a very tiny part could have found its way into the pockets of the unknown authors of many of them.

The ballad trade, then, consisted of the authors who sought

their recompense, however trifling, for a product which was short-lived in the extreme; the sellers who felt a pressing commercial need to reach as wide a public as possible in order to earn a meagre living; and the printers, who were the only ones who did reasonably well out of it – and even then Catnach's success was unusual and due partly to the fact that he exploited other markets with skill. In such circumstances it seems scarcely likely – and indeed there is no evidence to suggest it – that anyone concerned in this trade set himself the task of forming attitudes in society. Rather, they seized upon events and followed them up in the way which, we can assume, reflected best the developing tastes of their working-class readers.

Street literature is, therefore, worth a closer scrutiny than it has yet received. A contemporary said of these ballads: 'they are almost all written by persons of the class to whom they are addressed.'[11] He urged that they were worthy of study because they provided 'one of those windows through which we may get a glimpse of that very large body of our fellow-citizens of whom we know so little'. This was the literature of the urban working class, and with all its defects it provides one of the few insights we have into their popular culture. Occasionally there are ballads which look back to a rural past, but these are few. In its format, even in its size, the Victorian street ballad perhaps bears a resemblance to the tabloid newspaper which in many ways – concern with sex, crime, royalty – it somewhat crudely anticipated. Only organized sport for a mass audience is missing.

This sense of looking forward to the tabloid newspaper of the twentieth century is further strengthened when the Victorian street ballad is contrasted with the eighteenth-century chapbook. The ballad sheet dealt with topical themes and exploited the news and events of the day. The chapbook, on the other hand, preserved the fragments of an older tradition in 'Guy of Warwick', 'The Seven Wise Masters', 'Old Mother Shipton' and others, together

11. Anonymous article, 'Street Ballads', in *National Review* (October 1861), p. 399.

with a good deal of folklore and many of the jests and rhymes which had earlier formed an important element in the oral lore of the English peasantry.

Clearly these differences between the popular literatures of the eighteenth and nineteenth centuries are evidence of a fundamental change in mass reading habits and in attitudes to life. But there is another reason for looking more searchingly at this kind of publication. Although we cannot be absolutely certain who bought and read such sheets, contemporaries suggested strongly that they circulated almost entirely amongst the poor,[12] and such circulation figures as we have are impressive. 'The Execution of F. G. Manning and Maria, His Wife' – based on a celebrated case in 1849 – sold two and a half million copies, and 'The Trial and Sentence of Constance Kent' one hundred and fifty thousand. These are considerable figures and not by any means unique for the street trade. Taken in conjunction with the enormous stocks carried by Catnach, they are a strong indication that such ephemeral literature was an important element in the development of the mass reading public. Like the chapbook in the eighteenth century, the street ballad provided the means by which those who could read – an ability not always gained easily by the nineteenth-century poor – could exercise this skill. Ballad sheets were readily available, and they were short. This latter point is an important one, for, as a London vicar pointed out: 'it needs more than an average love for reading to be able to turn with interest or profit to books, when mind and body are wearied with a long day's toil.'[13]

Through street literature we are able to penetrate, however vicariously, the world of feeling of the urban poor – and the ephemeral nature of the street ballad could be taken to symbolize the precarious quality of their lives.

12. An example of this is provided in C. J. Montague, *Sixty Years in Waifdom; or The Ragged School Movement in English History* (1904), pp. 17–20. (Reprint published in 1969 by Woburn Press.)

13. Robert Gregory, *Sermons on the Poorer Classes of London* (1869), p. 109.

'PENNY' FICTION AND CHEAP NON-FICTION

During this time fiction became of increasing importance in popular literature, and its growth, at a romantic and sensational level, amongst unsophisticated and working-class readers was phenomenal. Well below the reach of the three-volume novel, the circulating library and the world of literature there existed an immense sub-literary public for novels which were sold in penny parts, and even at a penny for a complete novel.

The career of Pierce Egan will serve as a convenient starting point. He was not the first writer of popular fiction, nor was he the best, but the variety of his writing anticipated more clearly than that of any other writer the way in which much popular literature was to develop.

Pierce Egan was born in 1772 and died in 1849. By 1812 he was a well-known sporting journalist with a reputation for producing impromptu songs and epigrams. Prize fighting was much in vogue at the beginning of the nineteenth century, and one of Pierce Egan's most successful undertakings was *Boxiana; or Sketches of Modern Pugilism*, which commenced serial publication in 1818. He included memoirs, portraits and descriptions of fights, and the work's success was such that it continued publication – running eventually to several volumes – until 1824.

Three years earlier he had commenced publication, also in serial parts, of what was to prove his most famous work. This was *Life in London*, each number of which cost one shilling – a price clearly beyond the reach of those who had to think twice before laying out a copper or two on a street ballad or a lurid piece of fiction. The theme of *Life in London*, however, proved irresistible, and the adventures of Corinthian Tom and his friend Jerry Hawthorn during their 'rambles and sprees through the metropolis' found an audience which was considerably greater than one composed only of those who could afford to buy each number as it appeared. Such indeed was the success of this venture that it sparked off various imitators and a number of stage versions.

Reading it today, one finds it difficult to see why the book achieved such extraordinary popularity. The coloured illustrations by Isaac Robert and George Cruikshank remain as delightful as ever, but the prose itself seems affected and to modern taste lacks texture and life:

On approaching the ROYAL EXCHANGE, TOM observed to JERRY, that they would just look in, and he would point out to him a few of the *primest* features of LIFE IN LONDON. 'My dear Coz,' said the CORINTHIAN, 'you are surrounded by *characters* highly worthy of your observation. Volumes would not contain half their talents; and to their honour be it recorded, the greatest part of them have been the architects of their own fortune. Believe me, JERRY, such a group of Merchants is not to be met with under the canopy of heaven: possessing never-tiring industry, and indefatigable to the end of the chapter, they may challenge all Europe for a comparison, and I will back them two to one; indeed, they have astonished all the world.'[14]

Whatever we might think of it today, readers in 1820 were taken by storm. Thackeray, writing in the *Cornhill Magazine* for October 1860, looked back to the time when he first read about Tom and Jerry:

... The style of the writing, I own, was not pleasing to me: I even thought it a little vulgar – well! well! other writers have been considered vulgar ... But the pictures! – Oh! the pictures are noble still! First there is Jerry arriving from the country ...[15]

Perhaps it was this pictorial quality which made *Life in London* so popular on the stage. The best of these adaptations was said to be that by W. T. Moncrieff, which opened at the Adelphi Theatre, London, on 26 November 1821 and ran for two seasons. The success of stage versions extended all over the British Isles and even to the United States. There was a revival at the Elephant and Castle Theatre, London, in 1886, where *Tom and Jerry; or Life in*

14. *Life in London* (reprint, undated, c. 1875), p. 317.
15. Reprinted in *Roundabout Papers* (1863), p. 124.

LIFE IN LONDON;

OR, THE SPREES OF

TOM AND JERRY;

ATTEMPTED IN CUTS AND VERSE.

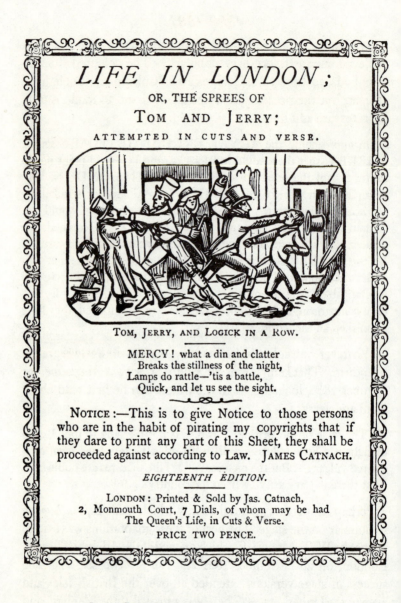

TOM, JERRY, AND LOGICK IN A ROW.

MERCY! what a din and clatter
Breaks the stillness of the night,
Lamps do rattle—'tis a battle,
Quick, and let us see the sight.

NOTICE :—This is to give Notice to those persons
who are in the habit of pirating my copyrights that if
they dare to print any part of this Sheet, they shall be
proceeded against according to Law. JAMES CATNACH.

EIGHTEENTH EDITION.

LONDON: Printed & Sold by Jas. Catnach,
2, Monmouth Court, 7 Dials, of whom may be had
The Queen's Life, in Cuts & Verse.
PRICE TWO PENCE.

13. James Catnach's twopenny version of a popular book

London was advertised with 'all the Original Music, Songs, Duets, Choruses, and Dances'.

The clearest indication that Pierce Egan's book achieved a vogue in the 1820s which made the phrase 'Tom and Jerry' a byword right across the social spectrum was the publication by James Catnach of a twopenny chapbook version. The production was crude enough, comprising twelve woodcuts very roughly adapted from the original illustrations, accompanied by verses which told part of the story:

> *Scene in a gin shop*
>
> HERE are some tumbling and jumping in,
> And some are staggering out;
> One pawned her smock for a quarten of gin,
> Another, her husband's coat.
>
> Behold, Mr Tom and Jerry,
> Have got an old woman in tow,
> They sluic'd her with gin, 'till she reel'd on her pins,
> And was haul'd off to quod for a row.[16]

> *Jerry in training for a swell*
>
> Now Jerry must needs be a swell,
> His coat must have a swallow-tail,
> And Mr Snip, so handy, O
> Soon rigg'd him out a Dandy, O
> They hey for Life and London Town,
> To swagger Bond Street up and down,
> And wink at every pretty maid
> They meet in Burlington Arcade.[17]

Part of Pierce Egan's popularity as an author sprang from the fact that he used the slang of fashionable men about town – Corinthians, Regency Bucks – with consummate skill. Then, as now, the appeal of slang was enormous. While its use in *Life in London* gives the book, for modern readers, a slightly

16. C. Hindley, *The True History of Tom and Jerry*, p. 56.
17. ibid., p. 15.

archaic flavour, there is no doubt of its attraction, in one form or another, for a very wide range of readers in early nineteenth-century England.[18]

With Pierce Egan, then, we stand at the threshold of the nineteenth century. He was both a successful journalist and a best-selling author. But before pursuing developments in popular fiction it is worth-while to digress briefly to another figure who, in quite a different field, found a large market for his writings in the years following the Napoleonic Wars. This is William Hone, publisher, author, editor, satirist.[19]

It was in the last of these roles that Hone became something of a *cause célèbre* at the end of 1817. He faced three separate trials on charges of blasphemy at Guildhall, London, and was acquitted at each one. Although his acquittal was regarded as a triumph by Radicals and their supporters, it had two widely ranging implications for the development of popular literature as well. In the first place, Hone was a leading protagonist in the struggle for a free press and, incidentally, for a very much more liberal and tolerant climate in which publishing and the dissemination of ideas could take place. Secondly, he exploited to an extent that had not been known previously the *illustrated* political pamphlet. The issues which moved him and the passions he felt seem now to be of less importance to us than his skilful exploitation of picture and print in mass publishing. It was Hone who commissioned George Cruikshank to illustrate a number of the pamphlets he published. Amongst these were *The Political House that Jack Built* (fiftieth edition, 1820); *The Political Showman – at Home!*

18. For a valuable glossary of Pierce Egan's slang, see Charles Hindley, *The True History of Tom and Jerry* (undated), pp. 151ff. ('Key to Persons and Places etc.').

19. See F. W. Hackwood, *William Hone His Life and Times* (1912); J. Routledge, *Chapters in the History of Popular Progress* (1876); H. M. Sikes, 'William Hone: Regency Patriot, Parodist and Pamphleteer', in Newberry Library Bulletin 5 (1961), pp. 281–94; V. E. Neuburg (ed.), facsimile of Hone's trial pamphlets, with Introduction (Frank Graham, Newcastle upon Tyne, 1970).

(sixteenth edition, 1821); *The Queen's Matrimonial Ladder* (forty-fourth edition, 1820); *A Slap at Slop* (1822). None of these was cheap – the first three cost one shilling each and the last one 2s. 6d. – but even at such prices all but one of the titles mentioned went through a number of editions. What is, however, especially worthy of note is Hone's anticipation of popular journalism in its widest sense. As we have seen, the political broadside ballad was not new; but Hone gave this kind of literature a new dimension, and his effect upon pictorial popular literature should not be overlooked.

William Hone and Pierce Egan have each an important place at the head of developments in nineteenth-century popular literature. The trends which they anticipated were, in the case of Hone, illustrated political journalism and, in the case of Egan, popular sporting journalism. These were, of course, separate from the more serious, didactic world of mechanics' magazines, penny magazines and similar publications, and from the probably more influential world of popular fiction. It is to the latter that we now turn.

The fiction which was to become such an important part of nineteenth-century popular literature had its origins in the late eighteenth century.[20] Two qualities characterize the novels of this kind which were published from about 1770 onwards – popularity and poor writing. The popularity was not, however, quite of the kind which ensured tremendous circulations for street ballads. It was restricted to those who could afford to buy them or could pay a subscription to a circulating library. Novels were not cheap: in the '70s they were usually advertised in three forms: 3s. a volume bound; 2s. 6d. a volume in stout paper covers; or sheets at 2s. a volume which could be bought by country libraries. By the '90s this practice had died out and the price of novels rose, volumes usually costing from about 3s. 6d. to 5s. each. Circulating libraries

20. See especially J. M. S. Tompkins, *The Popular Novel in England 1770–1800* (1932); and Dorothy Blakey, *The Minerva Press 1790–1820* (Bibliographical Society, 1939).

would supply their subscribers, but the rates were well beyond the pockets of the poor. A. Todd, at his circulating library at 2 St Patrick's Square, Edinburgh, charged £1 1s. per year or 3s. 6d. per month, while non-subscribers could have new volumes at 4d. per day and old ones for 1d. per day. William Lane, who founded the Minerva Press, also ran a circulating library in Leadenhall Street, London, and we find that his subscriptions rose from £1 1s in 1798 to £2 2s. in 1814. He could accommodate those who could not afford an annual subscription, but they were required to deposit the cost of the books they took away and to pay a borrowing fee as well.

It is worth noting that Lane became a wealthy man as a result of his publishing and circulating-library enterprises. At least two of the novels which he first published in 1796, *The Children of the Abbey* by Regina Maria Roche and *The Farmer of Inglewood Forest* by Elizabeth Holme, remained in print in cheap editions for something like one hundred years. At their original publication these novels appeared in four volumes; indeed, it was far from uncommon at this time for novels to be published in two or more volumes. There was the anonymous *Charles and Charlotte* (two volumes, 1777); *Wilmot* (1782) appeared in four volumes; so too did *Anna; or the Memoirs of a Welch Heiress* by Mrs A. M. Bennett (1785); while Mrs Gunning's *Anecdotes of the Delborough Family* was published in five volumes in 1792, and its popularity was such that it was reprinted in the same year.

In terms of price and the time spent in reading them, these novels were demanding. From the researches of J. M. S. Tompkins and Dorothy Blakey it seems beyond doubt that popular novel reading at this period was essentially an occupation for the middle classes and beyond. Besides the factor of cost, the sheer physical difficulty of reading a two-volume, or still more a five-volume, novel in an urban slum or labourer's cottage would have been almost insuperable.

The process by which fashionable novels became the popular wares offered to working-class readers by mass publishers several generations later is a complex one. In part it can be explained by the continuing spread of literacy and a heightened sense of sophistication on the part of working men and women in the nineteenth century, but it is also explicable in economic terms. These novels were available and had once been popular, and it was not too much of a risk to gamble upon the appeal of a romantic novel to a fresh generation of readers who were concerned in their reading with an escape from a reality which was often squalid and poverty-stricken. The theme of escape from reality is one which we meet over and over again in nineteenth-century fiction. Out of the late eighteenth-century 'gothic' romance had come the ingredients for a popular novel based upon romance and sensation – fiction of a kind which offered this escape, and which was read very widely.

The world of the gothic novelist bore no relation to reality. The air was thick with the smell of putrefying corpses on lonely gibbets, and picturesquely ruined castles were inhabited by bats and mad nuns. Generations of virtuous but insipid heroines languished in dark and dreary dungeons from which they were rescued by impeccable heroes, while a fitful moon shone through a break in the clouds after the storm with which so many of these novels opened. It was almost a convention of such tales that the hero should be cheated out of his rightful inheritance by some moustached and scheming relative who had first murdered the boy's parents. A secret closet was opened, and the ghosts of the murdered ones shocked the villain into discomfiture. The rightful heir was restored to his estates, having first rescued his beloved from the unwelcome attentions of the villain.

This kind of plot, with slight and occasional variations, was the model for gothic novels. So far from being a test of the reader's endurance, many of these novels enjoyed an amazing popularity! Jane Austen mentioned this kind of fiction in *Northanger Abbey*:

'I will read you their names directly; here they are in my pocket book. *Castle of Wolfenbach, Clermont, Mysterious Warnings, Necro-*

mancer of the Black Forest, Midnight Bell, Orphan of the Rhine, and *Horrid Mysteries.* Those will last us some t.me.'

'Yes; pretty well; but are they all horrid? Are you sure they are all horrid?'

'Yes, quite sure; for a particular friend of mine, a Miss Andrews, a sweet girl, one of the sweetest creatures in the world, has read every one of them . . .'

Perhaps the best known of these novels was *The Mysteries of Udolpho* by Mrs Ann Radcliffe, which was first published in 1794 in four volumes. It was her fourth novel and the most successful tale she wrote. An officer serving with Wellington's army in the Peninsular wrote home that his billet was 'as full of long passages, iron gratings, and trap doors as any locality ever selected by Mrs Radcliffe for her theatre of monstrosities'.[21] Nearly seventy years after its first appearance it was a well-established shilling novel published by Milner & Sowerby in the Cottage Library. Milner was an astute businessman, and his belief that what had been popular with one generation of middle-class readers was likely to appeal to a lower stratum of readers in a later generation was triumphantly vindicated. In turning this belief to his advantage he issued cheap editions of several other gothic novels -- there was, for example, *The Farmer of Inglewood Forest, The Children of the Abbey* and Jane Porter's *Scottish Chiefs.*

When it first came out *The Mysteries of Udolpho* attracted much critical acclaim. Sir Walter Scott praised it highly; so too did Sheridan and Fox, while it is said that Dr Joseph Warton sat up half the night to read it. 'The very name,' wrote Scott, 'was fascinating; and the public, who rushed upon it with all the eagerness of curiosity, rose from it with unsated appetite.'[22]

A host of novelists rushed to cash in on the success of Mrs Radcliffe. The gothic novel had arrived and was enormously popular.

The story was not unlike that of an earlier novel, *The Romance*

21. Quoted in Antony Brett-James, *Life in Wellington's Army* (1972), p. 45.
22. *The Lives of the Novelists* (Everyman edition, undated), p. 216.

of the Forest, by the same author. Sir Walter Scott wrote of the heroines: 'Both are divided from the object of their attachment by the gloomy influence of unfaithful and oppressive guardians, and both become inhabitants of time-stricken towers, and witnesses of scenes now bordering upon the supernatural, and now upon the horrible.' The superiority of *Udolpho*, thought Scott, arose from the fact that 'its interest is of a more agitating and tremendous nature; the scenery of a wilder and more terrific description; the characters distinguished by fiercer and more gigantic features.'

The novel-reading public seemed to agree with this, and eventually it was published sufficiently cheaply to bring it within reach of the large and increasing readership who could afford neither to purchase the four-volume edition nor to subscribe to a circulating library, but who could afford to buy it in weekly parts or in a cheap one-volume reprint.

It should be emphasized that Mrs Radcliffe was not the first gothic novelist, but it was this novel which was instrumental in creating a demand for more of its kind. Despite the horror piled upon horror, these were essentially moral stories, and the closing paragraph of *Rosina; or, the Village Maid*, by Louisa Jones, epitomizes the attitude implicit in this kind of fiction:

> I have now brought these memoirs to an end. and I intend to leave them as a legacy to the youth of my sex generally, but more especially to country maidens, who, like myself in youth, may possess beauty, but be diffident in experience. My life will teach such, that however vice may seem to prosper for a time, it will at last be found that virtue and happiness are inseparable.[23]

Some of the earlier gothic novels survived to be reprinted time and again by enterprising publishers who exploited the growing market for cheap books. At its best the gothic novel was literature, but as a literary form it eventually disintegrated into a vulgarization known as the 'blood'. The line between the two is not, of course, always easy to draw and, as Michael Sadleir has put it, 'the

23. I quote from a cheap edition published by J. S. Pratt in 1843.

Published Weekly, Price 2d

Each Number embellished with a spirited Engraving.

Engraving to No. 1.

THE

Terrific

REGISTER.

—

ADDRESS.

It has been observed that whatever relates to man must be interesting to man. While we admit this as an obvious truth, it must also be admitted that there are some circumstances with which he may be surrounded, some things in which he may be engaged, some events in which he may be involved, much more calculated to rouse attention and affect the feelings than others. It appears to us that those awful calamities by which he is frequently overtaken by the fiat of heaven, or the resolves and decrees of bloody minded men, are of this description. The afflictions which our fellow creatures have been obliged to embrace, and the manner in which they have conducted themselves in their extremity, have always been objects of natural curiosity and deep and melancholy interest, and ever will remain so while man is " made of penetrable stuff." Sympathy is the characteristic of our better natures, and he whose mind is rightly constituted, whose heart, to use a homely phrase, " beats in the right place," must, from the very necessity of his nature, joy with the joyous, and sorrow with the sorrowful. Sensible of this truth, we were satisfied that a work in a cheap form, that presented the public from time to time with a body of human misery, such as was never before brought under one head, would excite a general and a lively interest, and meet with their sanction and support. Our expectations have not been disappointed, for a patronage has attended our efforts we believe unprecedented.

[*Turn over.*

14.   Sensational fare. A forerunner of the 'blood'

Contents of Eight Numbers.

Printed by T. Richardson, 98, High Holborn, London.

Published by SHERWOOD, JONES, & Co. Paternoster Row;

AND W. HUNTER, EDINBURGH;

And Sold by all Booksellers and Newsmen.

spirit of melodrama and of terror (which is only in rousing guise the spirit of escape) persisted unsubdued and persists to this day.'[24]

The field of Victorian cheap fiction and 'the blood' is very largely uncharted. The problem is mainly one of extent – so many novels written by a host of authors whose names are forgotten. Some of the writers concerned were extremely prolific – for example, J. F. Smith, J. M. Rymer, Pierce Egan Junior, T. P. Prest, Emma Robinson. All have an extensive and complex publishing history.

A good deal of this fiction was repetitive, and it was usually offered to the public in weekly or monthly parts. If we look at two or three typical authors and the leading publisher in this field, it should be possible on the one hand to avoid unsubstantiated generalizations and on the other to provide a synoptic view of the subject. Thanks to the work of Louis James, Margaret Dalziel and Montague Summers,[25] we have some guidance here.

G. W. M. Reynolds, who was born in 1814 and died in 1879, wrote a very large number of novels and made the fortune of one publisher. Originally destined for the army, he found Sandhurst uncongenial, and when his father died a substantial legacy enabled him to start a literary career in Paris. He invested capital in an Anglo-French newspaper called the *London and Paris Courier*; he opened 'The French, English and American Library'; and in 1835 he published his first novel, *The Young Imposter*. These literary enterprises cost him his fortune, and he returned to London, where he continued to write. A novel, *Grace Darling*, came out in 1836; he contributed to *Bentley's Miscellany* and edited the *Monthly Magazine*, besides producing various other novels, including *Pickwick Married* (1840), a three-volume study of French literature, translations and a 'teach yourself' French instructor.

It was in 1845 that he commenced his career as a best-selling author. Up until then there had been little to distinguish his

24. Quoted in Montague Summers, *A Gothic Bibliography* (undated), p. ix.
25. See Bibliography, pp. 285–6.

novels, despite his other literary activities, from those of countless hacks who produced sensational fiction; but in that year *The Mysteries of London* became available in weekly numbers at one penny or in monthly parts costing sixpence. There were four series, although Reynolds wrote only the first two, a total of four volumes. The third and fourth series were written by Thomas Miller and E. L. Blanchard. George Vickers, the publisher, died in 1846, but the business continued under the direction of his widow and his sons. Reynolds, however, then moved to another publisher, John Dicks, whose fortune was made as a result. Besides *The Mysteries of London* and other publications, Dicks took over *Reynolds' Miscellany of Romance, General Interest, Science and Art*, which had been started in 1845. The *Miscellany*, in fact, provides a view of Reynolds and his work.

In the preface to the first number – which, incidentally, carried the initial instalment of *Wagner : the Wehr-wolf* by Reynolds – the author stated that he intended to steer a course between magazines specializing in fiction and those which were purely instructional. In his weekly article addressed to 'the industrial classes' he put forward the Chartist views[26] for which he was known. There were articles on physiology, and on the provincial press; but it is the 'Notices to Correspondents' which are most revealing. From them came the information that the *Miscellany* was selling 30,000 current numbers a week plus 10,000 back numbers. Reynolds's *The Mysteries of London* went on selling under the new imprint at a rate of nearly 40,000 copies per week, and back numbers were kept in stock.

Between 1841 and 1856 more than thirty full-length novels appeared under Reynolds's name, but it must have been *The Mysteries of the Court of London* which most delighted Dicks. Reynolds had collected a good deal of material for the third series of *The Mysteries of London*, and it was this that he utilized for the

---

26. See R. G. Gammage, *History of the Chartist Movement 1837–1854* (Newcastle upon Tyne, 1894; reprinted by Frank Cass, 1969), pp. 293, 308, 354, 377.

new project. It commenced publication in September 1848 and, like its predecessor, was available in penny weekly numbers or sixpenny monthly parts. It ran altogether to four series of two volumes each and contained, according to one estimate, four and a half million words, the equivalent of about forty-eight modern novels. At the end of the second volume of the fourth series (Vol. VIII), Reynolds wrote in a postscript:

Every week, without a single intermission during a period of eight years, has a Number under this title been issued to the public. Its predecessor *The Mysteries of London* ranged over four years.[27] For twelve years, therefore, have I hebdomadally issued to the world a fragmentary portion of that which, as one vast whole, may be termed an Encyclopaedia of Tales. This Encyclopaedia consists of twelve volumes, comprising six hundred and twenty-four weekly Numbers. Each Number has occupied me upon an average of seven hours in the composition ... four thousand three hundred and sixty-eight hours.[28]

It is this regularity of routine, he continues, which 'will account to the public for the facility with which I have been enabled to write so many other works during the same period, and yet to allow myself ample leisure for recreation and for healthful exercise'.

Whether or not Reynolds had help with his enormous output,[29] there is no doubt that his achievement was a considerable one. Even amongst the prolific authors of nineteenth-century popular fiction he was outstanding.

Reynolds left little to the reader's imagination. As E. S. Turner says:

His slums were incestuous, pox-ridden hells in which pigs ate the bodies of newly dead babes and hardened undertakers' men fainted at the sights which met their eyes. Hump-backed dwarfs, harridans and

27. Reynolds, of course, ignored the work of Miller and Blanchard.
28. Quoted in Montague Summers, op. cit., p. 151.
29. See Louis James, *Fiction for the Working Man* (Oxford, 1963), p. 41. (Also Penguin University Books, 1974.) I am greatly indebted to Dr James's work for the details of Reynolds's life and work.

grave-robbers groped past against a background of workhouses, jails, execution yards, thieves' kitchens and cemeteries. His readers could depend on him to bring in the theme of maiden virtue rudely strumpeted as often as possible.[30]

How are we to assess Reynolds's work? As a novelist he was, as we have seen, extraordinarily prolific, and there is some reason to conclude that he had a greater taste for realism in his novels than did many of his contemporaries. In two respects he was totally untypical: he was avowedly both a religious sceptic and a political radical. J. M. Wheeler, in *A Biographical Dictionary of Freethinkers* (1880), has the following entry: 'Reynolds (George William MacArthur), English writer; author of many novels. Wrote *Errors of the Christian Religion*, 1832.'

Reynolds's religious scepticism is apparent in some of his novels. One of the main characters in *The Mysteries of London* is Reginald Tracy, a clergyman, who after being seduced by a lady of fashion becomes a libertine. This is how he sees another character: 'At a glance he scanned the fair form of Ellen from head to foot; and his imagination was instantly fired with the thoughts of her soft and swelling charms – those graceful undulations which were all her own, and needed no artificial aids to improve the originals of nature!'[31] Later he peers at Ellen through the bathroom keyhole, but before she is completely naked he is interrupted.

Tracy is not the only errant clergyman. A prison chaplain is shown as unfeeling and materialistic, while a dissenting minister becomes so drunk that he has to be taken home in a wheelbarrow.

Presumably this kind of thing did not shock the readers; at all events, sales did not seem to be affected. Perhaps much of the public for which Reynolds wrote shared his cynicism about religion and its advocates?

His radicalism is even more pervasive – although not always

30. E. S. Turner, *Boys Will Be Boys* (new and revised edition, 1957), p. 25. (Also Penguin, 1976.)

31. Quoted in Margaret Dalziel, *Popular Fiction 100 Years Ago* (1957), p. 41.

convincing. Implicit in the view he takes of working girls who are seduced is the question, what alternative did they have to selling themselves? Clearly there is an indictment of the system here, and occasionally Reynolds became so indignant about the plight of the poor that he introduced digressions into his work:

It was New Year's Day, 1839. The rich man sat down to a table crowded with every luxury; the pauper in the workhouse had not enough to eat. The contrast may be represented:

Turtle, venison, turkey, hare, pheasant, perigood pie, plum pudding, mince pies, jellies, blanc-mange, trifles, preserves, cakes, fruits of all kinds, wines of every description.	half pound of bread, four ozs bacon, half pound potatoes, one and a half pints of gruel.

And it was New Year's Day, 1839. But to proceed . . .[32]

Again, he draws a comparison between the income of the Sovereign at £500,000 per year and that of the Member of the Industrious Class who earns £20 in the same period (the Priest, by the way, is assessed at £7,500 per annum!), and asks: 'Is this reasonable? Is this just? Is this even consistent with common sense?'[33]

There is of course substance in George Orwell's comment: 'Of course no one in his senses would want to turn the so-called penny dreadful into a realistic novel or a Socialist tract. An adventure story must of its nature be more or less remote from real life.'[34]

But what was the reaction to Reynolds, and to the popular fiction of his time, of the more serious Victorians who were not disposed to be diverted by these extravagances? In the main it was felt that literature and its provision was a moral issue, and that a more wholesome approach was required if readers of little

32. Quoted in Turner, op. cit., pp. 26–7.
33. ibid., p. 26.
34. 'Boys' Weeklies', reprinted in *Critical Essays* (1946), p. 79.

education were to be saved from 'extravagant and horrible fiction' which, so right-thinking commentators from the middle class thought, could only debauch them and destroy their moral sense with atheism and radical politics. The cry, of course, was not a new one: ballads, chapbooks and fiction had all long been subjected to attack from those who saw popular literature as a threat to established values. Several attempts, which we shall note later, were made to 'purify' it.

John Parker, in an essay entitled 'On the Literature of the Working Classes',[35] acknowledged that Reynolds's novels were 'well penned' and 'artistically wrought', but claimed that their appeal was to young men and women of 'imperfect moral education'. Parker had in mind *The Mysteries of London* and *The Mysteries of the Court of London*, which he described as consisting of 'all the disgusting facts which have from time to time, during the last fifty years, been brought to light, and exposed in the public journals, as reports from police courts, criminal trials, and cases of seduction and adultery, from our ecclesiastical courts and courts of common law'.

'These,' he went on, 'are artfully and cleverly dressed up and aided by the depraved pencil of an artist skilled in depicting the sensual and the horrible; and while they interest the tale devourer, they, at the same time, fearfully stimulate the animal propensities of the young, the ardent and the sensual.'

Moral issues apart, Parker also felt that there were political dangers in this kind of fiction. He was at pains to point out the dangers of filling the minds of young readers with 'false social and political economy'. He was, however, a more perceptive observer of popular fiction than these extracts might lead us to think. He saw quite clearly that many of the penny romances were descended from the gothic novel, and that the penny versions were not necessarily inferior to their three-, four- and five-volume predecessors.

35. Published in *Meliora: or, Better Times to Come*, ed. Viscount Ingestre (Second Series, 1853; reprinted by Cass, 1971), p. 186.

Henry Worsley, writing some years earlier, did not mention Reynolds by name but almost certainly had him in mind:

The reader who may desire accurate information on this point [i.e. the content of popular fiction] may enter one of the shops in our large towns, in which ballads, cheap publications, novels, etc., are sold to the poor; and by inspection of this class of literature, he will easily perceive how the blush of modesty is laughed away, all sense of religion laughed at, and infidelity and socialist principles inculcated by those who have little more talent in the use of words, or more effrontery, certainly a greater depth of vice and obscenity, than their contemporaries of the same order. The character of the literature is uniformly both cause and effect of the general moral character and taste of the age.[36]

This was a very much less informed comment on popular literature than those by Parker, and by its sheer comprehensiveness it blunted the edge of an attack which many contemporaries might have supported.

Occasionally this kind of blanket condemnation recoiled upon itself. In the course of three articles entitled 'The Literature of the Lower Orders' which appeared in the *Daily News* between October and November 1847, Hepworth Dixon attacked a novel called *Gretna Green*. At the end of the final piece there appeared a brief postscript:

We have received a letter protesting against Mrs S. F. Reynolds' work of *Gretna Green* being included in the list of popular works being described as marked by 'looseness, warmth of colouring in criminal scenes and the false glow set around guilty indulgence'. We must admit that *Gretna Green* does not merit this; and that, whatever its faults, it certainly contains nothing derogatory to the character or delicacy of a lady writer.[37]

Mrs Reynolds was G. W. M. Reynolds's wife, and Dixon's disclaimer reveals at least some awareness that there were varieties of popular fiction.

36. *Juvenile Depravities* (1849), p. 113.
37. The *Daily News* (9 November 1847).

The novels of Susanna Frances Reynolds do indeed represent a more romantic and much less robust and realistic vein than that of her husband – and this is, in fact, the one from which women's magazine fiction developed. Mrs Reynolds stands directly in the tradition of the gothic novel, which to a great extent has survived until today. The literary antecedents of novels like *Whispering Palms* or *Winds in the Wilderness*, both by Rosalind Brett, or *The Legend of Roscano* and *Serenade of Santa Rosa*, by Iris Danbury – to mention only four of the popular romances which were being advertised in March 1973 – stretch back in an unbroken line to the last decades of the eighteenth century.

Mrs Reynolds wrote far fewer novels than her husband. Typical of them, and in fact representative of the whole range of such fiction, is her serial *The Poacher's Daughter*, which ran in the *Weekly Magazine* from 26 February 1848 until it was concluded in the final number which appeared on 1 July in the same year. It is the story of Evelin Grantley and Edith Freeland, who eventually marry. Edith's father, Ephraim Freeland, is a poacher, and as the story opens Evelin's father is 'sternly prosecuting' him for having shot a favourite buck. Inevitably, after various adventures and mishaps, the story ends happily with Evelin as master and owner of Ravenhurst Manor, the ancestral home, and Edith as Lady Grantley. Her father becomes a warden of the New Forest, and eventually dies after many years of faithful service during which he shows 'a discretion that tended much to repress the practice of poaching'. No irony was intended here and it is very doubtful whether contemporary readers would have suspected it.

The description of the heroine is worth quoting as a specimen both of Mrs Reynolds's writing and of the stereotyped characterization which was such a feature of these novels. Edith's beauty is in sharp contrast with the appearance of her 'hard-featured and scowling parent':

Yet what beauty in spite of her trouble and humble attire was there in the countenance and conduct of Poor Edith! Nature surely never formed a creature of more artless and winning loveliness. She had deep blue eyes, fringed by long silken lashes: her hair, of a dark auburn, fell in abundant ringlets about her snow white brow; and had it not been confined behind by a comb, would almost have covered the whole of her person. Her features prevailingly illumined by a modest smile, even amid the crystal drops that rained down her cheeks, – a smile which deepened the coy dimples there planted, – and the severed lips, when she whispered, by the side of which the reddest coral would have looked dull, were but emblems and the fitting tokens of the still more exquisite charms which, as Evelin felt assured, belonged to her heart.

Thus the heroine at Winchester Quarter Sessions, where her father is on trial for poaching.

Mrs Reynolds's support for radicalism is unmistakable, though very much more muted than that of her husband, and she does not allow political digression to hold up the action of her novels as he did. Indeed, it might be argued that her occasional political asides – 'fox-hunting parsons', 'rampant Toryism', or even the introduction of Arthur Thistlewood and the Cato Street Conspiracy – were little more than devices for gaining the sympathy of the reader.

Edwin F. Roberts was another prolific author who was connected with Reynolds. No complete bibliography of his work exists. According to Montague Summers, he wrote a number of novels, and biographies of George Washington and Napoleon, between 1848 and 1853; but this is only a part of what Summers called 'the immense literary activity of E. F. Roberts'.[38] His novel, *The Count of Crisono*, was published as a serial in the *Weekly Magazine*, the first instalment opening on page one of the initial number. The Italian background is reminiscent of the heyday of the gothic novel, and the sub-title, 'A Story of the Passions', was pretty run-of-the-mill. The story itself, while competent enough, rarely rises above the prosaic.

Very much more interesting are Roberts's short stories, which were sometimes used to fill spaces in the *Weekly Magazine*. Writers like Isaac Crookenden had written long short stories,

38. Montague Summers, *A Gothic Bibliography* (undated), pp. 160–61.

published at a few pence a time, in the early years of the nineteenth century. Few of them have survived. Summers describes them as 'chap books with horrific titles',[39] but they were in fact gothic novels in miniature, and in any case very much shorter than Roberts's short pieces. In the final number of the journal in which *The Count of Crisono* appeared, Roberts published a short story called 'A Romance of the Palais-Royal', of which the opening page is reproduced below. It cannot be claimed that it is the best thing he wrote, but it is typical of his style and of the kind of fiction for which some readers in the nineteenth century had an enormous appetite. Indeed, it is probably true to say that human nature at most periods craves some sort of melodrama and likes to identify with something larger than life. It is only the form taken by this melodrama which changes – we may think, for example, of the popularity of many of Dickens's characters.

Fiction of this kind, as both serial novels and short stories, had a long life. As already indicated, it still flourishes; while the more sensational kind of penny fiction formed the basis for a vigorous boys' literature of 'penny bloods' which flourished at the end of the century.[40]

Vice was always a particularly saleable ingredient in mass publishing – particularly when framed by admonitions to virtue. The preoccupation of nineteenth-century readers with violent crime is well known; *The Newgate Calendar*,[41] together with newspaper reporting of 'Jack the Ripper' crimes,[42] laid hold upon public imagination in a way that reprints of Shakespeare or Milton never could.

The best-known edition of *The Newgate Calendar*, edited by

39. Summers, op. cit., p. 32.

40. See E. S. Turner, *Boys Will Be Boys*, *passim*, for a readable account of early boys' fiction.

41. The earliest version of it had appeared in about 1774.

42. See *Jack the Ripper, a Bibliography and Review of the Literature* (1973). Alexander Kelly compiled the bibliography, and Colin Wilson contributed an introduction.

15. A journal edited by Mrs Reynolds in 1848

Andrew Knapp and William Baldwin, was originally published in parts in the earlier decades of the century. The four volumes, which appeared bound up in three between 1824 and 1828, maintained their popularity for many years. The illustrations were vivid and left little to the imagination. This publication was one of the source books for some of the fiction published by Edward Lloyd (see pp. 170–74.). Ostensibly, like an earlier work by John Reynolds, *The Triumphe of God's Revenge Against the Crying and Execrable Sinn of Murther* (seventh edition, 1704), the *Calendar* was a moral work:

> Next to the necessary example of punishment to offenders is to record examples in order that such as are unhappily moved with the sordid passion of acquiring wealth by violence, or stimulated by the heinous sin of revenge to shed the blood of a fellow creature, may have before them a picture of the torment of mind and bodily sufferings of such offenders. In this light *The Newgate Calendar* must prove highly acceptable to all ranks and conditions of men; for we shall find, in the course of these volumes, that crime has always been followed by punishment; and that, in many instances, the most artful secrecy could not screen the offenders from detection, nor the utmost ingenuity shield them from the strong arm of impartial justice.[43]

In fact, of course, it gloried in both the crimes and the punishments which attended them. There are nearly 2,000 pages in this edition, and its popularity was such that it circulated in one form or another throughout the century. There was even a pocket edition by Charles Cavendish which came out in 1840.

There were, however, novelists who had a more serious purpose than merely to amuse. From at least the 1880s there were 'Christian' novels which aimed, by implication, to provide popular reading of a wholesome, vaguely evangelical and entirely moral character, relying for their effect upon impeccable virtue rather than violence or sensation.

It is of course true that virtue generally triumphs over vice in popular fiction – a convention which was never seriously called into question even by authors who saw highwaymen and pirates in a more favourable light than middle-class, respectable commentators liked. The moral novelists, however, would have no truck with anything approaching a sympathetic view of vice in any

43. *The Newgate Calendar*, Preface, Vol. I, p. iv.

shape or form. Amongst these writers was an American, Timothy Shay Arthur, whose cause was total abstinence from strong drink. In support of it he wrote so many novels that one critic has said that he was responsible, single-handed, for one fifth of all the volumes of fiction published in the United States during the 1840s.[44] His novels enjoyed very considerable popularity in this country as well.

T. S. Arthur was born near Newburgh, Orange County, New York, in 1809. He settled in Philadelphia in 1841, and died in 1885. In 1852 he founded *Arthur's Home Magazine*, which he edited until the year of his death. Forty-nine separate works from his pen are listed in S. A. Allibone's *A Critical Dictionary of English Literature*,[45] and several contemporary comments are quoted: 'Mr Arthur writes very unexceptionable tales, illustrative of American and domestic life and adapted to the capacities of the young and uneducated classes. All his stories inculcate a moral...' So said the *New York Literary World*.[46] In the *New York Criterion* his writings were said to be 'not of a very high order...' *Godey's Lady's Book*, on the other hand, said categorically: 'the most popular of all our American writers on domestic subjects'. One of his English publishers wrote of him thus in a catalogue:

T. S. Arthur's moral novels
T. S. Arthur as an author

The world is greatly indebted to such authors as T. S. Arthur. He may truly be styled one of the first of its social reformers, for he has written for the people's welfare, both morally, socially, and religiously. His stories always improve the reader, in the highest sense of the word. He has done more to strengthen the morals and cultivate the religious faculties of his readers than a great many clever authors of the present day. None need fear the introducing of his books into the home circle; in fact they ought to be welcomed as the best aids to a moral and religious home training, that can be obtained. His efforts are always

44. J. D. Hart, *The Popular Book* (New York, 1950), p. 109.
45. Vol. 1 (Philadelphia, 1882), p. 71; Supplement, Vol. 1 (1891), p. 54.
46. ibid. Vol. 1, p. 71.

lively, and interesting, with sound principles running through the whole of them. He has lived and laboured to leave the world a better place than he found it.[47]

Three of Arthur's novels which were popular in England are *Anna Lee; or the Maiden, Wife and Mother*, said by the publisher to have 'a high moral tone'; *Cast Adrift. A Story of New York* ('The heroine is found in the lowest state of society, and by virtuous behaviour in the midst of vice, wins her way into upper circles'); and *Righted at Last. A Story of New England Life*, said by the publishers to be 'but another instance of the truth, that virtue and goodness will ultimately triumph though the time of triumph may be long delayed'.

Perhaps his best-known books were the temperance novels, *Ten Nights in a Bar-room* and *Three Years in a Man-trap*, first issued in America in 1854 and 1872 respectively. The former was dramatized by W. W. Pratt in the sentimental song, 'Father, Dear Father, Come Home With Me Now', which, together with successive reprints of the novel both here and in the United States, kept the title alive for many years.

Three Years in a Man-trap was written as a complement to the earlier temperance novel. The edition in front of me measures three inches by five inches and contains 315 pages of text followed by five pages of publisher's advertisements. The imprint is William Nicholson & Sons, Wakefield, and the general appearance, together with the ornamental binding, suggest that this was a cheap edition; other publications by Nicholson indicate that cheap books were the stock-in-trade of this firm. This copy, undated, probably belongs to the late 1870s or early 1880s.

The novel purports to be the experiences of a bar-keeper who eventually goes to prison and becomes so sickened of his trade that he decides to become a preacher, despite the sneers of his erstwhile companions. The villain of the piece is, of course, the demon drink, and the author loses no opportunity to drive home

47. Catalogue of books published by Milner & Co. Ltd, London and Halifax (undated).

his message. In the courtroom, trials of petty criminals go on: 'One after another was convicted and sentenced, until I found myself in the midst of a wretched crew – thieves, roughs, and vagabonds of the meanest class, and nearly all of them smelling of whiskey.'[48] One man, who spent 'half his wages in drink', had a miserable death: 'The man lived with his wife and three helpless children in two rooms on the second floor of a miserable house in a narrow dirty street. There was little furniture in the rooms. The sick man lay on a hard straw bed . . .'[49]

Arthur's *Tales of Married Life* had the same high moral tone as everything else he wrote. The English edition I have is undated and was issued by Milner & Sowerby. It consists of three short novels in one volume and runs to nearly 400 pages.

There is no literary merit in T. S. Arthur's work, but its sheer volume and the fact that he was so popular in his own day are worthy of note.

THE PUBLISHERS AND THEIR EXCURSIONS INTO THE POPULAR MARKET

The problem of quantity makes any discussion of nineteenth-century popular fiction difficult, and it would be impossible to generalize about it if so much of it were not repetitive. The authors I have mentioned are typical; but in order to see the entire field in perspective, it becomes necessary to alter the angle of vision and look at some of the publishers involved. It was they who gauged the public taste and issued their publications accordingly. The lists of what they published are surprisingly informative and reveal a vast world of sub-literary fiction, much of which is unexplored.

Just as William Dicey and James Catnach respectively dominated the eighteenth-century chapbook trade and nineteenth-century street-ballad trade, so there were several publishers who were pre-eminent in popular fiction. Like Dicey and Catnach, they did have rivals and imitators, but men like Edward Lloyd, John

48. T. S. Arthur, *Three Years in a Man-trap*, p. 249.
49. ibid., p. 109.

Dicks and William Milner were extremely influential and made large sums of money from the production of cheap popular books.

Edward Lloyd was born in Surrey in 1815. While still in his teens he opened a stationer's shop in Curtain Road, Shoreditch, and in 1836 he went into publishing. When he died in 1890 he was a very wealthy man. He founded several newspapers and established a large paper-making factory in Kent; his fortune, however, was derived primarily from the publication of cheap fiction, and when in later life he wished to live this down he made attempts to buy up stocks of his sensational publications and destroy them. It is interesting, too, that the *Dictionary of National Biography*[50] makes no mention of penny fiction in connection with Edward Lloyd.

He carried on this kind of business from a variety of addresses in London – Wych Street and Holywell Street, besides Curtain Road – but it was from 12 Salisbury Square, Fleet Street, that most of his stories were published. Two hundred titles of varying lengths were issued between 1836 and about 1856,[51] and this total is probably not complete. The stories were published in penny numbers, usually in a uniform demy octavo. Earlier titles were in single column, later ones in double column. Titles were reissued, sometimes with additional illustrations. John Medcraft has described Lloyd's output as including:

... historical tales of the type popularized by Harrison Ainsworth, Gothic horrors in the style of Ann Radcliffe, and so-called 'domestic' romances. The high proportion of the last was due to an extensive *feminine* following amongst the readers and in deference to their 'gentler' natures Lloyd eliminated highwaymen and vampires, added an innocuous title, and confined himself to the milder themes of pirates and smugglers, murder and rape, seduction and abduction.[52]

Some of Lloyd's earliest titles were unauthorized Dickens

50. Vol. XI, p. 1298.

51. J. Medcraft, *A Bibliography of the Penny Bloods of Edward Lloyd* (200 copies, Dundee, 1945).

52. ibid.

plagiarisms.[53] There was *The Post-humurous* [sic] *Notes of the Pickwickian Club*, edited by 'Bos'. Better known as the 'Penny Pickwick', this ran from 1838 to 1842, consisting of 112 numbers in double column, two illustrations per number. Its popularity was enormous, and there seem to have been at least two slightly different issues. In 1840 there was *Memoirs of Nickelas Nicklebery* by 'Bos'. This ran to forty numbers; and Lloyd published others.

Best known of the romances was perhaps *Ada the Betrayed; or, the Murder at the Old Smithy*, which came out in fifty-six numbers during 1847. The author, Malcolm J. Errym, wrote many similar tales; while another of Lloyd's authors was Thomas Prest, who, amongst many romances, wrote *Geraldine; or the Secret Assassine of the Old Store Cross* (1844), in twenty-six numbers.

Despite the fact that he was active in other spheres of publishing, Lloyd was for a time the leading publisher of cheap fiction. Sweeney Todd, the renowned 'demon barber', villain of countless melodrama performances, first made his appearance in a romance by Prest, which Lloyd issued in ninety-two numbers, starting in 1850, as *The String of Pearls, or, the Barber of Fleet Street*.[54]

Lloyd's methods were simple. Thomas Frost has left a picture of them as given to him by Lloyd's manager, 'a stout gentleman of sleek costume and urbane manners':

> Our publications circulate among a class so different in education and social position from the readers of the three-volume novels that we sometimes distrust our own judgement and place the manuscript in the hands of an illiterate person – a servant, or machine boy, for instance. If they pronounce favourably upon it, we think it will do.[55]

Such a method laid the foundation of Lloyd's fortune and was the basis upon which the immense popularity of the 'Salisbury

53. Against which, of course, Dickens fulminated in vain!

54. See J. Medcraft, 'Sidelights on Sweeney Todd', the *Collector's Miscellany*, Fourth Series, no. 2 (Winter 1941).

55. Thomas Frost, *Forty Years Recollections* (1860). Quoted in E. S. Turner, *Boys Will Be Boys*, p. 18.

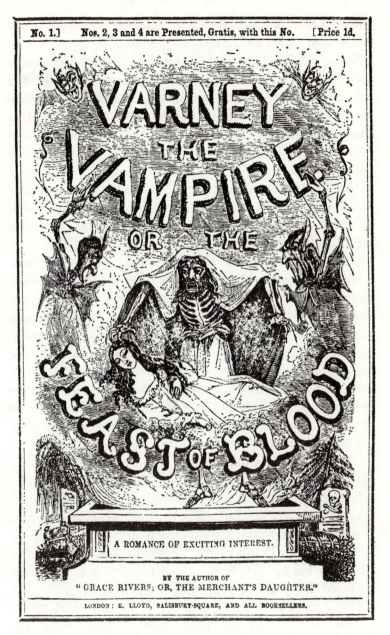

16. A typical penny dreadful

Square School' of writers was built. And it was this which he tried to live down in his later, 'respectable' years.

George Vickers, who died in 1846, was another publisher of cheap fiction. Reynolds was connected with him for the first volume of *The Mysteries of London*; but, as has been mentioned, after Vickers's death Reynolds transferred the publication of his work to John Dicks, then a small publisher in Warwick Square. As a result of this, Dicks became in the 1850s one of the largest publishers in London.

Very little is known about Dicks, but it can be said that his list of publications is extremely impressive in terms of quality, and he published a great deal outside the realms of fiction. There were the 'Standard Plays': in 1892 1,200 items in this series were advertised, each '. . . admirably illustrated . . . and issued in a coloured wrapper for the small sum of one penny each'. Another line consisted of Sir Walter Scott's Waverley novels, which were available at prices which ranged, at various times, from threepence to one shilling per volume. Amongst Dicks' English Classics, the works of Shakespeare, Byron and Pope could be had for one shilling each in stiff paper covers, or two shillings in cloth. Cheaper were the works of Goldsmith, Burns, Milton, Cowper, Wordsworth and others. Some of the books were illustrated, nearly all included a memoir and a portrait, and few paper-covered editions cost more than sixpence each.

The series Dicks' English Novels ran to over 240 separate items. It was advertised as 'An Illustrated and Unabridged Edition of the most Popular Works of the Best Authors, each Work containing from Ten to Twelve Illustrations, and issued in a stiff attractive wrapper. Price sixpence each'. Amongst the authors were W. H. Ainsworth, Charles Dickens, Lord Lytton, Theodore Hook, Paul de Kock and many others. Inevitably, G. W. M. Reynolds was very strongly represented.

Dicks' English Library of Standard Works each contained several novels in one paper-covered volume, costing 1s. 6d. The orange cover of one volume is shown here. The contents were

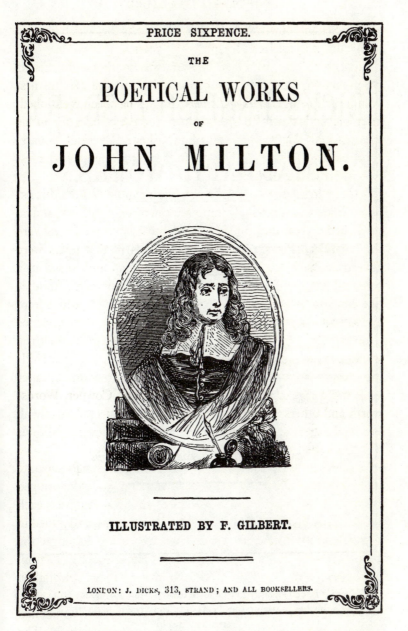

PRICE SIXPENCE.

THE

POETICAL WORKS

OF

JOHN MILTON.

ILLUSTRATED BY F. GILBERT.

LONDON: J. DICKS, 313, STRAND; AND ALL BOOKSELLERS.

17. Milton was only one of several poets whose works were issued cheaply

PRICE 1s. 6d.—COMPLETE.

DICKS' ENGLISH LIBRARY

OF

STANDARD WORKS.

CONTAINING

FIVE COMPLETE NOVELS.

CONTENTS:

MATHILDE. BY EUGENE SUE. ILLUSTRATED BY C. NANTEUIL.

THE MODERN DON QUIXOTE; OR, THE ADVENTURES OF SIR LAUNCELOT GREAVES. BY TOBIAS SMOLLETT. ILLUSTRATED BY GEORGE CRUIKSHANK.

REAL LIFE IN LONDON IN THE TWENTIES. ILLUSTRATED.

ANDRE THE SAVOYARD. BY PAUL DE KOCK. ILLUSTRATED BY BERTALL.

THE IRISH SKETCH-BOOK. BY MICHAEL ANGELO TITMARSH (W. M. THACKERAY). WITH NUMEROUS ILLUSTRATIONS BY THE AUTHOR.

ONE HUNDRED AND FORTY ILLUSTRATIONS.

LONDON: JOHN DICKS, 313, STRAND.

18. Novels issued cheaply in this form offered value for money and enabled the publisher to use up the sheets of titles issued in parts which had remained unsold

originally issued in monthly parts, each containing an instalment of the five stories listed. Presumably the sheets remaining at the end of the run were put up in wrappers in this way and offered for sale as single volumes containing a number of stories. This enterprise was still under way in 1891 and indicates that Dicks's success in the 1850s was no mere flash in the pan.

The typography left much to be desired – these novels were printed in small type, three columns to the page; but they were cheap, and the illustrations were often striking. The scope of the vast publishing empire over which Dicks presided in the second half of the nineteenth century awaits investigation. He has not been thought worthy of a place in the *Dictionary of National Biography*, but the range of his publishing activities suggests that the task of unravelling their pattern would be a complex and difficult one.[56]

John Dicks, then, issued both sensational popular fiction and cheap editions of the classics; but he was not the first to exploit the rising market for books in this way. William Milner, a York-shireman born in 1803, did so as well, although in a rather different way: he concentrated on cheap books bound in cloth and avoided the kind of penny fiction in which Lloyd, Vickers, Dicks and others specialized. He undertook the continuing reissue of gothic novels – *The Children of the Abbey*, *The Farmer of Inglewood Forest*, *The Mysteries of Udolpho*; and he produced numerous novels by English and American writers – T. S. Arthur was one – who specialized in the kind of fiction which was both popular and eminently respectable.

In his late teens Milner set up in business as a general dealer, and in 1836 he became a jobbing printer in Halifax. A year later, having found that the production of political pamphlets and handbills provided a scanty living, he went into fiction and

56. See 'John Dicks', in the *Bookseller* (March 1881), p. 231. For a superb example of how problems in this field have been tackled, see A. Johannsen, *The House of Beadle and Adams* (Norman, Oklahoma; Vols 1 and 2, 1950; Vol. 3, 1962).

founded the Cottage Library, which established both his fortune and his reputation as a publisher. These little books, bound in cloth, measuring about three inches by five inches (Royal 32mo), cost one shilling each, and the series ran for more than fifty years, covering an immense range of titles. Included in it were not only the old and tried favourites such as those mentioned above, but also various handbooks – *Every Man His Own Farrier*, *American Receipt Book* – and editions of Byron, Coleridge and Moore. Several volumes of Bunyan's works were included, of which *The Pilgrim's Progress* was only one.

The Cottage Library proved so successful that other series were started. There were the New Novelist's Library, costing 1s. 6d. a cloth-bound volume, and the Wide, Wide World Library, costing 1s. 3d. or 1s. 6d. according to binding and containing both fiction and non-fiction. Juvenile books were published in large numbers at various prices, mostly at 1s. or 6d. a time, and some titles were issued in paper wrappers. For 3d. a *Manual of Croquet* could be had, and a *Hieroglyphical Bible* with nearly two hundred woodcuts was available in cloth at 1s. or in paper at 6d. There was a strong evangelical flavour about many of the non-fiction titles: all kinds of devotional books were published, and three temperance reciters appeared in catalogues towards the end of the century.

William Milner died in 1850, but the business continued very successfully. A London office was opened and expansion continued, new projects including a 'Moral and Religious Series' and an 'Instructive and Entertaining Series'.

The business methods of the founder were summed up in his own phrase, 'small profits and quick returns'. In pursuance of this, William Milner himself stumped the country with a stock of books. In towns like Bristol, Glasgow or Norwich he would take a shop for a week or two and sell off his stock in a lively fashion – he held an auctioneer's licence – before returning to his native Yorkshire. Towards the end of the century the firm could say:

ESTABLISHED OVER HALF-A-CENTURY!

In every part of the world – wherever the Anglo-Saxon language is spoken, *Milner & Co's Publications* are, and have been read by thousands of the people for a great number of years. They are acknowledged by all to contain the greatest quantity of reading for the small amount charged; – also the most durable in Binding; and the neatest in appearance of any Books published at the low price at which they are issued. Your special attention is particularly drawn to the wonderful cheapness of the *One Shilling Novels! They are the only Standard Romances Bound in Cloth that are issued at that Price*, and are unequalled by any other House in the Publishing Trade! This series contains the choicest productions of Charles Dickens, Charlotte Brontë, Lord Lytton, Henry Cockton, Captain Marryat, William Makepeace Thackeray, Samuel Lover, Charles Lever, &c., &c., as well as the best works of the cleverest American authors.

TO OUR NUMEROUS READERS EVERYWHERE

Ladies and Gentlemen,

It is no empty boast when we say that we have more successfully suited the varied tastes of our innumerable readers in every part of the globe, for a longer period than most of the Publishing Houses now in existence.

The especial features of our Publications are their cheapness, completeness, and durability. There are thousands of our volumes in the homes of the people today, in very good condition, which were bought ten, fifteen, twenty, thirty, and forty years ago; they have given education and entertainment to the purchasers most completely, and at a price at which no other Publishing House has ever offered them.

We have added, in the following Catalogue, a large number of New Novels, by the best English and American Authors, Religious Works, Juvenile Story Books, School and Temperance Books, &c., &c., any of which may be had of the Booksellers, or by sending postage-stamps to the amount of the published price, and One Penny on the Shilling extra for Postal delivery to your own homes, to

Milner & Co., Publishers, Halifax, Yorkshire, or,
16, PATERNOSTER ROW, LONDON

179

PEOPLE'S EDITION.

DICKS' ENGLISH NOVELS.

SKETCHES BY "BOZ."

By CHARLES DICKENS.

Complete, from the Original Edition.—Forty Illustrations.
LONDON: JOHN DICKS, 313, STRAND.

PRICE SIXPENCE.

19. A popular novelist like Dickens was published in many other cheap editions

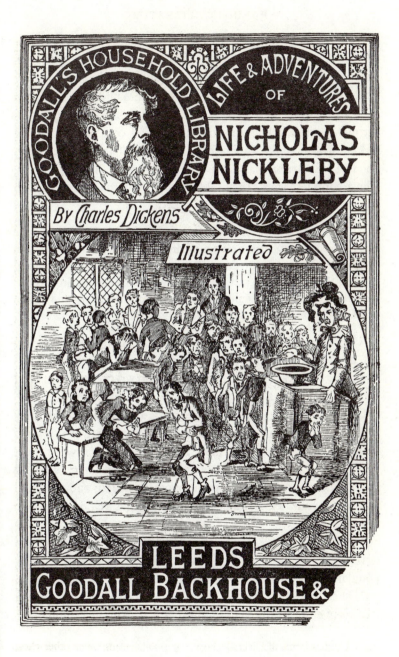

GOODALL'S HOUSEHOLD LIBRARY

LIFE & ADVENTURES OF NICHOLAS NICKLEBY

By Charles Dickens

Illustrated

LEEDS
GOODALL BACKHOUSE &

Much of their trade was done with the colonies. Partly because of this, and partly because the firm welcomed direct sales to readers, catalogues of current titles were often bound with the books themselves. Although most books were undated, much can be learned from these catalogues. The earliest tended to be descriptive, while later ones often included comment upon the writers whose books were offered for sale. What they had to say about T. S. Arthur has already been quoted. Charles Dickens, whose complete works they sold at 1s. per volume,[57] is given high praise:

He has never had a compeer who at all approached him in the graphic and faithful descriptions of the characters which abound in the multifarious walks of life, to be found in the thickly populated 'modern Babylon'. The scenes he portrays are so life-like in description, that if the reader could be transported to the places and scenes of which he has written, then he would find them 'true to the letter'.

The reader, it is claimed, is brought 'face to face with the low life of the metropolis'. Captain Marryat, too, was praised unstintingly – 'a practical son of the sea', who wrote 'humorous and instructive sea-tales'.

Comments upon lesser-known writers are perhaps more valuable. There was, for instance, Mary Bennett, author of *The Jew's Daughter*, *The Broken Heart*, *Jane Shore; or, the Goldsmith's Wife*, *The Cottage Girl*, and *The Gipsy Bride*. 'Varied in their styles and plots,' said the publishers, 'the aristocratic villain and the cruel poacher are alike condemned, and their crimes held up to public reprobation.'

Mrs Mary Jane Holmes and Miss Dupuy were American novelists who figured in Milner catalogues. The former was a very popular author who was born in Massachusetts and whose novels, published between 1858 and 1887, sold over two million copies in American editions which her publisher bound up in lots of 50,000

57. The reprinting of Dickens's novels in one cheap edition or another was almost a minor literary industry. See illustrations on pp. 180–81.

at a time.[58] 'A particularly fascinating writer,' said the Milner catalogue. 'Her master mind has grasped the wants of the day.' Amongst the novels available in England were *Edna Browning*, *Edith Lyle*, *Ethelyn's Misfortune*, *Lena Rivers*, *Marian Grey*.

Miss Dupuy – she is referred to without initials in the Milner catalogue – must be, I think, Eliza A. Dupuy, who came from an old-established Huguenot family in the United States, and whose novels seem to have been originally published in the 1850s. One of them, *The Conspirator*, sold over 24,000 copies, and six of her novels were advertised by Milner at one time. 'She has the gift,' said the publisher's blurb, 'of raising the mind to that pitch of excitement which our own female writers are seldom able to do.'

There was a vast literature of popular romantic fiction in the nineteenth century, and I have done little more than indicate its existence by pointing to the tip of a very substantial iceberg. Novels of this kind are still popular in the 1970s. The firm of D. C. Thomson of Dundee issues a number of weekly magazines which specialize in stories which bear a striking resemblance to those written by Mary Jane Holmes, Eliza A. Dupuy, Mary Bennett and many others.

Let us examine some sales figures. Although fiction formed the bulk of Milner's lists, he did sell very substantial numbers of his editions of the classics and it is worth looking at some circulation figures for his books which have survived. Down to 1895, the number of copies of poets printed ran as follows:[59]

Burns	183,333	Longfellow	63,092
Byron	126,514	Moore	58,322
Milton	85,296	Cowper	51,926
Pope	69,296	Wordsworth	25,811
Bloomfield	65,550	Shelley	22,022

58. J. D. Hunt, *The Popular Book* (New York, 1950), p. 97.

59. In Stock Book of Messrs Milner & Co. Ltd, quoted by H. E. Wroot in 'A Pioneer in Cheap Literature. William Milner of Halifax', the *Bookman* (March 1897), p. 174.

Dryden	17,926	Coleridge	8,150
Scott	17,050	Butler	4,250
Hemans	13,100	Heber	3,550
Thomson	12,100	Keats	3,500
Kirk-White	10,450		

Milner's edition of Burns's poems was one of the earliest books published by him. It consisted of 10,000 copies in 1837, and by 1839 about 30,000 copies had been sold.[60] The sales of Robert Bloomfield and Mrs Hemans illustrate changes of taste. Of the former's works, 60,050 had been sold by 1866, and Mrs Hemans's works had sold 12,000 copies by 1864. Walter Scott is fairly low down on the list, probably because a cheap 'Edinburgh' edition was also available.

As far as fiction was concerned, the runaway best-seller was *Uncle Tom's Cabin*. Milner's edition came out in 1852 and cost 1s. His presses ran day and night for six months to keep up with the demand, and 25,000 copies were sold in fifteen months. It should be remembered, too, that eight or ten other English publishers were selling the same book at prices which ranged from 1s. 6d. to 12s. per copy.

There are figures for other novels which sold well over a period of time. *The Children of the Abbey* sold over 75,000 copies. *The Farmer of Inglewood Forest* did even better. The continuing sales of these novels in cheap editions indicate very clearly an unchanging tradition in some kinds of romantic fiction; and they indicate also that titled aristocracy – about half the characters in the former novel fell into this category – were an attraction so far as popular novels were concerned. However, characters did not have to be drawn from the nobility to catch the imagination. The interminable saga of Trueman Flint in Maria Cummings's *The Lamplighter* was published in America in 1854, and 40,000 copies were sold in eight weeks. In England, the Milner edition – not the only

60. These and the following sales figures are from Milner catalogues in the possession of the author.

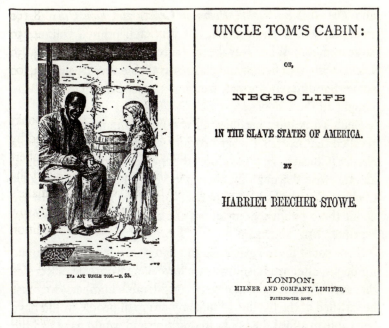

UNCLE TOM'S CABIN:

OR,

NEGRO LIFE

IN THE SLAVE STATES OF AMERICA.

BY

HARRIET BEECHER STOWE.

LONDON:
MILNER AND COMPANY, LIMITED,
PATERNOSTER ROW.

EVA AND UNCLE TOM.—P. 53.

20. Milner's edition of the best-known American novel

one available in this country – sold 119,700 copies over a period of forty years.

Upon figures like these a successful business was founded, and it seems odd, in view of the extent of Milner's popularization of books amongst the poor, that he does not rate an entry in the *Dictionary of National Biography*.

William Milner was the most successful among publishers who exploited the market for cheap books in a small format; but others included J. S. Pratt of Stokesley in Yorkshire and William Nicholson of Wakefield in the same county. Both, like Milner, opened London offices and, although we cannot be too precise about dates, the little that we do know about these publishing houses indicates a considerable area of mass publishing. Books from firms like this were cheap, portable and popular. The quality of their fiction was for the most part extremely low; but, in addition to this, editions of the poets were readily available at a small price, and *The Arabian Nights*, *Robinson Crusoe* and *Don Quixote*, for example, sold in these small, not very well-printed volumes in large numbers. When we take into account the enterprise of John Dicks, with both fiction and classics available very cheaply but in somewhat different format, we cannot escape the question: who bought all these books?

Such a question becomes all the more important when it is recalled that neither Richard Altick, whose *The English Common Reader* (Chicago, 1957) explores the theme of popular reading in an otherwise thorough manner, nor Michael Sadleir in his *XIX Century Fiction* (Vol. II, London, 1951) had very much to say about these publishers, or about the authors whose works they reprinted time and again.

To account for the existence and nature of a purchasing public for books, after establishing as we have done from sales successes that such a public existed in very considerable numbers, we must be satisfied of the likelihood that any group of people would have been able to afford the books in question and would have had the degree of literacy and leisure necessary to read them; and we must also look for confirmation from those who have left us a contemporary picture of life.

The books which I have described were certainly available for small sums; and I suspect that, fairly stoutly bound as they were, copies could quite readily have been available from second-hand shops and also from subscription libraries. Literacy, as I have suggested in the previous chapter, had already reached a substantial proportion of the working class by 1800; and during the century which followed, supported by an ever-growing government involvement from 1833, the work of reformers and educationalists was providing more and more people with at least a basic literacy. Leisure is perhaps more difficult to assess. It must be stressed that much romantic popular fiction was written by women for a female audience; but to be specific about the shadowy 'general reader' of either sex is by no means justifiable. Clearly, however, it was in the main to members of the working class,

T. S. ARTHUR'S MORAL NOVELS.

T. S. ARTHUR as an Author.

THE world is greatly indebted to such authors as T. S. ARTHUR. He may truly be styled one of the first of its social reformers, for he has written for the peoples' welfare, both morally, socially, and religiously. His stories always improve the reader, in the highest sense of the word. He has done more to strengthen the morals and cultivate the religious faculties of his readers than a great many clever authors of the present day. None need fear the introducing of his books into the home circle; in fact, they ought to be welcomed as the best aids to a good moral and religious home training, that can be obtained. His efforts are always happy, lively, and interesting, with sound principles running through the whole of them. He has lived and laboured to leave the world better than he found it.

Anna Lee; or, the Maiden, Wife, and Mother.

THIS beautiful novel is written in a truly natural strain; it is not highly coloured with romantic tints, but its pictures of life are portrayed with so vivid and striking a truthfulness, that the social ties of the domestic hearth are seen in all their pristine loveliness. Its high moral tone and virtuous teachings will enable it to win its way in the families of all classes of the community. It comes from the pen of one of the best American writers, T. S. ARTHUR, whose reputation on both sides of the Atlantic, as a most excellent, truthful story-teller, is universally admitted.

Cast Adrift. A Story of New York.

THE most fastidious parents need not have the least fear of introducing the Works of T. S. ARTHUR into their families. They are full of instructive moral lessons, and are written in a very attractive style. "Cast Adrift" is a story of life in New York City. The heroine is found in the lowest state of society, and by virtuous behaviour in the midst of vice, wins her way into upper circles.

Righted at Last. A Story of New England Life.

THERE is a common proverb "Every dog has its day;" by the hand of retribution with which Providence almost invariably lays hold upon the evil-doer, and punishes him severely, when he has persisted in his wicked courses of oppression and the exercise of tyranny upon the weak and defenceless. We see many things that are wrong "righted at last," and this charming story by T. S. ARTHUR is but another instance of the truth, that virtue and goodness will ultimately triumph, though the time of triumph may be long delayed.

21. How Milner Company presented a best-selling author to the public. A page from one of their catalogues, undated but probably issued in the late 1880s.

22. (a) Inside a shop which carried a small stock of fiction for lending to customers at a low fee

artisans or clerks, that the great entrepreneurs of popular publishing addressed their wares, and fiction of the sensational or romantic kind did, of course, offer a ready escape from the harsh realities of a daily existence which was bounded by work, crowded conditions and poverty. Such stories could be read at odd moments – ten minutes snatched on the journey to work, or during meal breaks – and this kind of reading pattern is not as

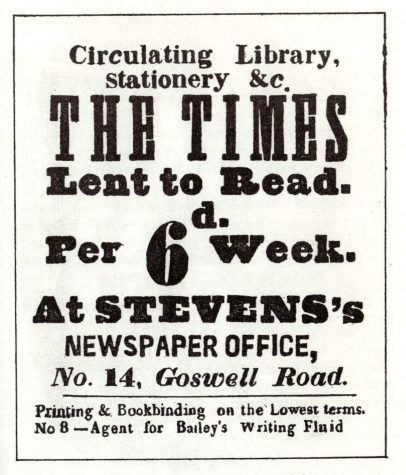

22. (b) A circulating library label, 1848

fanciful as it might appear, according to at least one Victorian writer:

The clerks and artizans, shopgirls, dressmakers, and milliners, who pour into London every morning by the early trains, have, each and every one, a choice specimen of penny fiction to beguile the short journey, and perhaps the few spare minutes of a busy day. The working man who slouches up and down the platform waiting for the moment of departure, is absorbed in some crumpled bit of pink-covered romance . . .[61]

Thus we can understand the reading of fiction; and it does not, for example, seem hard to imagine opportunities for reading, however brief, during the housewife's day. Nevertheless it must be said that, despite the impressive publication figures of William Milner's firm and the immense success of John Dicks, reading even of light novels was not necessarily a majority activity.

Who bought, and presumably read, all those editions of Burns, Byron, Scott, Milton and other poets, and of the classics? To give added sharpness to this question, we must think also of Cassell's Penny Shakespeare – the plays published towards the end of the century at one penny each, with a coloured cover. The archetypal purchaser of these must surely have been the kind of man described by Mrs Gaskell in her novel, *Mary Barton*:

There is a class of men in Manchester, unknown even to many of the inhabitants, and whose existence will probably be doubted by many, who may yet claim kindred with all the noble names that science recognizes. I said 'in Manchester', but they are scattered all over the manufacturing districts of Lancashire. In the neighbourhood of Oldham there are weavers, common hand-loom weavers, who throw the shuttle with unceasing sound, though Newton's *Principia* lie open on the loom, to be snatched at in work hours, but revelled over in meal times or at night.[62]

The author was describing Job Legh, who was the sort of man who would have bought cheap editions of the poets. As Mrs Gaskell implies, he was not alone, and it is, I think, no mere coincidence that Milner first set up his business in the north of England. Indeed, the figure of the 'self-taught man' – and I can think of few other working men who would have read Milton for pleasure – is an important one in the nineteenth century. Such a man exists in the pages of several autobiographies, of which those

61. Agnes Repplier, 'English Railway Fiction', in *Points of View* (1895), p. 209.

62. Penguin Books (1970), p. 75.

" The street lamps were his study-lights, while he read and re-read the books lent him by Mr. Danvers."—*Page* 59.

23. The pursuit of knowledge under difficulties! Mr Danvers was the master of a National School, and the boy he helped, Walter Benn, hero of Grace Stebbings's novel of this name (undated, ?1890), went on to become super-intending engineer of an Indian railway

by Thomas Cooper, W. E. Adams and Samuel Bamford are obvious examples; but he is seen more clearly and certainly in a contemporary light in what I can only describe as the 'literature of self-made men'.

THE SENSATIONAL.

News-vendor—" Now, my man, what is it ? "
Boy—" I vonts a nillustrated newspaper with
a norrid murder and a likeness in it."

24. At the point of sale

G. L. Craik set the fashion in *The Pursuit of Knowledge under Difficulties*, first published in two volumes in 1830 and several times reprinted. Unlike Alton Locke, Adam Bede, or even Mr Polly, who were fictional characters, Craik dealt in actual people, and his book was intended to show by examples drawn from real life that it was possible to succeed, according to nineteenth-century ideas of attaining fame and fortune, through one's own efforts in which education, notably reading, played an important part. Craik cast his net wide, and his two volumes are a treasure-house of self-made men. The notion of holding up as examples individuals who rose above their humble beginnings became irresistible, and a very minor literary industry developed. Among such books were *Self-help*, by Samuel Smiles (first published 1859 and went through many editions), *Self-made Men*, by William Anderson (second edition, 1865), and two anonymous, undated books, *Small Beginnings or the Way to Get On* and *Biography of Self Taught Men*.

If we are to judge from the sheer volume of cheap serious literature which was available throughout the nineteenth century, books like those mentioned above were either an encouragement to artisans to read or a reflection of a situation which existed. The self-taught man, or even woman, was becoming accepted as a reality.

This kind of reader was the object of a great deal of attention from both reformers and publishers during the nineteenth century. An obsession with the distribution of tracts gave way in the Industrial Revolution to an equally strong desire to educate the poor. In part this was an extension of evangelism and the desire to 'improve' the unprivileged through the agency of the printed word;[63] but to a growing extent there was a demand from working men and women for an education which would more easily enable them to take their places in an expanding industrial society in which, for many, the traditional skills of an agricultural economy were seen to be increasingly irrelevant.

Incoherent as such a demand for education may have been, several publishers responded to it vigorously throughout the century, and the resulting popular literature, largely unexplored, stands as a testament to the enlightened self-interest, not un-

63. We should remember, too, that novels were frequently given away as Sunday-school prizes – but they had to be moral and wholesome!

25.   (a) Reading below stairs

mixed with a degree of philanthropy, which characterized the
work of such men as Charles Knight, the Chambers Brothers and,
finally, John Cassell.

Knight was not a pioneer. Thomas Kelly, whose premises in
Paternoster Row were opened in 1809, published large editions of
a family Bible sold in weekly parts. Altogether he sold about
230,000 Bibles in various editions, besides other works. The
secret of Kelly's success was that the payment for his books, sold
in parts, was gradual, and he was shrewd enough to organize
throughout the country an effective network of agents to handle
his publications. The problem facing the publisher who wished
the poor to buy his books was that such people might go only
rarely into bookshops. How, then, were the books to be distributed
effectively? William Milner, as we have seen, used a combination
of temporary premises which he supervised for himself and direct

25.   (b) Reading light novels

sales; while before him popular literature had been available in single sheets and small booklets from sellers in the streets, and the eighteenth-century chapman had not only supplied local dealers but had also offered his stocks in fairs and markets, at farms and cottages. The sheer mechanics of distributing a more substantial popular literature and persuading people to pay for it presented problems at the outset of the nineteenth century – and, I suspect, at other times as well. Then, as now, it is only a minority of the population which ventures into a bookshop.

Charles Knight held that the organization of book clubs by local groups offered the best solution, and in an article entitled

'Book Clubs for All Readers' published in the *Penny Magazine* on 11 May 1844 he set out his views. Before we examine them, something must be said of the man himself.[64]

He was born in 1791, and had a long career in publishing up until his death in 1873. He was also an author in his own right, and an editor. In 1825 he was planning a 'national library' which was to comprise a series of cheap books containing information available only in more expensive volumes. The project came to nothing, and after varying fortunes in trade he undertook in 1828 to supervise the publications of the Society for the Diffusion of Useful Knowledge, which Lord Brougham and others had founded some months earlier. As publisher to the Society, Knight was involved in a number of educational enterprises, the most important of which was the *Penny Magazine* from 1832 to 1845. By the end of its first year the magazine had a sale of 200,000 in weekly numbers, but by the mid forties the circulation had fallen to 40,000 and costs of production were barely covered.

Quite apart from the fact that neither political discussion nor fiction were allowed to sully its pages, the *Penny Magazine* never apparently reached the public for which it was intended. It had 'only to a limited extent,' said an active member of the Society,[65] 'reached the humblest classes of this country, but other classes have been found who were in want of the information contained in these works, and have benefited by them.' What contributed mostly to the downfall of the magazine was its preoccupation with facts – something which might have pleased Mr Gradgrind, but was not entirely to the taste of a working-class readership.

Knight published a number of instructional works, including a 'Pictorial Shakespeare', and in 1844 he began his series, Knight's Weekly Volume for All Readers. The first volume was his own

64. See his own autobiography, *Passages of a Working Life During Half a Century* (three vols., 1864–5); also the entry in the *Dictionary of National Biography*, XI.

65. B. F. Duppa, quoted in R. K. Webb, *The British Working Class Reader* (1955), pp. 78–9.

life of Caxton, and every week for the next two years a new title appeared. For two years more there was a monthly volume. The books cost 1s. paper-bound and 1s. 6d. in cloth. The range of subjects was limited: Vol. XI was devoted to *Bird Architecture* and Vol. XV to *The Elephant*, while Vol. XXX was a series of *Pictures of English Life*, gathered from Chaucer. The series paid its way, and many of the books in it were excellent; but Knight did not reach the mass market.

Indeed, his importance for this study lies not in the fact that he was a successful publisher of popular non-fiction works – for he was not – but rather in his concern with persuading people to buy books for themselves and his awareness of the necessity of cheap editions. The fact that he was hardly successful in reaching the market which he felt sure existed does not in any way obscure the further fact that he had some very interesting things to say about the distribution of books and about cheap literature in general.

In the article on book clubs already referred to, Knight advocated the setting up of local groups which could purchase on a communal basis one book per week and then run a lending library. It was to this end that he started the 'Weekly Volume' series, and he offered in addition, gratis, to supply any group which applied to him with forms which could be stuck into the front of each book as a record of loan and return.

With his usual thoroughness Knight traced the history of book clubs and claimed that the earliest which was both cheap and successful had been started by Robert Burns when he was living at Mauchline. Knight, like Lord Brougham,[66] argued strongly that people should set up their own reading societies, or book clubs, but, somewhat exceptionally, Knight was ready with practical advice:

> The principle of voluntary association for the purchase of books has scarcely been called into action; and the reason is pretty obvious. The machinery by which such associations are worked is too cumbrous. We have before us the rules of a Reading Society in a village some ten

66. *Practical Observations Upon the Education of the People* (1825).

miles from London. Here we have all the array of president, vice-president, secretary, honorary members, and subscribing members. There are quarterly meetings and annual meetings, balloting for new members, minutes, notices of motion – in a word, all the complex contrivances by which the management of such matters is kept in the hands of a directing few. But the great difficulty of all is the choice of books; and this is a difficulty which cannot be got over without some new arrangements. If a collection of books were published at a sufficiently rapid rate, and at so low a price as very soon of themselves to be capable of being the foundation of a library – always provided that such books were unexceptionable in their morality, interesting as well as instructive, and containing an abundant provision of truly national literature – it is evident that all the troublesome arrangements of proposing books and of approving books, to say nothing of the difficulty of getting the best books sufficiently cheap, would be effectually got rid of. If a subscription of a penny a week by twelve individuals would place at their command fifty-two volumes in the course of a year, in which, from the nature of the subjects and their modes of treatment, the majority should feel an interest, it is evident that no machinery would be required to set such a plan in action but the association of twelve such individuals. and the choice of one amongst them as secretary, who would receive the subscriptions quarterly, purchase the books week by week as they came out, paste within their covers the rules of the Club, with a list of the names of the members in alphabetical or other order, and then send a volume to the first person on the list, who should keep it for a limited time, passing it on to the next, till it had been circulated through the whole number, and returned to the custody of the secretary. A few books of reference might be purchased by a small extra subscription, and deposited in some place of common access. The books might form a permanent library, or be sold amongst the subscribers at the end of each year.[67]

An interesting sidelight upon such book clubs was provided by William Lovett, the Chartist, who wrote to Francis Place on 17 November 1834:

[67] 'Book Clubs for All Readers', an 8-page leaflet bound into many numbers of Knight's Weekly Volume for All Readers, originally published in *Penny Magazine* (11 May 1844).

Sir, about twelve years ago, chance introduced me into a little society composed of intelligent, and chiefly young men, who hold their meetings at a house in the vicinity of Leicester Fields. They by a trifling weekly subscription had accumulated a Library of the most choice and to me valuable books ... By their conversation and discussion together with the books I read I acquired a taste for mixing with companions of this description ...[68]

In an article published in his book, *Once Upon a Time* (1854), Knight wrote about 'the beginnings of popular literature', and what he had to say revealed on the one hand the narrow view he took of the subject and on the other that he seriously overestimated the importance of the circulating library. The narrowness of his view is demonstrated by the fact that he seems to have had no inkling at all of the vast public which had enjoyed both chap-books and street ballads; and he made extravagant claims for circulating libraries in these terms:

What a revolution was that in popular literature! How this new planet appeared above the earth ... There it was – this great economizer of individual outlay for books – in most market towns at the beginning of this century. The universal adoption of the name is the best proof of the common recognition of the idea. It changed the habits of the old country booksellers. It found them other occupation than keeping a stall in the market-place, as did their worthy forefathers. They dealt no longer in tracts and single sermons. It sent the chap-books into the villages. It made the 'Seven Champions of Christendom' and 'The Wise Masters of Greece' vulgar. It created a new library of fiction. It banished 'Robinson Crusoe' to the kitchen, and 'The Arabian Nights' to the nursery.

The euphoria of this reaction led Knight seriously astray, both in his estimate of circulating libraries and in his judgements about achieving a wide sale for his books through such institutions. His failure as a publisher was, however, not altogether due to these factors. Leaving aside his inability to select books which were

68. British Museum ADD MS 27,827, Place Papers Vol. XXXIX, Leaf 29ff.

going to sell in large numbers, he was hampered crucially by the fact that he did not have adequate distribution arrangements for his publications. It was the primitive state of the book trade that led him to place undue reliance upon other outlets, notably book clubs. The fact is that self-help, however enterprising and energetic, was no substitute for an efficient trade organization. This was lacking in the early nineteenth century and unless, like James Catnach, one could rely largely upon hawkers and street sellers the problems of circulating all over the country large numbers of bound books, as opposed to magazines and journals, were well-nigh insuperable – as Knight found to his cost.

Of course there were successful booksellers. James Lackington (1746–1815) was one and Thomas Tegg (1776–1845) another. Both set new fashions in bookselling, and their respective careers demonstrated to those who came after them that the market for cheap books was potentially enormous. Each was a pioneer, and his experience foreshadowed future patterns in the selling of books that were later to be more successfully exploited. In particular, W. H. Smith was able to learn from the experience of these earlier men and also to see clearly for himself the new opportunities for retail distribution which the coming of the railway, together with an increasing need for bookshops open to all, was to offer.

James Lackington was born in the West Country and first showed his capacity for business when he was ten years old, as an itinerant pie-seller. After this he sold almanacs in the streets, and in 1773 he went with his wife to London. In the following year he spent a guinea on a sackful of old theological books and combined the running of a bookstall with a shoemaker's shop. In six months, having borrowed five pounds from 'Mr Wesley's people', the value of his stock had increased so much that he was able to give up shoemaking and devote himself entirely to books.

Lackington continued to prosper, and in 1779 his firm brought out a catalogue of 12,000 volumes. His shop, one of the sights of London and called 'The Temple of the Muses', was situated at

TEMPLE OF THE MUSES

An interior view of the extensive Library of
LACKINGTON, ALLEN & Cº. FINSBURY SQUARE, LONDON
where above Half a Million Volumes are constantly on Sale.

26.   Inside a famous eighteenth-century bookshop

one corner of Finsbury Square. It contained an enormous stock, displayed for sale in a series of ascending galleries. The higher one went, the cheaper and shabbier the books became. Lackington's practice – one upon which he built a considerable fortune – was to sell for cash, pricing his books as cheaply as possible.

By 1784 his stock had reached 30,000 volumes. He broke with the established trade practice of destroying all but a few copies of books which did not sell, and would sell off the entire stock at a knock-down price. In 1791 he reckoned to be selling 100,000 volumes a year at a profit of £4,000; and still his turnover increased. He was, it seems, the first bookseller to realize the importance of the remainder trade. He sold both from his premises and from the catalogue, and his success was clearly due to the fact that he met a very real need for cheap books – and saw bookselling in economic rather than literary terms.[69]

Thomas Tegg was apprenticed to a Scottish bookseller when he was nine years old; but his master treated him badly, so he started out on his own selling chapbooks. Eventually he moved to London, where he opened a bookshop which failed because his partner was a drunkard. After a brief career as a book auctioneer in the provinces he returned to London and opened a shop in Cheapside where he sold large numbers of books which he produced himself.

His earliest publications were pamphlet abridgements of popular works. There were 200 of these, some of which sold up to 4,000 copies. With the death of Nelson at Trafalgar, Tegg rushed a sixpenny biography onto the market and sold 3,000 copies. He had other successes of this kind, and his reputation rested chiefly upon cheap reprints and abridgements of popular works; but he was also extensively engaged in the trade of publishers' remainders and made a great deal of money out of this.[70]

What both Lackington and Tegg had in common was a sense of professionalism and a quick eye for opportunities in the selling of books. For the most part they lacked the altruism of Charles Knight, but they were able to judge very much more readily what was saleable. Both men were important in the development of the book trade. They belonged to the long line of successful nineteenth-century entrepreneurs, while Knight was much more like a gentlemanly bookseller of the preceding century.

A very determined effort to reach a mass public with cheap 'improving' publications was made by the Edinburgh brothers, William and Robert Chambers (1800–1883; 1802–71). The first number of their periodical *Chambers's Edinburgh Journal* was published on 4 February 1832, price three halfpence. It was

---

69. For Lackington see his own *Memoirs* (1791); also the *Dictionary of National Biography* XI.

70. For Tegg see H. Curwen, *A History of Booksellers* (undated), pp. 379–98; also the *Dictionary of National Biography* XIX.

successful, and the circulation soon rose to 80,000 copies, although
the extent to which it was genuinely popular amongst the poor is
highly questionable, since the price was more than they could
afford to pay. Its readership consisted almost certainly of the more
skilled and aspiring artisan who was keen to better himself, to 'get
on', in the tradition which Samuel Smiles was later to popularize.
The ideas behind the magazine were described by William: 'In
the beginning of January, 1832, I conceived the idea of a cheap
weekly periodical devoted to wholesome popular instruction
blended with original amusing matter, without any knowledge
whatever of the *Penny Magazine*, or even hearing that such a
thing was in contemplation.'[71]

The difference between the Chambers's enterprise and that of
Charles Knight and the Society for the Diffusion of Useful
Knowledge is highlighted in the phrase 'original amusing matter'.
William and Robert Chambers were very much more realistic
about the contents of their publications and saw clearly that
fiction, though not of a sensational kind, was a necessity if they
were to reach a really wide public. All the same, the proportion of
fiction to fact in their publications was pretty small.

Also among their publications was a series entitled *Chambers's
Miscellany of Useful and Entertaining Tracts*, which ran to ten
volumes. Another work which ran eventually to ten volumes was
Chambers's Encyclopaedia, which came out between 1859 and
1868; while *Chambers's Educational Course*, which commenced
in 1835 with a three-halfpenny infant primer, went on to
cover grammar, a dictionary, historical and scientific themes,
and cheap editions of standard authors, both foreign and
classical. This enterprise was a splendid example of putting
the means of education into the hands of readers at a very
moderate price.

In 1855 the firm issued reprints of stories which they had
published in the *Journal* in 32-page numbers at a penny or twopence each; and thirty years later it was still thought worth-while

71. Quoted in Curwen, op. cit., p. 244.

to issue tales published earlier in the century as sixpenny paper-backs.[72]

Odd volumes of *Chambers's Miscellany* can still be picked up in second-hand bookshops and exemplify the kind of material put out by this energetic firm. Volume 8 of an undated 'New and Revised Edition' contains reprints of sixteen of the original 'instructive and entertaining tracts'. There is a life of William Hutton – himself a notable self-educated man and book-seller – with a portrait; a selection of Byron's poems; two stories by Mrs S. C. Hall; the Crusades; a tale entitled 'The Sister of Rembrandt'; and other tracts covering archaeological subjects, biography and popular science.

With such a mixture the Chambers were remarkably successful in reaching a popular market. Towards the end of his life William speculated upon the reasons why the *Penny Magazine* and its associated publications had not been as successful as their sponsors had hoped. They were, he said,

... on the whole too technical and abstruse for the mass of operatives; they made no provision for the culture of the imaginative faculties; and, in point of fact, were purchased and read by persons considerably raised above the obligation of toiling with their hands for their daily bread. In a word, they may be supposed to have been distasteful to the popular fancy.[73]

There was a great deal of truth in this criticism, and Chambers's view of popular literature was a very much more realistic one than that of Charles Knight. He had, for example, a good deal more to say about chapbooks:

Let us look into the matter historically, saying a few words in the first place regarding the oldest cheap literature of all – the Penny Chap Books, consisting of coarsely printed sheets, duodecimo, embellished with equally coarse frontispieces, aimed at no sort of instruction, such as we now understand by the term; yet they furnished amusement to

72. See Michael Sadleir, *XIX Century Fiction* (2 vols, 1951), Vol. II, p. 25.
73. William Chambers, *Memoir of Robert Chambers* (sixth edition, 1871), p. 245.

the humble fireside. They appealed to the popular love of the heroic, the marvellous, the pathetic, and the humorous. Many of them were nothing more than an embodiment of the legends, superstitions, ballads, and songs, which had been kept alive by oral tradition before the invention of printing.[74]

There are limitations in this viewpoint, but on the whole it is a remarkably shrewd assessment of chapbook literature and it provided a sound theoretical basis for the Chambers to specialize in the provision of cheap instructional literature while not altogether ignoring the claims of more imaginative material in the form of novels and poetry. In any case their formula was successful, and it was this Edinburgh firm which laid the basis of a didactic popular literature which was widely circulated and which avoided the worst excesses of exhortation and moralizing.[75]

The market that Knight had revealed and the brothers William and Robert Chambers had exploited with such skill was considerable and constantly expanding. In 1836 a young man called John Cassell (1817–65) came to London from Manchester to seek work as a carpenter. For some time before this he had been involved with the temperance movement as a lecturer, and he continued with these activities in London. By 1847 he had become a tea and coffee merchant – beverages which he sold because they were alternatives to alcoholic ones. He advertised widely, and one of his slogans, 'Buy Cassell's Shilling Coffee', was a household word.

The following year he issued the first number of the *Standard of Freedom*, a weekly newspaper costing 4½d. a copy. The editorial policy was broadly a liberal one, the paper standing for religious, political and commercial freedom; but it was, of course, bitterly opposed to intemperance. The comparatively high price meant that, despite the success of this venture, it did not reach the lower sections of the popular market. But the founder had once said in another context: 'I have it! The remedy is Education! Educate

74. ibid., p. 232.
75. For the Chambers brothers see also W. Chambers, *Story of a Long and Busy Life* (1882); and the *Dictionary of National Biography* IV.

the working men and women, and you have a remedy for the crying evil of the country. Give the people mental food and they will not thirst after the abominable drink which is poisoning them.'[76]

It was in this spirit that he drifted into publishing. Even before launching the *Standard* he had been the anonymous proprietor of the *Teetotal Times*, so he came not entirely as a beginner. It was with social causes that he was first concerned. There was, for example, *The Financial Reform Almanac for 1850*, the circulation of which was put at 20,000. Cassell's weakness for almanacs is reflected in the number of them, together with annuals of various kinds, which his firm issued during the nineteenth century.

In 1850 he turned to the provision of educational reading matter, and in January the first number of a penny weekly, the *Working Man's Friend and Family Instructor*, appeared. The keynote was 'instruction and rational amusement'. While the emphasis was upon such serious themes as a history of the Cromwellian period, ethnology, politics, biography and law – to name only a few of the subjects dealt with fairly early on – there was also fiction, and Mary Howitt contributed a serial. After a year Cassell claimed that he was selling 100,000 copies a week.

Cassell soon became involved in the movement to restrict the 'taxes on knowledge', as they were called – newspaper stamps, advertisement duty and paper duty which forced up the price of established newspapers and periodicals. The $4\frac{1}{2}$d. charged for the *Standard* was forced up to 5d., and Cassell's opposition was natural enough for a man of his nonconformist and radical views.

Also in 1850, he commenced a sixpenny monthly periodical 'expressly for working men', entitled *John Cassell's Library*. In the first year the contents included a serialized book on maritime exploration, a biographical dictionary and a work which was described as 'the cheapest and most complete history of England ever issued from the press'. Each serialized work was later issued in a cloth binding as a complete book. John Cassell had moved into book publishing.

76. Simon Nowell-Smith, *The House of Cassell 1848–1958* (1958), p. 9.

From then on, the progress of the firm was spectacular. In a wide range of books, periodicals and serial publications Cassell was giving practical expression to his exhortation regarding education and 'mental food'. His death in 1865 made little difference to the policy of the firm which he had founded. Popular education was the overwhelming characteristic of what was issued. There were, for instance, *The Biblical Educator*, commenced in 1853; a family Bible illustrated by Doré; a whole range of timetables, maps and guidebooks (in the '90s Cassell's firm was the publisher of official guides to all the principal railway companies); books of self-help; books of instruction; religious books. All these were issued, usually very cheaply in weekly parts, by the house of Cassell.

From amongst such a wealth of material two undertakings stand out as especially relevant to the general theme of didactic popular literature. The first of these was *Cassell's Library of English Literature*, a series of summaries and extracts from the classics with a commentary by the editor. When it began in 1875 it was issued in sevenpenny monthly numbers, and it ran for nearly six years. Its success was such that it was reprinted at a cheaper price, and later as a five-volume collection. Altogether there were 282 separate parts to this edition, and a comprehensive index, plus a dated list of contents, was available. The range is staggering, and runs from pre-Beowulf poems to George Eliot and Robert Browning. Practically every writer of note is included, and some very minor ones find a place in these volumes. The arrangement was as follows:

I   Shorter English poems
II   Illustrations of English religion
III English plays
IV   Shorter works in English prose
V   Sketches of longer works in English verse and prose.

There were illustrations throughout, and the scope of this collection remains extraordinarily impressive after almost one hundred years.

This was probably the most successful popularization of English literature for a mass market ever undertaken in the days before radio and television. The editor was Henry Morley, Emeritus Professor of English Literature at University College, London. As an academic he appears to have put his services at the disposal of more than one publisher, and in these various enterprises his skill deserves recognition. For the firm of Routledge he edited, between 1883 and 1888, *Morley's Universal Library*, a series which covered world literature in sixty-three volumes costing 1s. or 1s. 6d. each. In an advertisement serving as an end-paper in some volumes of the *Universal Library* Morley wrote: 'Messrs George Routledge & Sons have found that there is in England a very large public demand for good books.' He had demonstrated the truth of this statement with both his *Library of English Literature* and *Morley's Universal Library*, and his next undertaking confirmed it even more conclusively.

Cassell's National Library was founded in 1886, and weekly 16mo volumes were issued at 3d. or 6d., according to binding, until 1890. It was described as 'a series of Standard Works in every branch of [world] literature, including travel, biography, history, religion, science, art, adventure, fiction, drama, belles lettres, and whatever else may be worth lasting remembrance'. It was the most ambitious of Morley's undertakings. Arnold Bennett remembered them, saying that the first book he ever bought was 'the first volume of the first modern series of presentable and really cheap reprints, Macaulay's *Warren Hastings* in "Cassell's National Library"'.[77] *Punch*, in a characteristic comment, said: 'The old proverb was "Every man's house is his castle"; in future this will be "Every Englishman's house has his Cassell"'.[78]

The publishers were perhaps more pleased with what they

77. Quotations are from Nowell-Smith, op. cit., pp. 109–10.
78. Quoted by the publishers in Marco Polo, *Voyages and Travels*, issued in the National Library series (1886).

described as a letter from 'a Lancashire working man':

I am very much pleased with the twenty-three Volumes already

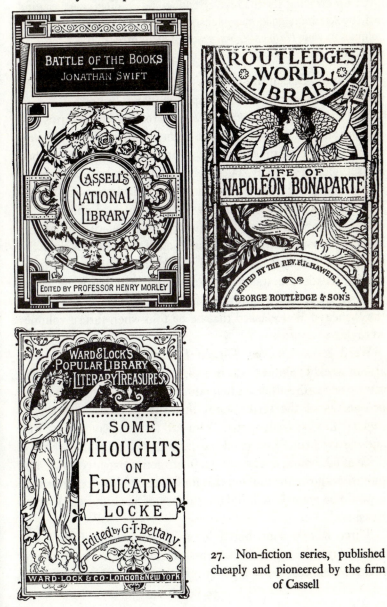

27. Non-fiction series, published cheaply and pioneered by the firm of Cassell

issued in your *National Library*. They have done a great deal of good even in my own neighbourhood, for several of my own friends have given up drinking for the sake of taking and reading your beautiful little books; and a good many subscribers have assured me that if the volumes in your *National Library* were issued three times a week, they would buy them as readily as they do one.[79]

A pity John Cassell did not live to read this letter! Can ever a publisher's intent have been so splendidly vindicated?

The success of the *National Library* prompted other firms into starting similar series. Routledge launched their *World Library*, weekly volumes of the classics at 3d. and 6d., and in this they had the services of the Rev. H. R. Haweis. Copies were apparently sent to prominent men and women, and their letters of acknowledgement were then printed as 'Letters to the Publishers' in some of the volumes. Queen Victoria was non-committal. Sir Henry Ponsonby, writing on her behalf, merely thanked the publishers and said that he had placed the volumes before the Queen. Gladstone was a little more forthcoming – he wrote wishing 'all success to your laudable undertaking'. A letter from the Prince of Wales asked that he be told when future volumes were due to appear.

Ward & Lock's *New Popular Library of Literary Treasures*, also in weekly volumes, was in a slightly larger format, but at the same price as the others. Their editor was G. T. Bettany, and the prospectus of the series states that the volumes of the *New Popular Library* 'will contain from 128 to 160 octavo pages, well and clearly printed on good paper, and will be sold at the low price of 6d. bound in cloth or 3d. in attractive paper covers'. The publishers go on to point out that for less than 6d. a week for a year it would be possible to build up a library of one hundred 'literary treasures'.

Three factors contributed towards the maintenance of low prices: first, the reprinting of classics had become a highly competitive business; second, the numbers of each title printed were

79. ibid.

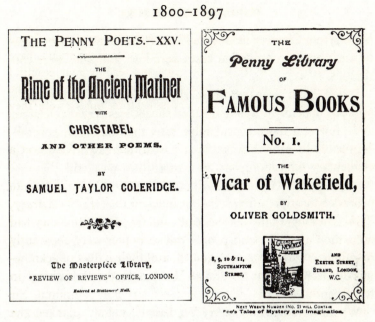

28. This was the cheapest price at which classics were issued!

large; and, finally, each series was subsidized by advertisers who took this opportunity to reach a wide and presumably serious-minded public. Amongst those firms using the books as an advertising medium were Beecham's Pills, whose slogan 'worth a guinea a box' was prominent in all three series, Mellin's Food, Keating's Powder, and Coventry Machinists' Co. Ltd, advertising their bicycles and tricycles. The frequent appearance of some kind of patent medicine among the advertisements reminds us that in the eighteenth century William Dicey and John Newbery had made a good deal of money out of publicizing pills and sundry nostrums.

By the close of the nineteenth century the provision of cheap editions of the classics had become a commonplace[80] – so much so that Frank Swinnerton could say: 'At the turn of the century nearly every publisher of note cheaply reprinted old and elderly

80. In 1896, for example, George Newnes started a series called *The Penny Library*, to be published weekly. No. 1 was *The Vicar of Wakefield*.

books, from Chaucer to George Eliot. He had no royalties to pay on such books; production costs were low; and sales were continuous.'[81]

It does seem clear that the market for cheap popular books, as opposed to penny novels and ballad sheets, was very much larger, and grew at a more considerable rate, than has been generally supposed. Its growth was due in part to increased facilities for elementary education, but even more to a powerful Victorian drive, descended from the Puritan ethos, to 'get on' – and in this process education, often self-education, was seen as a vital part. The autobiographies of several nineteenth-century working men show that working people did own books. George Meek mentions a radical shoemaker in a Sussex village who 'had quite a decent library',[82] and we may conclude that he was not too exceptional.

Where were books bought? We have one clue – and it is certainly no more than this – in the kind of notice which is reproduced on p. 189. This was stuck into a book published in 1848, and there was a network of such small shops. It is not too difficult to imagine that premises like these would have carried a stock of cheap books. Then we find, for example, an advertisement by H. Gearing, a bookseller and stationer in Lindfield, Sussex: 'Any Books supplied to order, H. G. having a parcel from London three times a week.'[83] This was in 1858; twenty-nine years later W. H. Brown, a bookseller in another country town, East Dereham, proclaimed: 'Daily parcels from London.'[84] While there is no doubt that much popular literature was borrowed for a small fee from private circulating libraries, many of these seem to have combined lending with selling. Yet another method of obtaining books was described

81. Editor's Preface to Arnold Bennett, *Literary Taste* (Penguin Books, 1938), p. 7.

82. *George Meek, Bath Chair-man, by himself* (1910), p. 34.

83. *Melville and Co.'s Directory and Gazeteer of Sussex* (1858), un-numbered advertisement leaf.

84. E. R. Suffling, *The Land of the Broads* (1887), un-numbered advertisement leaf.

by George Meek. He was born in Eastbourne in 1868, and when he was eight or nine the family used to buy 'Book' tea: 'You bought so many pounds of tea and then you received a book in return for the coupons attached to each package.'[85] How far such commercial sponsorship of books went in the nineteenth century it is difficult to tell.

In the shops of newsagents or confectioners, or from a market stall, serial fiction and novelettes were available for the odd copper or two, along with editions of the classics for perhaps a few more pence. As we have seen, customers could also order direct from William Milner's firm, although this may have represented a barrier to those readers who had no incentive to make the effort. Nevertheless, both fiction and the classics had to be quite deliberately purchased, as against the even more readily available ballads which were hawked about the streets with their contents spilling over into a shared spoken experience. I do not believe that cheap serious literature was ever in direct competition with these street ballads; and, to take this further, neither do I believe that the didactic strain in popular literature was in real conflict with the entertainment angle. Romantic novels and adventure tales, together with murder broadsides, outsold the more serious fare, however competitively priced.

How did the newsagent himself see the situation? We have a pretty good idea of what was likely to be found on his counter – penny novelettes, comics, sporting papers, competition journals, newspapers – but we know rather less about the attitudes and preferences of purchaser or shopkeeper.

J. H. Haslam visited a number of newsagents in Manchester, and offers views from both sides of the counter.[86] 'What they want here is love and romance,' said the owner of a shop in Ancoats. Customers confirmed this. 'What sells best with me,' said a woman, 'is penny novels ... These yo' know is good stories; no silly kissin' and lovin' about 'em. Of course, they is all

85. Meek, op. cit., p. 30.
86. J. H. Haslam, *The Press and the People* (1906).

stories about love, but it's proper love – sensible like – an' all ends happy – an' that kind o' thing.' Another said: 'It is the chief pleasure of my life to read these tales – they're lovely.'

There in Ancoats sporting papers rivalled the penny novelettes, and in Salford things were much the same. A penny edition of Tennyson's poems had remained unsold, according to one shopkeeper, for two years.[87] A small minority of readers wanted something serious – a self-educator in instalments, a Labour magazine – but purchases of this kind were few.

Harpurhey proved more rewarding to the investigator. Here he found a wider range of publications on sale. Sixpenny paper-covered novels were bought, and so were fashion magazines; there was also a brisk trade in guidebooks to various pleasure resorts – a sure indication of higher wages and more holidays. In summer the reading of newspapers and magazines fell off considerably, and even the day-to-day weather could affect sales. One newsagent in this area was specific about this: 'I like a wet Set'dy afternoon and reet. There's a big rush for pappers then; I allus sell up.' Penny novels and journals like *Tit-bits* were chiefly in demand on these occasions.

What did strike Haslam as odd when he went into several newsagents' shops in the East Manchester area was the lack of interest shown in Labour papers or anything touching on social, industrial or political reform. 'Garn!' he quotes a customer as saying. 'Too much preachin' about reform in that paper. We want no bloomin' reform, guvnor.' Similar comments were made by other customers. 'Oh, there's too much Labour in this', or 'too much reform in that', 'too much Socialism', and so on. Such attitudes are a far cry from those of working men who were committed politically. At about this time, for example, George Meek was distributing copies of *Clarion* and *Merrie England* in Eastbourne. Between the apathetic and the activist there existed

87. Presumably this was one of W. T. Stead's series of *The Penny Poets*, another late Victorian attempt to provide literature cheaply.

a whole range of attitudes and responses which make glib general-izations about the working class extremely dangerous.

There is, of course, no way of telling how typical or otherwise Haslam's experiences were. This is the nearest we can get to knowing something about readers and readership in some Manchester working-class areas at the end of the nineteenth century, and it may have been the same in other large towns. However, this kind of evidence is too narrow to draw conclusions about the stratification of the popular reading public.

These views of purchasing and reading habits in the town lead us to consider the country reader. Is it, in fact, valid to make a distinction between urban and rural readers? One writer on rural affairs at the end of the nineteenth century thought there was a difference, and held that the rural reader was in some respects less fortunate than his urban counterpart. This writer was Richard Jefferies, whose observations based upon his native Wiltshire invite comparison with those made by Haslam in Manchester:

To read everything and anything! The cottagers in faraway hamlets, miles from a railway station, read every scrap of printed paper that drifts across their way, like leaves in autumn. The torn newspapers in which the grocer at the market town wraps up their weekly purchases, stained with tallow or treacle, are not burned heedlessly. Some para-graph, some fragment of curious information, is gathered from the pieces. The ploughman at his luncheon reads the scrap of newspaper in which his bread-and-cheese was packed for him. Men read the bits of paper in which they carry their screws of tobacco. The stone-pickers in spring in the meadows, often women, look at the bits of paper scat-tered here and there before putting them in their baskets. A line here and a line yonder, one to-day, one to-morrow, in time make this material equal to a book.[88]

Jefferies took the wish to read for granted. The problem, as he saw it, was how country people obtained their reading matter. For newspapers there was no difficulty: 'Not a hamlet but has its

88. Richard Jefferies, *The Life of the Fields* (1884), 1908 edition, p. 186.

newspaper agent, often at the little shop where tobacco, snuff and lollipops are retailed . . .'[89] It was not, however, daily papers that Jefferies referred to here. What he had in mind were weekly papers for perusal on Saturday night and Sunday. Anything more than a newspaper was to be had either from a pedlar or hawker calling at the cottage door or from a shop in the local market town. Jefferies' comments need to be treated with some care, because of his tendency to romanticize about the countryside; but this does not necessarily invalidate his findings.

When Jefferies was writing the pedlar was still a figure to be met with in the countryside:

> The pedlar does not confine himself to one district, and he sells for his own profit. In addition to the pins and ribbons, Birmingham jewellery, dream books, and penny ballads, the pedlar now produces a bundle of small books, which are practically pamphlets, though in a more convenient form than the ancient quartos. They are a miscellaneous lot, from fifty to one hundred pages . . . Dream books and ballads sell as they always did sell, but for the rest the pedlar's bundle has nothing in it, as a rule, more pernicious than may be purchased at any little shop. Romantic novelettes, reprints of popular and really clever stories . . .[90]

Door-to-door selling of this kind in the country is confirmed by George Bourne, recalling 'Jack the Matchman', who, besides retailing kettleholders and executing small commissions for the villagers, had 'pallats' for sale. These were ballad sheets, with two songs printed on very thin paper. Some prized them greatly, folding them carefully after purchase to carry away in their pockets.[91]

To buy books was very difficult indeed for the country-dweller. Village stores would not stock them, and even at the

---

89. 'Country Readers', in *Field and Farm* (1957), p. 48; this essay was first published in 1877.

90. Richard Jefferies, *The Life of the Fields*, pp. 190–91.

91. George Bourne, *William Smith, Potter and Farmer, 1790–1858* (1920), pp. 216–17.

cheaper stationer's shops in the local town little was on display beyond stationery, paper-covered novelettes and newspapers. It is precisely this lack of connection between the publishing trade and the countryside that Richard Jefferies stressed. For the better-educated there was always access to the middle-class book-shop and circulating library, but the villagers felt out of place in such premises, and in the shops they did use 'the shopkeeper does not know what they want, and they cannot tell him. They would know it if they saw it; but till they see it they do not know them-selves.' The contrast is made, therefore, between a countryside where those of the poor who want to buy cheap books cannot do so and the towns where books are readily available to all. Jefferies perhaps overstated his case to some extent; but this is of less importance than the fact that we are able to glimpse from his pages what country people read and how they obtained it.

CONTEMPORARY DISCUSSION OF POPULAR LITERATURE

Reference has already been made to the Victorian view that literature and its provision was a moral issue. Needless to say, this view was – with certain exceptions noted earlier in this chapter – most liable to be expressed by those not actually in-volved in publishing, selling or purchasing popular fiction!

Contemporary comment, therefore, tended to spell out warn-ings of the effect which fiction could have upon its readers. Charles Mackay, in contributing to these warnings, may in fact have had in mind such publications as *The Newgate Calendar* when he wrote of 'popular admiration of great thieves'.[92] The conclusion he drew was that villainy in stories or upon the stage had a bad effect upon the young – a point which was echoed by the anony-mous author of *The Blade and the Ear*,[93] a book of guidance for young men:

Let us warn the young man against what may well be called the

92. *Memoirs of Extraordinary Popular Delusions* (3 vols., 1841, and subse-quent reprints).

93. Undated, perhaps *circa* 1880.

'Satanic Literature' of the day. The cause and effect of reading pernicious books is a moral scepticism. It is said that Byron ridiculed the
idea of anyone being seriously injured by reading a book ... His
occasional beauties – the effusions of genius – are, for this reason, all
the more dangerous. No one can peruse impure books without
vitiating his taste, and losing all interest at last in whatever is written
to elevate and improve. Such works lower the tone of the moral
susceptibilities ... and often render plain-dressed virtue a cheap
undesirable thing.

He went on to criticize the imaginary world in which heroes and
heroines engage the sympathies of readers more than the suffer-
ings of their fellow beings – 'Much of the literature of the day is
addressed to the lower sentiments of our nature'– and he deplored
the fact that so many people read fiction and nothing else.[94]

One does not have to search very far to come across similar
criticisms.[95] Sensational fiction – in fact, the whole range of
popular fiction – was a good Aunt Sally for the moralist, as ballads
and stories had been in the sixteenth and seventeenth centuries.
Much of the comment throughout these periods rarely rose above
the level of outraged orthodoxy or evangelical special pleading.

Several contemporary commentators and critics did, however,
take a more reasonable view. An anonymous writer in *The Eclectic
Review*[96] had some interesting things to say in the course of a long
review article about the reading of 'the clerk, the milliner's
apprentice, the shop-boy'. He went out of his way to emphasize
the role of circulating libraries in making popular fiction available
to people 'whom the extension of education and the circumstances
of social life have of late years made readers . . .' The author was
critical of the process, but his strictures were couched in terms
far removed from the comments already referred to. Without
circulating libraries, he claimed, 'the reading of the most trashy,

94. *The Blade and the Ear*, pp. 140–41.
95. Louis James, *Fiction for the Working Man* (1963), lists several. See pp.
212ff.
96. Vol. LXXXII (1845), pp. 74–84.

meretricious, highflown, and maudling [sic] class of novels could have found no circulation . . .'; and, although he went on to describe circulating libraries as 'these gin palaces of the reading world', the entire piece is a very serious attempt to discuss a subject which was clearly of concern to many Victorians.

J. Hepworth Dixon contributed three articles on 'The Literature of the Lower Orders' to the *Daily News* on 26 October and 7 and 9 November 1847. Condescension, mixed with a belief that the publications with the largest circulation were the most mischievous in their effects, gives these articles a rather quaint period atmosphere. Is this really what many Victorians thought?

In the *Companion to the British Almanac* for 1873 J. P. Harrison wrote a paper of more than twenty pages on 'Cheap Literature – Past and Present', combining some fairly shrewd comment with the customary censoriousness of the age. What lifts this essay above mediocrity is the fact that Harrison provides facts, figures and extracts from the fiction he condemns. His conclusion that there was a growing demand for a more serious – his word is 'superior' – popular literature was at least an optimistic one, and partly true.

The debate on what working men and women read – and it was debate rather than merely a desultory discussion – is, I think, best epitomized by three articles which cover most aspects of popular literature. The first of these, 'On the Literature of the Working Classes', by John Parker, was published in 1853.[97] This was a widely ranging survey, and one which was free from aggressive moralizing. The *Reasoner*, G. J. Holyoake's freethinking journal, is mentioned as running at a loss because working men did not buy it. Temperance journals, on the other hand, were well subscribed: 'To enumerate the weekly and monthly temperance publications known as "Intelligencers", "Advocates", "Essayists", "News", "Reviews", "Chronicles", etc., would occupy too much space; suffice it to state, that not only have these had a

97. Viscount Ingestre (ed.), *Meliora: or, Better Times to Come*, Second Series (facsimile reprint 1971), pp. 181–97.

wide circulation among working men, but that without exception, the whole are based on Christian principle and conducted
by Christian men.'

Was there, perhaps, a hint of exultation over Holyoake's difficulties? Probably yes; but the keynote of the entire piece is
optimism about the future. Great things were to be expected from
a wholesome popular literature, and fiction was not excluded.
One of the functions of fiction was to give the members of one
class information about members of another: 'The rich become
more familiar with the habitudes of the poor, and the poor are
made better acquainted with the rich.' In a similar way the un-
tutored reader could learn much about foreign countries and the
lives of their inhabitants from well-written stories. Despite the
somewhat bland assumptions which are made, there are valuable
insights. The most surprising is the admission that fantasy is
more popular with most people than reality – a point of view
which was in sharp contrast with that held by Lord Brougham and
other champions of popular education.

Rather more magisterial is Chapter XII of J. A. St John's book,
The Education of the People.[98] 'The conviction,' he writes, 'is fast
spreading, that, to create an intelligent people, books must be
used as the chief instrument.' St John speaks well of lending
libraries, and discusses book hawkers and their wares, making a
distinction between religious tracts which were given away and
sensational ballad sheets which were sold. Of the latter he says:

The poor ... buy them by the millions and thus introduce mischievous ideas into their minds, these do ferment and prepare them
for the commission of crime. Depraved prints and handbills also
circulate largely among the working classes, together with cheap
blasphemous books, which tend at once to destroy their religion and
their morals. It is said that of this class, nearly thirty millions are
circulated annually, which is almost equal to the issues of all the
Religious Societies put together.

The way to combat this state of affairs, St John argues, is to put

98. Published in 1858. It was reprinted in facsimile in 1970.

good cheap books within reach of those who are reading rubbish. Such books would be most effectively distributed by hawkers, for the poor would be too readily inhibited from going into bookshops. Books mentioned as being found in the humblest cottage are *Robinson Crusoe*, *The Pilgrim's Progress* and *Paradise Lost*. Editions of all three were sold in very large numbers by Milner and other publishers, so there is almost certainly something in what St John says.

St John writes, of course, as an educationalist, and sees the circulation of cheap good books as an extension of the school experience, and as productive of nothing but good in society. Even the housewife, he is careful to point out, can benefit greatly from books. If his optimism is more muted than that of John Parker, he does reflect, faithfully I think, the attitude of the many who believed that reading had a considerable part to play in making better men and women amongst the working classes. Undoubtedly there was a strong element of patronage and condescension in what he had to say, but certainly many contemporaries would have agreed wholeheartedly with him, sharing his assumptions about 'us' and 'them' in a society where the poor were expected to know their place.

Oddly, perhaps, in view of the countless volumes of popular fiction written by women, few of them joined in the nineteenth-century discussion. In fact, the only one I have come across who did so was Agnes Repplier, an American, whose essay upon 'English Railway Fiction' was both perceptive and well written.[99] Because she had no specific educational or ideological axe to grind, and perhaps because she was not English, she took a very much less high-minded view of popular literature in this country than her male predecessors, who had discussed the subject with a good deal of seriousness and occasionally pomposity.[100]

99. Published in a volume of her essays, *Points of View* (1895).

100. I. D'Israeli, for instance, who wrote: 'The courtly favourites of a former age descended from the oriel window to the cottage-lattice; perpetuated in our "Chap-books", sold on the stalls of fairs, and mixed with

What chiefly impressed Agnes Repplier was 'the wonderful dullness of penny fiction', and in support of this view she quoted James Payn, himself a well-known popular novelist, who, she said, 'found in them [i.e., cheap novels] neither dramatic interest, nor even impropriety'. She also referred to Thomas Wright, who found that 'the lovely heroines of these stories are virtuous even to insipidity, and their heroes are so blamably blameless, as to be absolutely revolting.' The dullness was due, she concluded, not to an absence of incident in the novels, but to the calmness with which situations and incidents were experienced. In one story, poor Bonny Adair finds herself taking tea with a lady whom she discovers to be the wife of the man who has proposed to her. When introduced to 'Mrs Alec Doyle', she withdraws and becomes a hospital nurse. The wife is killed in a subsequent hunting accident and Bonny re-establishes her claim to the bereaved husband. 'Well-bred indifference', was Agnes Repplier's summing up.

Elfrida's Villainy, which she also quoted, has a villainous lover – thwarted – and a virtuous lover – rewarded. In the course of this novel there is an abduction; but the wrong girl – the vicar's daughter – is carried off by the rogues. Her mother is barely perturbed. 'Rupert,' she says to her son, 'it is your place to go and look for your sister.'

In *Golden Chains* the heroine, Ernestine, marries a scoundrel in order to oblige a friend. This is Captain Beamish, an English officer, who immediately imprisons her in a ruined castle situated 'on a lonely hillside looking down upon a blue Mediterranean'. Eventually he leaves her there to starve quietly in a dungeon, from which she is rescued by the accidental arrival of her lover, Linden, who is travelling in Southern Europe and has a taste for exploring ruins. He discovers Ernestine in a comatose condition, 'but beautiful still', though 'her youthful roundness was gone forever'. He 'lifts the fair head upon his arm' and gives her a shot

the wares of "the Chapman", they became the books of the people...'
('Books of the People', in *Amenities of Literature*, Routledge's Excelsior Series, undated, p. 138).

of brandy. As she comes to, he asks, 'Dearest, do you know me?' There is a faint affirmative, and Linden goes on: 'All is well, Nessa. You have been cruelly used, but all is well. You are safe with me. Tell me, dear one, you are glad to see me.' Captain Beamish has by now been accidentally drowned, so presumably Ernestine and Linden live happily ever after.

Stories of this kind – and there were many – made up what Agnes Repplier called 'the wilds and deeps of penny fiction'.

It is with an obvious sense of relief that no 'socialistic tendency' is found in these stories. Neither is there 'any disposition to exalt the lower orders at the expense of the upper'. The real villains, says Agnes Repplier, were the self-made businessmen or scheming lawyers. One of the latter, John Farlow, urges offers of friendship and cash upon an impoverished landlord:

The colonel shudders, as he gazes, half wearily, half scornfully, at the shapeless, squat figure of the Caliban-like creature before him. That he, Courtenay St Leger Walterton, late in command of Her Majesty's Lancers, should have to listen respectfully to the hectoring of this low city rascal, while a horsepond waits without, and a collection of horsewhips hang ready for instant application on the hunting rack in the hall within! Yet it is so; he is wholly at this man's mercy, and the colonel, like the humblest of mankind, is obliged to succumb to the inevitable.[101]

It is the convention of these novels that low city rascals deserve to be horsewhipped by blue-blooded country squires. Is there an echo of Cobbett's radicalism in all this? This is doubtful. The fact is that such a convention was by no means new at the close of the nineteenth century, and in a somewhat less crude form is still acceptable and popular in similar tales today. It is the working-class character who was then, and still is today, barely a credible figure in popular fiction.

101. Agnes Repplier, 'English Railway Fiction', in *Points of View* (1895), pp. 225–6.

MOVING TO A MASS READERSHIP

As we come into the last years of the nineteenth century and find Agnes Repplier writing of one publishing company claiming a weekly sale of seven million copies for its penny novelettes, popular literature verges upon a mass public. Those who bought the novels she discusses were doing so in the years following the Education Act of 1870. The reading public had continued to grow, and so indeed had the population: the market for popular literature was buoyant.

The sensational novels published by Edward Lloyd had become the stuff of boys' stories, while romantic tales continued to find favour with female readers. The sheer volume of publications destined for the popular market at the close of the nineteenth century is daunting. For one year taken at random, 1885, I have traced forty-six monthly and weekly publications featuring fiction, and the list is certainly far from complete. Amongst those on sale weekly were the following:

> *Family Circle* (Tuesday edition of the *Christian World*). Established in 1877, price one penny. It specialized in 'entertaining and elevating tales and fiction'. Circulation 50,000.

> *Family Herald Supplement*, price one penny. It published a complete tale in each issue. Circulation 232,000.

> *Fireside Novelist*, price one penny, established in 1881. A journal designed for female readers. Circulation 18,000.

> *Penny Illustrated Paper*, established 1861. Circulation 200,000.

> *Penny Pictorial News*, price one penny, established 1877. Circulation 95,000.

> *Weekly Budget*, price one penny, established 1860. Circulation 350,000.

Amongst the monthlies were these:

After Work, price one penny, established 1874. Circulation 8,000. 'Home reading for the working classes'.

Catholic Fireside, price one penny, established 1878. Circulation 40,000.

Crystal Stories, price one penny, established 1880. Circulation 35,000. 'Temperance tales'.

Home Words, price one penny, established 1870. Circulation 100,000.

There is clearly a problem in putting these figures into context, involving questions about the kind of readership to which the publications appealed and an analysis of the contents. Further, most of these figures were gleaned from publishers' advertisements, and to this extent may be questionable. However, the dates quoted do indicate in most cases that these periodicals had been in existence for some years; and, whatever the reservations, these figures do seem impressive.

These were some of the cheapest journals available; and, of those mentioned, *Family Herald Supplement* is of especial interest. Its circulation was large, and from it developed a whole series of cheap periodicals devoted to novels and novelettes. The publishers, William Stevens Ltd, of 421 The Strand, exploited the market with a great deal of skill. There was *Monthly Magazine of Fiction*, which cost 3d. and contained a full-length novel, *Sixpenny Magazine of Fiction*, *Family Pocket Library of Short Stories*, costing one penny – but these began to spill over into the twentieth century.

The quality of the fiction was not high, although possibly better than the strictures of contemporaries might lead us to believe. *Juno*, whose front cover is reproduced overleaf, was one such novel, published anonymously in November 1886. Here are the opening paragraphs.

She lived all alone now. There was no one near to cheer her loneliness

PRICE THREEPENCE.

Monthly Magazine of Fiction.

No. 19.] **NOVEMBER, 1886.** [VOL. 4.

∴ Contents ∴

JUNO:

A HUNTING STORY

A COMPLETE NOVEL

BY A NEW AUTHOR

LONDON:
WILLIAM STEVENS, LIMITED, 421, STRAND.

29. Some popular novels like this one were romantic rather than sensational

during the long dark winter nights, to welcome her on her return from work, or to share the small two-roomed hovel built on the edge of the moor. Two miserable little rooms they were, into which the rain dripped plentifully on wet nights – and they are many up in that land of hills and lakes – making pools on the uneven floor, and sending little streams coursing about the damp, dreary cottage. The rent was trifling, and, as the present tenant made no complaints, the landlord did not see the use of putting himself to the needless and unasked-for expense of re-thatching the humble dwelling, but let the roof grow year by year more out of repair. The bricked floor had become broken and uneven from constant coming and going over the narrow space. One needed to be accustomed to its ups and downs to prevent stumbling, and a stranger would have found it difficult to cross the tiny kitchen without accident.

But it did not matter now. No stranger ever set foot in the house, so why repair the rugged floor? Its solitary inmate knew every ridge and furrow; had learnt them all in childhood; and for old acquaintance' sake held them dear, and would not have changed them for the brightest, softest carpet in the land.

Both rooms boasted a window – just two small panes of glass in each. There was very little furniture scattered about, even for the modest needs of one person, and she not a very exacting individual.

In the kitchen was a round deal table and a brown-painted settle. There was also, carefully put by in a far corner, an armchair, never sat in or brought forward for common use, yet scrupulously rubbed and dusted each morning. Lastly, a venerable eight-day clock, decorated with devices representing the sun, moon, and its attendant satellites, but grown so rusty with age that its croaking voice could scarcely tell out the hours, as the hands travelled slowly and with spasmodic jerks round the discoloured face. Still it kept time, that staunch old servant, and ticked off the whole twelve hours as faithfully and methodically as ever it had done in its palmiest days, though its voice had grown husky and asthmatic, and its machinery stiff and laboured by long service. A shelf or two, garnished with a modest supply of coarse crockery, a row of china cups, cracked and broken, hanging from one of them, formed the whole of the kitchen furniture; while that of the bedroom was hardly less mean. A small wooden bedstead, a straw-stuffed mattress, a thin patched blanket, an old tartan plaid shawl – these,

with a black oak chest, in which she kept her meagre treasures and
scanty change of clothes, formed the whole of the furniture of Roona's
sleeping-apartment.

Altogether it was the sort of place few would have cared to live in
from choice; dire necessity alone might compel one to accept it as a
last resource. It was an abiding-place fit only for a pariah or outcast of
society.

In sheer volume of different series and titles published, Milner
& Sowerby led the field so far as cheap literature was concerned;
but in terms of the *numbers* of each title printed, they were probably outdone by W. B. Horner & Son, London and Dublin,
publishers of 'Horner's Penny Stories for the People'. By about
1889 they were advertising 147 different tales, and new ones came
out on the first and third Tuesdays in each month. These novels
were constantly being reprinted, and a list in my possession shows
that the numbers of each one issued ranged between 150,000 and
450,000.

'As forceful, fresh, and fascinating as they are wholesome,' said
the *Congregational Magazine*, quoted by the publishers. There
was nothing in these novels that even the most sensitive reader
could take exception to. Several of the stories were available as
'services of song'.[102]

A typical novel is *Until Seventy Times Seven*, 'a farmer's
daughter's story' by Emily Searchfield. The copy in front of me
is the fifth edition, 250th thousand. Undated, it consists of sixteen
pages printed in double column with some illustrations. It is a
story of unfulfilled love, of fidelity and resigned happiness. The
closing sentences exemplify both tone and style:

... so he and I live on here in the dear home, an old maiden and a
bachelor, full of whims and fancies, with the sunset of life about us,
changeful with all sweet lights and colourings, the pains and rapture
gone by, for us, for ever. And in that light which surely must be a

102. The service of song was popular in some Nonconformist chapels. The
reading of an edifying story would be interspersed with appropriate hymns
and solos.

Until SEVENTY TIMES SEVEN.

A Farmer's Daughter's Story

By

Emilie Searchfield.

30. A typical Horner novel

foreshadowing, so to speak, of the morning – or wherefore its all but satisfaction of peace? – I watch for my life-crowning, which here had but its counterpart of pain and chastening. Yes, walking by faith and not by sight, I feel David Grey is waiting for me there, among the mists shutting out the eternal morning, as he often surprised me among the real misted earth in the early morning of the dear long ago.

Plots were simple, characters were clearly defined, and sales to women readers were enormous. The overwhelming impression of this particular novel and of others like it – *Molly Darling* by Fanny Eden (350,000 copies), *His Brother's Keeper* by Sydney Watson (200,000 copies), *Charlie Coulson* by Dr Rossvally (450,000 copies, and available as a service of song) – is one of cosiness and resignation. Preoccupation with the past and hope for future bliss meant that the present could be endured. This is what romance readers wanted – a story which would take them out of the present, out of crowded homes and poverty. A penny was not too high a price to pay for such escape from reality. Certainly some of this material was very overtly moral, and there were rather artless religious attitudes implicit in it. These characteristics may reflect some of the conventions of the Victorian age, and subsequently the evangelical religious movement may have helped to create a climate for the flourishing of this kind of fiction. Does this conflict with the rather different appeal – also escapist – of the more violent gothic romances? On reflection, it does not. Popular fiction has, in fact, always been fairly moral, in the sense that so far as the story is concerned virtue has triumphed over vice; and the continuing acceptance of the dichotomy between violence and morality seems to be reflected in contemporary journalism. The readers of the more sensational Sunday newspapers appear to find little difficulty in accepting the most salacious details of murder and sex crimes together with the highly moral fiction offered, for example, in women's magazines.

It is with publications like the penny novels that the dividing line between a paper-covered book and a periodical becomes blurred. Probably to the buyers and readers no such distinction existed; and to an increasing extent publications specializing in fiction had to compete with magazines covering sport and including competitions. One Salford newsagent is recorded as saying: 'Reading don't matter that much. What does count is the chance of getting something for nothing, £10 notes for tram tickets, gold watches for naming football winners.'[103] This was clearly a reference to the new family magazines, *Tit-bits*, which George Newnes had founded in 1881, and *Pearson's Weekly*, started by Cyril Pearson (who had once worked as a clerk in the *Tit-bits* office) in 1890. These two men, together with Alfred Harmsworth, brought about a further revolution in the popular sphere, this time in cheap journalism. In doing so they created a public which could be numbered in millions, and which was to be catered for by the cinema, the wireless and television – each of which in turn was to dominate the mass market in a way that printers had been unable to do. Their importance cannot be over-estimated, although any account of it must lie outside the scope of the present study. Let just one fact suffice: in 1897 *Pearson's Weekly*, in which a competition was run, reached a circulation of one and a quarter million copies. There was a new dimension in popular literature – the mass audience.

Such an audience can perhaps best be examined by considering the phenomenon of Ally Sloper. This comic character was invented in about 1870 by C. H. Ross, who was then a young clerk in the Admiralty. Ross became editor of a rival to *Punch*, entitled *Judy*, and introduced Ally Sloper cartoons into the pages of his paper in 1878 or 1879. From this a twice-yearly annual developed entitled *Ally Sloper's Komic Kalendar* and *Ally Sloper's Summer Number*. These little publications sold extremely well, and in 1884 a weekly called *Ally Sloper's Half Holiday* was launched. It was a comic journal which continued to be published, with minor interruptions, until 1923.

From the first it proved most popular, and a number of famous artists contributed to it, among them Bernard Partridge, later a

103. J. Haslam, *The Press and the People* (1906).

31. The famous Victorian comic character

Punch cartoonist, and H. K. Browne, better known as 'Phiz', one of Dickens's illustrators. George R. Sims, chiefly recalled now for his ballad, *Twas Christmas Day in the Workhouse*, wrote in the early years of *Ally Sloper* a serial called 'How the Poor Live'.

The magazine's success gave rise to further publications, and the founder's son claimed that Sloper publications of all kinds amounted to over 52 million copies in the 1890s.[104] Ally Sloper became a household word, and onto the market came Ally Sloper umbrellas, walking sticks, pipes, watches, toys, sweets, kites, fireworks. Ally Sloper was played as a character in a Drury Lane pantomime, *The Forty Thieves*, and there was a set-piece Ally Sloper display in fireworks at the Crystal Palace.

When compared with the Beatle explosion of the 1960s it all seems pretty trivial, but in a world unused to this kind of commercial exploitation the Ally Sloper craze was, as the first of its kind, to cast its shadow right down the twentieth century to the days of special offers and endorsements of sundry products by celebrities. The vogue was in one sense the climax of Victorian popular publishing for a wide audience and in another the beginning, in this country, of an era in which the comic strip has played an enormous role in popular literature – and continues to do so. In his grotesqueness and his general ethos Ally Sloper belonged to the nineteenth century: as a favourite character whose name and likeness were exploited, he belonged emphatically to the twentieth.

Both *Chips* and *Comic Cuts*, weekly comics which Alfred Harmsworth founded in 1890, owed much to *Ally Sloper's Half Holiday*, except that the Harmsworth comics cost a halfpenny each, half the price of Ally Sloper.[105]

Cyril Pearson's million and a quarter readers stood, unknowingly, at the threshold of a new age. No thoughts of coming developments in the mass market, from the gramophone,[106] the

104. Unpublished MS, *Brief Notes re. Ally Sloper*, in the possession of the writer. I am deeply grateful to the late Mr Charles Ross, son of Ally Sloper's creator.

105. For these early comics, see G. Perry and A. Aldridge, *The Penguin Book of Comics* (revised edition, 1971), pp. 47ff.

106. See, for example, the article by Laura Alex Smith entitled 'Games for Winter Evenings' in the *Lady's Realm* (January 1898), in which she refers to the possibilities offered by the gramophone.

cinema and radio to television, can have crossed the mind of the 'common reader' as he or she rummaged through the stock of a newsagent's shop.

Inevitably we have moved from popular literature to its common readers. Ever since printing began these shadowy figures have been given reality almost entirely through the surviving evidence of what they have chosen to read for pleasure. Broadside, ballad, jestbook, chapbook, song-sheet, sensational novel, romantic novelette; cheap editions of the classics; novelists whose names are almost forgotten; tattered, flimsy sheets; precious collections of highly ephemeral publications; shabby copies of Milner novels (still to be met with in second-hand shops) – these are the stuff of popular literature. From material of this kind we can learn something of the mental universe of unlettered men and women in the past. All too often the outline we sketch of their reading lacks definition; but if we look at what they read and how it developed, then I believe that the outlines become very much more precise.

FIVE

THE ORAL TRADITION: SOME NOTES ON SURVIVAL

One a penny, two a penny, hot Cross Buns!
One a penny, two a penny, hot Cross Buns!

Maids, I mend old Pans or Kettles,
Mend old Pans or Kettles, O!

Muffins, O! Crumpets! Muffins today!
Crumpets, O! Muffins, O! fresh today!

Clothes Props! Clothes Props! I say, good wives
Clothes Props, all long and very strong, today.
                        London street cries

'... Penny Readings have rapidly grown into general popularity, and have done an incalculable amount of good. They have familiarized with the treasures of our literature many who formerly had as little inclination possibly as opportunity to read for themselves.'
                        Tom Hood, *Standard Penny Readings* (1871)

My old man said 'follow the van'...
Victorian music-hall song

THE printed popular literature with which this book is concerned represents only part – although a very important part – of a total popular culture; and because the printed word has, by its very nature, so often survived, there may be a tendency to see it somewhat out of context.

To be aware of this fact is a start. We must, however, consider what is meant by the oral tradition which, together with the printed one, makes up a considerable element in the mental universe of ordinary men and women. Men and women have been talking through the centuries, and what they have said – important or trivial, affectionate or abusive – has reflected their attitudes, their values. How are we to retrieve some part of this experience? The actual words, of course, are almost always gone for ever; but we can, as Keith Thomas has so brilliantly shown,[1] enter partially at least into the world of popular ideas. A great deal more work is required in this direction, and there is no doubt that a detailed survey of William Hone's *The Every-day Book*, *The Table Book* and *The Yearbook*[2] – superb repositories of *reported* oral culture – would yield an authentic picture, however fragmentary, of the mental world of eighteenth-century and early nineteenth-century men and women. Equally, the three substantial volumes by John Brand, *Observations on the Popular Antiquities of Great Britain*,[3] together with *British Popular Customs* and *Folk-lore of Shakespeare*[4] by T. F. Thiselton Dyer, represent an impressive source of similar material which is yet to be ransacked and exploited.

It is also relevant to consider the experience of ordinary men and women at, for instance, the hands of the law. What was said in defence of poaching?[5] What were popular attitudes to theft and outlawry? To riot? There was, as we know, a good deal of interest in the reporting of crimes of violence, but how did this relate to everyday life? There were those who made their living at fairs and markets. There were the craftsman, the shopkeeper, the labourer. How did their attitudes to authority differ? How, too, did they regard the problems of earning and spending?

I take the term 'popular culture' to mean the values, assumptions and attitudes of the unprivileged, and some light may be shed upon these by our tracing of the ways in which relaxation,

---

1. *Religion and the Decline of Magic* (1971). See also R. W. Malcolmson, *Popular Recreations in English Society, 1700–1850* (Cambridge, 1973).

2. 4 vols, 1826–7.

3. Bohn edition, with additions by Sir Henry Ellis (1849).

4. 1876; 1883; facsimile reprint, 1966.

5. See *James Hawker's Journal: A Victorian Poacher* (1961), a valuable counterbalance to the more orthodox view put forward in *The Autobiography of an English Gamekeeper*, by John Wilkins (1892).

entertainment and knowledge were sought. In general, popular literature has represented an imaginative escape from the drabness of everyday lives. The background against which we set the kind of questions that I have suggested was largely shaped by the variable cycle of the agrarian year, and it incorporated the daily round, the public house and the gin shop, popular songs and traditional tales, transgression and punishment, violence, poverty and crime, rather than church or chapel or the spurious stability which existed only in the minds of those who believed quite literally in the ideal of a contented peasantry.[6] In considering popular culture within an urban and industrial setting, we must remember that the earliest workers in factories came from the country, and there is no reason to suppose that they shed their traditional mental baggage at the factory gates. For how long did the notions and beliefs of a rural past remain with them? Clearly there are no easy answers. An introductory study of urban and industrial folklore is long overdue,[7] and the fact that at present we lack such a work underlies the difficulty of discussing popular culture in anything but the vaguest terms.

'It is,' wrote E. P. Thompson, 'one of the peculiarities of the English, that the history of the "common people" has always been something other than – and distinct from – English History Proper . . .'[8] A similar view was expressed by W. G. Hoskins in a broadcast talk entitled 'Harvest and Hunger':

Most English historians are snobs. They write only about 'top people', to use a nasty but convenient expression. Yet these are very limited social classes. In Tudor England, for example, the whole of the gentry from the peerage down were only about two per cent of the population. In the towns the merchant class amounted to only two or

6. For example, the anonymous author of *Sketches of Rural Affairs* (1848).

7. For instance, George Korson's two excellent books, *Minstrels of the Mine Patch* (1938 and reprints), and *Coal Dust on the Fiddle* (1943, reprinted 1965), concern the culture of American miners.

8. 'History from Below', in the *Times Literary Supplement* (7 April 1966), p. 279.

three per cent. So some ninety-seven per cent of English people escape the attention of the historian altogether, except when they rush upon the stage in brief rebellion, and then they are usually disposed of in a line or two as 'the mob'.[9]

Something of the oral tradition of this vast majority of Englishmen can be gleaned from folklore, ballads, traditional tales, nursery rhymes, proverbs, catch phrases and jokes, in so far as these found their way into print, and even from brief moments of social protest to which W. G. Hoskins referred.[10] In particular, the oral tradition in popular literature maintained a vigorous life throughout the nineteenth century in two respects – popular song and penny readings.

The words of songs which were whistled and sung about the streets of towns and in country places were usually printed in pocket songsters during this period. Unlike the ballad sheets which covered crime, comment and news besides popular songs, it was in the latter that these little books specialized. They had the advantage of offering more songs for the money, and they were in a more convenient form, for they could be carried in the pocket without folding. On the other hand, of course, they were never so eye-catching nor so topical.

There must have been a ready sale for these pocket songsters. Many of them are known to us only through publishers' catalogues, for all too often the flimsy booklets were read to pieces. They did not, of course, originate in the nineteenth century. Cluer Dicey and Richard Marshall were offering eight-page collections of songs in their 1764 catalogue, but it was during the following century that songsters became outstandingly popular. Most of them were undated, and their contents comprised for the most part songs which were sung at concerts, at home, and later in the

9. Printed in the *Listener* (10 December 1964), p. 931.

10. See for instance A. W. Smith, 'Some Folklore Elements in Movements of Social Protest', in *Folklore*, Vol. 77 (Winter 1967), pp. 241–52. *The Established Church and Popular Religion 1750–1850* (1971) by the same author is both valuable and suggestive.

music hall. The immense world of nineteenth-century popular song is very largely uncharted. Its themes varied, and represent the shifting and imprecise point at which printed and oral popular literature meet. Song sheets and pocket songsters represent (as did chapbooks in the earlier century) a living oral tradition literally transfixed in the fastness of the page.

George Korson described his quest for the songs of miners: 'My research was not limited to oral sources. Broadsides, pocket songsters, local newspapers, and the files of the "United Mine Workers Journal" yielded ballad texts . . . These printed sources give continuity by filling gaps . . .'[11]

In regard to the popular song of nineteenth-century England, continuity is perhaps less evident in the topical and music-hall songs of the day, but the practice of printing the words of songs goes back almost to the beginning of printing. According to Harry B. Weiss,[12] a London printer, T. Passinger, issued in 1686 *The Loyal Garland, as a Choice of Songs, Highly in Request, and Much Esteemed in the Past and Present Times*. Printed in black letter, it contained the words of 83 songs. Earlier than this was Deloney's *The Garland of Good Will*, the earliest extant edition of which is dated 1631, although it probably first appeared some thirty-five years before; and in 1663 there was *Robin Hood's Garland*.

The term 'garland' stuck to these books throughout the eighteenth century, and the word 'songster' came to be used at some point during the following one. Novelty titles of the former included 'The Maidenhead's Garland', 'The Duke of York's Garland', 'The Cuckold's Cap Garland', and so on. Few of these early publications have survived, but their popularity is hinted at in a statement found in the Dicey and Marshall catalogue which has been referred to: 'NB Each Time of Re-printing the above Song-Books, the Songs therein are always changed for New.'[13]

11. *Coal Dust on the Fiddle* (1965), p. xvii.
12. *A Book about Chapbooks* (1942), p. 75.
13. Dicey & Marshall Catalogue (1764), p. 97.

During the real heyday of pocket songsters they could cost one penny for as many as 32 pages, twopence or threepence, and occasionally more for substantially bound books like the one 'published for the booksellers' by Milner, which cost one shilling and ran to 382 pages, of which twelve formed an index to the 'several thousand favourite songs and popular toasts'. *The Vauxhall Comic Song-book*, edited by the Musical Director of Vauxhall Gardens, J. W. Sharp, was issued in the same format some years earlier. Two series were bound together – altogether 432 pages of popular songs in a volume measuring three inches by five inches! If dumpy little books like these have become scarce, the ephemeral paper-bound pocket songsters are even harder to find. One of them is illustrated on p. 241.

The contents were varied. In *Yankee Palmer's Go A-head Comic Songster*, for instance, the traditional maypole song 'Come Lasses and Lads' was in company with more contemporary pieces like 'Mrs Muggins's Maid' and 'I Never Says Nothing to Nobody'. J. Wood of Holywell Street, who was the publisher, advertised in it:

Now Publishing, in Penny Numbers and Sixpenny Parts
Bartr's
Illustrated Book of Songs
Containing the most varied, and best selected collection of Sentimental and Comic Songs, Glees, etc., etc., ever submitted to the public.
No. 17 will be published on the 1st of October, with which will be reissued No. 1, price One Penny each.

Although undated, this enterprise can be ascribed to the 1850s, since the publisher also advertised *Uncle Tom's Song Book* in six penny numbers. Harriet Beecher Stowe's novel was published in London in 1852, and the song book was clearly an attempt to exploit the popularity of a well-known fictional character.

Later in the century, when music hall was established,[14] songsters were published containing the words of songs associated

14. A social history of music hall is much needed. Harold Scott, *The Early Doors* (1946), is still the best study of origins.

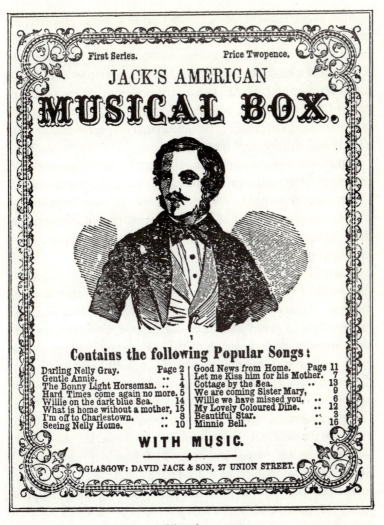

32. A Victorian songster

with the stars of the day – George Leybourne, Sam Cowell, Arthur Lloyd and others. Usually only the words were reproduced, although *Jack's American Musical Box*, of which there were eight series at twopence each, was advertised as 'Containing the following Popular Songs WITH MUSIC'. These clearly

241

printed songsters emanating from Glasgow were, however, an exception. Illustrations, too, were uncommon. *The British Songster* (undated) did have some woodcuts amongst more than one hundred separate items; but for the most part the pocket songsters costing no more than a copper or two were undistinguished in appearance, and their general lack of visual appeal makes it easy to overlook their importance in preserving in print a lively and shifting oral tradition.

Penny readings were quite different. They represented a conscious effort on the part of the middle class to woo the working classes away from public houses and music saloons by providing a more wholesome kind of entertainment. In suitable premises there were readings of extracts from English literature, often interspersed with music.

When the scheme was set on foot by Charles Sulley, editor of the *Ipswich Express*, meetings were free, local supporters meeting the cost. At one gathering in Liverpool a member of the audience proposed that a penny should be charged for admission, and this was carried with enthusiasm. Thus the 'penny reading' movement became increasingly popular throughout the country; and if in some cases a modest profit was made, it was also claimed that people of differing classes mixed socially at these functions: 'Wealthy manufacturers have been seen reading to their workmen, and the delicately trained and accomplished lady has thrown aside reserve, and played and sung to her humbler neighbours.'[15] Some sort of mingling may indeed have taken place, but it seems more likely that in many instances penny readings gave an opportunity for the charitably minded to exercise good offices on behalf of working men and women, rather than providing a point where all might meet on more equal terms. 'The likes of them' and 'the likes of us' were phrases which defined attitudes which were pretty rigidly adhered to by both sides. At the same time it must be said that, for a time at least, penny readings were successful and

15. Quoted in Oliver Edwards, 'All for a Penny', in *The Times* (24 November 1966).

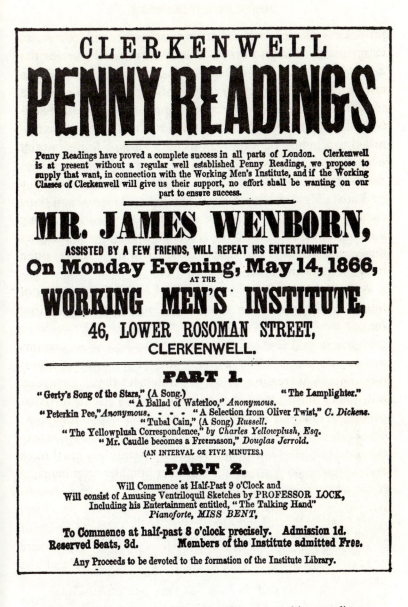

CLERKENWELL
PENNY READINGS

Penny Readings have proved a complete success in all parts of London. Clerkenwell is at present without a regular well established Penny Readings, we propose to supply that want, in connection with the Working Men's Institute, and if the Working Classes of Clerkenwell will give us their support, no effort shall be wanting on our part to ensure success.

MR. JAMES WENBORN,

ASSISTED BY A FEW FRIENDS, WILL REPEAT HIS ENTERTAINMENT

On Monday Evening, May 14, 1866,

AT THE

WORKING MEN'S INSTITUTE,

46, LOWER ROSOMAN STREET,

CLERKENWELL.

PART 1.

"Gerty's Song of the Stars," (A Song.)   "The Lamplighter."
"A Ballad of Waterloo," *Anonymous.*
"Peterkin Pee,"*Anonymous.* - - - "A Selection from Oliver Twist," *C. Dickens.*
"Tubal Cain," (A Song) *Russell.*
"The Yellowplush Correspondence," by *Charles Yellowplush, Esq.*
"Mr. Caudle becomes a Freemason," *Douglas Jerrold.*

(AN INTERVAL OF FIVE MINUTES.)

PART 2.

Will Commence at Half-Past 9 o'Clock and
Will consist of Amusing Ventriloquil Sketches by PROFESSOR LOCK,
Including his Entertainment entitled, "The Talking Hand"
Pianoforte, MISS BENT,

To Commence at half-past 8 o'clock precisely.   Admission 1d.
Reserved Seats, 3d.   Members of the Institute admitted Free.

Any Proceeds to be devoted to the formation of the Institute Library.

33.   Penny readings, advertised like this, often attracted large audiences

did draw audiences where lectures, scientific and otherwise, conspicuously failed to do so. Whether or not they were the 'complete success' claimed by the poster shown on p. 243 is open to question. The preference of working men and women for a lighter kind of entertainment could quite simply be attributed to the fact that after a long day's work it was pleasanter to be moved to laughter or tears than to follow a long lecture which might have been inexpertly prepared. As a contemporary who compiled three volumes of extracts suitable for reading aloud put it: 'The standard works of English literature, ill read or well read, would be worth all the gaseous gabble of the scientific, all the ultra-Johnsonian diction of the academic, and all the buffoonery of the comic lecturer.'[16]

Contemporary discussion seemed to confirm Hood's view – six or seven reciters could offer something very much more to the taste of working men and women than the didacticism of the lecturer.

What was read at these meetings? There were, of course, the masterpieces – Milton's 'Lycidas' and 'Hymn on the Nativity', Emerson on Shakespeare, Disraeli on the Prince Consort, pieces from Locke and Carlyle. But the tone was not always so lofty; variety was the great thing, and it is, I suspect, amongst the forgotten gems of the nineteenth century that we will find the reasons why people turned up to the readings. Purple passages from Shakespeare were a draw, but who could resist, say, Charles Kingsley's 'The Last Buccaneer', which was a favourite:

> Oh England is a pleasant place for them that's rich and high,
> But England is a cruel place for such poor folks as I;
> And such a port for mariners I ne'er shall see again
> As the pleasant Isle of Avès, beside the Spanish main.
>
> There were forty craft in Avès that were both swift and stout
> All furnished well with small arms and cannons round about;
> And a thousand men in Avès made laws so fair and free
> To choose their valiant captains and obey them loyally.

16. Tom Hood, *Standard Penny Readings* (a new edition, 1871), p. vi.

This paradise of pirates – the narrator himself is one – had everything that might be wished for:

> And the negro maids to Avès from bondage fast did flee
> To welcome gallant sailors, a'sweeping in from sea.

Eventually Avès is attacked by 'the King's ships'. Wounded, the pirate flees in a small boat:

> Nine days I floated starving, and a negro lass beside,
> Till for all I tried to cheer her, the poor young thing she died;
> But as I lay a'gasping, a Bristol sail came by,
> And brought me home to England here, to beg until I die.[17]

It is not difficult to see why this kind of thing, with its theme of a 'golden land', and undertones of violence and even exotic sex, went over so well. Other favourites included 'The Inchcape Rock' and 'How They Brought the Good News from Ghent to Aix'.

The nine small volumes of *Carpenter's Penny Readings* were the great standby for organizers, and there were also the three volumes selected by Tom Hood mentioned above. There were, too, very much humbler sources than these several-volume selections – humbler and, for this reason, more ephemeral. Nicholson of Wakefield, a noted publisher of cheap fiction, issued various 'reciters', including *Penny Readings and Recitations*, two series, costing 1s. 6d. each. The compiler was 'Professor Duncan', who was responsible also for *The Temperance Orator*, which cost 6d. and comprised speeches, readings, dialogues and illustrations of the evils of intemperance. Other titles published by this firm offered extracts which were variously described as entertaining, pathetic, witty, humorous, instructive or interesting.

To what extent were readings and recitations a part of social gatherings? The penny readings proper seem to have possessed an underlying structure and purpose, but there is no reason to suppose that the same kind of thing did not go on at less formal

17. Charles Kingsley, *Andromeda and Other Poems* (second edition, 1858), pp. 91–4.

social occasions. Certainly the number of 'reciters' and selections of readings offered by publishers was considerable. Milner's firm was offering three different kinds of temperance reciter at the end of the century, and the implication is that readings and recitations formed a prominent element in popular temperance propaganda.

The distinctions between the meeting at which one penny was paid for admission, the temperance meeting and the more *ad hoc* gathering at which guests were expected to 'say their piece' is hard to draw. Clearly there was an element of 'self-help' in party entertainments, while propagandist meetings and formal readings had a strong element of 'us to them'. These activities, taken together with the preoccupation in elementary classrooms of the nineteenth century with learning poems by heart, and with the number of books, cheaply produced, which contained suitable extracts, do indicate that the spoken word maintained a vigorous life in the enjoyment of 'literature' – however widely defined – at this period.

The decline of the penny-reading movement has not been satisfactorily explained. For a time it fulfilled a real need, but it is possible that the element of patronage implied in it contributed to its ultimate downfall. Less formal readings and recitations within the family circle proved very much more resilient and had, if one's own family experience is anything to go by, a much longer life.

Ultimately, of course, it was the gramophone and the bioscope which spelled out the end of oral enjoyment of literature. The two most striking survivals were the family party and the Nonconformist service of song.[18] The oral thunder of Wesley had become a whisper in such circles by about 1897.

The persistence of an oral tradition into the nineteenth century is a theme which requires investigation. In a world increasingly dominated at all levels by the printed word and cheap publications, its survival is of more than academic interest, and the fact that men and women of this time did show a liking for the spoken word in part, at least, of their entertainment provides us with a

18. See p. 228 above.

thread of tradition running from the days of Homer to the late Victorian age.

Perhaps the most unconsidered example of an enduring oral tradition is that of merchants' street cries. If today their voice has become muted, there was a long period when the strident, cajoling tones of huckster, pedlar and hawker contributed to a very real popular literature – a folk rhetoric which people took so much for granted that they were hardly aware of it.

RELIGIOUS TRACTS

HOUSEHOLD TRACTS FOR THE PEOPLE. *FOUR MILLIONS*
of these popular tracts are now in circulation in
Great Britain and the Colonies, and the demand is
increasing. They are adapted for gifts or loan;
are eagerly listened to at Public Readings at
Lecture Halls and Schoolrooms; and are worthy of
the attention of all who promote the moral,
sanitary, and religious improvement of the people.

TWOPENCE EACH.

> Advertisement for tracts published
> by Jarrold & Sons, 12 Paternoster
> Row (undated, about 1872)

It cannot be claimed that religious tracts were ever popular in the
sense that large numbers of the people into whose hands they fell
actually *bought* them. They were, however, distributed in great
numbers, and they represent in a tangible form what politicians,
bishops, influential evangelists and philanthropists thought that 'the
lower orders' ought to want to read. In these tracts the recipients were
constantly counselled to accept with humility and gratitude long hours
of work, low wages and poverty. These, their betters were at pains to
point out, were ordained by God, who had called the poor to their
humble station in society. Unsatisfactory as such a social doctrine was,
it is impossible not to be astonished by the extraordinary resilience
with which it was peddled over nearly two centuries.

Strictures of this kind cannot, however, be levelled at the first
religious tract, which was *The Souldier's Pocket Bible*, a sixteen-page
pamphlet published in 1643. Tradition has it that every soldier in
Cromwell's army was given a copy. Whether this is literally true or
not, it does seem that this little publication marks the first attempt at

tract distribution. The motives which lay behind it were far from those which prompted others in the eighteenth and nineteenth centuries. *The Souldier's Bible* was intended solely to provide Parliamentary troops with a readily portable version of the Scriptures. In an army deeply convinced of divine support for its cause it was a valuable adjunct to the religious and military ardour exemplified by Cromwell's remark, 'Trust in God, and keep your powder dry.'[1]

It was not until the outset of the eighteenth century that a concerted effort was made to commission the writing of religious tracts for mass distribution. The Society for Promoting Christian Knowledge was founded in 1698, and early in its life it turned its attention to this matter. The closing decades of the seventeenth century had seen the formation of various societies concerned with the reformation of manners, and from this general concern for the godlessness of society there grew the many-sided activities of the Society for Promoting Christian Knowledge, including the reformation of Newgate and other prisons, the spiritual needs on plantations in North America and the West Indies, the establishment of libraries, and the foundation of charity schools.[2]

To initiate their tract programme, the Society commissioned Dr Josiah Woodward, who had been a member since 1699, to write several short works. The choice of Woodward as an author was not surprising. He had been involved in evangelical work, and in 1698 his *An Account of the Religious Societies in the City of London* had been published. His view of Christianity was made explicit in its pages:

It is true, the Christian Religion is one of the most mild and gentle Institutions in the whole World, and the fullest of Mercy towards Sinners; but not to insolent and obstinate Sinners, but to the Humble and Penitent. The Gospel itself is Thunder to the impudent and impenitent Transgressor...[3]

As minister of Poplar, and later of Maidstone, he was a working clergyman; and he made very clear what he saw as the tasks confronting him. Small wonder, then, that at the SPCK's meeting on 21

1. A facsimile edition of this pamphlet, with a preface by Field Marshal Viscount Wolsley, was issued in 1895.

2. See Rev. E. McClure, *A Chapter in English Church History: Being the Minutes of the Society for Promoting Christian Knowledge for the Years 1698–1704* (1888), Preface, p. iii.

3. ibid., p. 66.

July 1701 it was 'ordered that Mr Hodges be desired to speak to Dr Woodward to compose a small Tract for the use of the Souldiers'.[4] The result – with a dedication to the Duke of Marlborough – was *The Souldier's Monitor*. This turned out, in fact, to be somewhat more substantial than its Cromwellian forerunner, and contained 72 pages. Moreover, it remained in print for a longer period – a thirtieth edition came out in 1802. 'If a Soldier Steals, Lies or Swears profanely,' wrote Dr Woodward, 'if he drinks to Excess, or does Violence to Man or Woman, he degrades himself and forfeits the honour due to his Station.'[5]

Further titles were commissioned. Later in 1701 the Society thanked Dr Woodward for writing a companion, *The Seaman's Monitor*[6] (by 1818 in its twenty-first edition). Other publications from his pen included *The Young Man's Monitor*, *Kind Caution to Swearers*, *Baseness of Slandering and Backbiting*, *Dissuasive from Gaming*, *Dissuasive from Drunkenness*, *A Present for Servants*, and so on. These tracts were designed to reach as wide a public as possible. At one meeting of the Society, held on 16 July 1701, it was reported that one group had 'dispersed above thirty thousand printed Papers throughout all the publick Houses in and about Westminster, and that all these Papers had been well received in all these Houses, tho' between six and seaven thousand in number, except in about twenty of them'.[7]

In 1704–5, 15,500 copies of *The Souldier's Monitor* were distributed to troops in Marlborough's army. They comprised, wrote Major R. E. Scouller, 'the only welfare service . . . which I have been able to trade'.[8] Admiral Benbow's fleet benefited from a distribution of *The Seaman's Monitor*, and eight hundred copies of the tract on swearing were given away to hackney coachmen in London.[9]

What is surprising about these tracts is not the dreary subject matter, nor one's doubts about whether the recipients ever gave them more than a second glance: it is the scale of the operation, and the assumption made by fairly hard-headed clergymen that masses of

4. ibid., p. 142.
5. *The Souldier's Monitor* (eighth edition, 1796), p. 8.
6. McClure, op. cit., p. 153.
7. ibid., p. 137.
8. *The Armies of Queen Anne* (1966), p. 289.
9. McClure, op. cit., p. 122.

people could at this period be reached effectively by means of the printed word. Even allowing for their enthusiasm, and a zeal which may have outrun reality, they were prepared to back their views with hard cash; and whatever view is held regarding the tract undertaking, the assumption that a mass reading public existed so early in the eighteenth century is significant.

Curiously enough, the Methodists under John Wesley did not follow the example of the Society for Promoting Christian Knowledge until much later in the century. It is hard to see why. Wesley had a very keen appreciation of the value of the printed word in spreading religion; but his disregard of the tract in the early days of his movement sprang partly from the fact that, where people in their masses were concerned, he relied to a tremendous extent upon a personal charisma which seems never to have failed him. Then, too, there was his innate and firm Toryism, which made it difficult for him to envisage a mass reading public at the bottom end of society. Nevertheless, his neglect of the tract is still puzzling, particularly in view of the fact that he was a best-selling author in his own right. Leaving aside his religious works, which sold extremely well – *A Collection of Prayers and Hymns* (1741 and subsequent reprints) and *The Character of a Methodist* (1742), often reprinted, are two examples – not even the favourable reception given to his *Primitive Physic* when it came out in 1747, leading to a twenty-third edition before his death in 1791, seems to have awakened his mind to the possibilities of the tract market.

The Society for Promoting Christian Knowledge appealed to specific groups in society with specially written works for soldiers, sailors, servants, coachmen, prisoners, farmers. The Methodist approach, when it came, was very much more general, although this same pattern was adopted in one series of tracts. A single sheet entitled 'A plan of the Society instituted in January, 1782, to distribute religious Tracts among the Poor' set out the rules and aims. Every member was required to subscribe half a guinea, a guinea, or more, each year. According to the subscription paid, he would receive tracts for distribution. Subscribers were allowed, if they wished, to choose their own titles from the list of thirty which the handbill advertised. Prices ranged from a threepenny version of *A Serious Call to a Holy Life* to a series which included *A Word to a Freeholder* (with similar tracts addressed to a smuggler, a soldier, a Sabbath-breaker, a prostitute and others), which cost between one shilling and two shillings per hundred copies. There was also a penny version of *A Collection of Hymns*. The enterprise was given Wesley's uncompromising approval:

> I cannot but earnestly recommend this, to all those who desire to see true scriptural Christianity spread throughout these Nations. Men wholly un-awakened will not take the pains to read the Bible. They have no relish for it. But a small Tract may engage their attention for half an hour: and may, by the blessing of God, prepare them for going forward.[10]

There is insufficient evidence to judge the success or otherwise of this enterprise. Having at last taken a first step, the Methodists seemed reluctant to take a second and they did not set up a Tract Committee until 1822. Before that, however, there were two events which must be mentioned – the publication of Cheap Repository Tracts and the foundation of the Religious Tract Society.

Hannah More, friend of Dr Johnson, who 'gallented it' round Oxford with her in 1782, was a formidable figure. Author and edu-cationalist, she was the 'blue stocking' lady *par excellence*. What brought her into tract writing was, indirectly, the French Revolution. The Bishop of London, Beilby Porteus, met her in Bath in 1791 and asked her to write something, in simple words, to counteract the evil effect of words like 'liberty' and 'equality' which were beginning to be bandied about. At first she demurred, but the idea stayed with her, and she wrote her first tract, *Village Politics, by Will Chip, a Country Carpenter*. Tom Hod, a mason, has been reading Paine's *Rights of Man*, and Jack Anvil explains to him the real meaning of the terms which have seduced him from patriotism:

Tom: And art thou very sure we are not ruined?

Jack: I'll tell thee how we are ruined. We have a King, so loving that he would not hurt the people if he could: and so kept in that he could not hurt the people if he would. We have as much liberty as can make us happy, and more trade and riches than allows us to be good. We have the best laws in the world, if they were more strictly enforced; and the best religion in the world if it was but better followed. While old England is safe, I'll glory in her, and pray for her, and when she is in danger, I'll fight for her and die for her.

10. I am grateful to the Rev. J. Bowmer for drawing my attention to this handbill, a copy of which is in the Methodist archives.

Tom: And so will I too, Jack, that's what I will. (Sings)
    'Oh, the roast beef of old England!'

The Bishop of London and some friends were so impressed with this tract as an antidote to revolution that they financed its publication. Jack and Tom turn up in 1795 in a political ballad by Hannah More, 'The Riot: or Half a Loaf is Better than No Bread'. Tom tries to incite Jack to riot:

> But though poor, I can work, my brave boy, with the best,
> Let the king and the parliament manage the rest;
> I lament both the war and the taxes together,
> Though I verily think they don't alter the weather.
> The king as I take it, with very good reason,
> May prevent a bad law, but can't help a bad season.
> > Derry down.
>
> And though I've no money, and though I've no lands;
> I've a head on my shoulders, and a pair of good hands;
> So I'll work the whole day, and on Sundays I'll seek
> At church how to bear all the wants of the weak.
> The gentlefolks too will afford us supplies,
> They'll subscribe – and they'll give up their pudding and pies.
> > Derry down.
>
> Then before I'm induced to take part in a riot,
> I'll ask this short question – What shall I get by it?
> So I'll e'en wait a little, till cheaper the bread,
> For a mittimus hangs o'er each rioter's head;
> And when of two evils I'm asked which is best
> I'd rather be hungry than hang'd I protest.
> > Derry down.
>
> Quoth Tom, thou art right; if I rise, I'm a Turk;
> So he threw down his pitchfork, and went to his work.

Village Politics and other writings of this kind proved so popular that a group of influential evangelists known as the Clapham Group agreed to underwrite another project – Cheap Repository Tracts. These were to be a series of readable ballads, tales, Bible stories and the like, produced with the definite aim of countering what the group believed to be the pernicious and dangerous effects of chapbooks, broadsides and other infidel publications. The first publication date was March 1795; before that, a circular announced:

PLAN FOR ESTABLISHING A REPOSITORY
OF

Cheap Publications, on Religious & Moral Subjects; which will be sold at a Halfpenny, or a Penny, and few to exceed Twopence, each.

After a patriotic beginning urging that Britain had always been distinguished by the special care she had shown to 'persons of the lower class', the proposal continued:

The object of this institution is the circulation of Religious and Useful Knowledge, as an antidote to the poison continually flowing thro' the channel of vulgar and licentious publications. These, by their cheapness, as well as by their being, unhappily, congenial to a depraved taste, obtain a mischievous popularity among the lower ranks. – It is not the impure novel or romance which attracts the common labourer's ear, or defiles his cottage: but his gross and polluted phrases may be often traced to those profane and indecent songs, and penny papers, which are vended about our cities, towns and villages, by hawkers: of whom it is a low statement to say, that more than 20,000 are employed in this traffic.[11]

There are two references to the size of the reading public which the tracts were designed to reach – 'vast numbers have now learned to read', and 'multitudes whose reading . . .'. The sponsors also insist that they prefer the contents to be 'striking' rather than 'merely didactic', and the first twenty titles advertised include *The Gin-shop or a Peep at a Prison*, *The Market Woman, a True Tale, in Verse*, and *Providential Detections of Murders by Henry Fielding, Esq*. There seems nothing aggressively moral or religious in these titles. Titles costing a penny each could be had at 4s. 6d. per 100, 2s. 6d. for 50 and 1s. 6d. for 25; those costing a halfpenny were available in bulk at half these prices.

Methods of distribution are clearly outlined. Sale is to be preferred to donation. 'Let the experiment be fairly tried,' the circular goes on. 'Let the substantial dealer – let the retailer of papers and songs in the obscurer parts of a town – let those who occupy a stall at a fair for the sale of books and ballads – let the poor woman who travels with her

11. *Plan for Establishing a Repository of Cheap Publications, etc.*

matches and her cakes – be all encouraged to try whether they cannot, at once, assist themselves and the cause of virtue.'[12]

Inevitably the wealthy bought the tracts in large numbers for distribution. The Archbishop of Canterbury, besides the Bishop of London, were active in promoting Cheap Repository Tracts. In one year over two million had been sold. Of the first 114 titles Hannah More wrote 49, and she took the task with such seriousness that she made her own collection of chapbooks so that she could learn the secret of their popularity. Certainly these tracts resembled chapbooks: they were printed on the same kind of coarse paper, and the texts were enlivened with similar woodcut illustrations. But there, of course, the similarity ended. Hannah More's tracts were well-written, a good deal of her material was drawn from life, and she possessed a unique blend of practicality and charm of style which lifted her work well above that of other Cheap Repository authors, amongst whom were the Rev. John Black, a Suffolk clergyman who signed his work 'S.S.' (Sappho Search, his pen-name), William Mason, Hester Chapone and William Gilpin. Hannah More's stories continued to be reprinted well into the nineteenth century, long after the work of the others had fallen into obscurity.

The best known of her tracts, *The Shepherd of Salisbury Plain*, was little more than an attempt to persuade the poor to be content with their lot in life and, delightfully written as it is, there is no escaping the bleak counsel that is offered in its pages. The burden of her political philosophy, so far as it informed her tract-writing, was fourfold. First, it was assumed that the gentry would always take care of the poor. Second, there was no connection between the government and conditions of poverty and want. Next, the common man should not attempt to meddle in government, this being no concern of his. Finally, God, who had created society as it was, knew what was best for everyone.

Views like this were convenient for those whose concern *was* with government – those who were able to dispense both charity and tracts to 'the meaner sort'. For the majority of the population they could hardly have been palatable, and the identification of political repression with the kind of Christianity peddled in tracts must have done a great deal to turn the minds of some working men to infidelity and atheism.

12. ibid.

W. H. Reid, who wrote about the radical societies at the close of the eighteenth century, concluded his critical account of them with a note of caution which developments in the nineteenth century were to justify:

> But though, in a moral view, the anti-religious opinions of Infidels must meet with accumulated contempt from the Christian world at large; yet as those who entertain them are all, without exception, tinged with revolutionary politics, and naturally detest every establishment, the utmost caution continues necessary on the part of government, to prevent any combustion or real grievance, of which these incorrigible members might avail themselves, to involve the community as agents in the prosecution of their invidious designs.[13]

Reid went further than most in defining the situation which tracts, it was hoped by their imitators and sponsors, would go some way towards remedying. Indeed, by 1803 the tract had become a weapon in the hands of those who, like him, urged the 'utmost caution' as a means of preserving the *status quo*. In that year appeared an eight-page pamphlet, *Popular and Patriotic Tracts*. The announcement on the front page set the tone:

> At the present important period, when the utmost energies of a *free* and *independent people*, will be necessary to repel the attacks of an *invading and implacable enemy*, it has been thought requisite to point out, by every means and in every shape, the *situation* in which *we stand*, the *character* of our *ambitious* and *tyrannical enemy*; and what may be *naturally expected* from *his success* on the British shores. With this view, many Gentlemen of intelligence and patriotism have written and published a series of animating and encouraging addresses on the most interesting topics which can at this crisis engage the public mind; together with certain *most striking* and *notorious facts*, illustrative of the *character* of the enemy . . .

The intention, clearly, was to stiffen resistance to the threatened invasion of Napoleon's forces by appealing to a sense of patriotism and loyalty amongst those who might have felt that they had little to lose by a change of master. The effectiveness of the tracts in whipping up patriotism or in diminishing disaffection was never put to the test. Presumably large numbers of them were bought for distribution, at prices ranging from 2s. 6d. per dozen to 6d. a hundred. Titles included

13. *The Rise and Dissolution of the Infidel Societies in This Metropolis* (1800; facsimile reprint, Woburn Press, 1971), p. 117.

Shakespeare's Ghost, a Cento of Loyal Passages from Our Inimitable Bard, Applied to the Present Crisis; A Letter to the Volunteers on Their Military System; and 'The French in a Fog', which was sung to the tune of 'Hearts of Oak'.

What is really surprising is that publications of this kind seem to have evoked so little reaction in print from radicals. One angry comment that I have found was written by William Hone in 1817, during the depression which followed the cessation of the Napoleonic wars. On two occasions in *Hone's Reformist Register* he turned with anger to the subject of Cheap Repository Tracts:

One of these, addressed 'to the Mechanics, Artizans, and Labourers of London and Westminster', and diligently stuck about the streets, has the impudence to say, that 'the evils under which *we all* (more or less) suffer, are wholly imputable not to the crimes of individuals, but to *natural* and *uncontrollable* causes'; and with unfeeling audacity, tells the poor famishing creatures who read it, that 'it becomes us to submit with Christian patience, to being put on short allowance'![14]

A fortnight later he returned to the same theme, and used even stronger terms:

This very week, when tens of thousands in London are out of work, a ballad is hawked about the streets, written by Miss Hannah More, to the tune of 'a cobler there was, and he liv'd in a stall', in which are the following verses.

Hone here quoted from 'The Riot: or Half a Loaf is Better than No Bread',[15] and then continued:

This is the dull lying consolation offered to the half-starved and miserable. We are already exhorted to be patient under affliction and to bear our crosses with humility; not to murmur or complain, or be fretful; not to be irritated or angry; but to submit ourselves as we ought, to the stations allotted to us.[16]

His was a lone voice, however, and the more orthodox view of tracts was expressed by Anna Buckland, who wrote a life of Hannah More in the nineteenth century[17] and described her efforts as 'bringing light

14. *Hone's Reformist Register*, no. 11, 5 April 1817.
15. The text of this ballad is given on p. 254.
16. *Hone's Reformist Register*, no. 13, 19 April 1817.
17. *The Life of Hannah More* (the Religious Tract Society, undated).

and help into lives sunk in sordid toil, or the deeper degradation of mere brutal existence'.[18]

There is no reason to doubt the sincerity of tract writers and publishers: the charge of hypocrisy would be hard to sustain. Religious tracts were an important element in the evangelical work practised by many believers in the nineteenth century. In its first decades local tract societies were formed in many areas, and the Religious Tract Society, founded in 1799, issued hundreds of tracts over the years, most of them illustrated and printed on good-quality paper.

The Methodists, as was mentioned earlier, instituted a General Tract Committee in 1822, and with characteristic thoroughness set about production. In 1830 they published a twelve-page pamphlet, *An Address on Tract Distribution with a Word to the Distributors*. One hundred copies could be had for three shillings and, although it was anonymous, the author was probably John Mason, Methodist Book Steward from 1827 to 1864, who was responsible for issuing an extremely large number of tracts. The pamphlet outlined the reason for distributing tracts – it was a method of reaching 'the poorer classes of Society'. It offered also a brief history of Wesleyan tracts, together with detailed instructions on how to form a tract society.

How effective was all this activity? Did people actually read tracts? On the evidence of the tracts themselves, which strike the modern reader as pretty dull, probably not to any great extent. Certainly none of the autobiographies of working men that I have come across mention them, while ballads and chapbooks are often spoken of with affectionate remembrance. Dickens's character, Mrs Pardiggle (in *Bleak House*), typified the well-meaning distributor of tracts, and she received a very dusty answer: '"Have I read the little book wot you left?" said the brickmaker. "No, I an't read the little book wot you left. There an't nobody here as knows how to read it; and if there wos, it wouldn't be suitable to me. It's a book fit for a babby, and I'm not a babby."'

Another contemporary had this to say:

Walking one day through a green lane in Somersetshire, I noticed a boy employed to watch a cow, seated amid wild flowers on the grass, with a number of tracts before him. I inquired if he had read them, and he replied

18. ibid., p. 94.

34. (a) A tract seller

that he could not read. When I further asked what he did with them, he pointed to two gentlemen, a short distance before me, who he said had thrown them to him as they passed. He added that I might have them if I liked, as they were of no use to him.[19]

Notwithstanding this, the tract industry continued to expand. In 1866 the Rev. C. H. Spurgeon founded the Metropolitan Tabernacle

19. J. A. St John, *The Education of the People* (1858; facsimile reprint, 1970), p. 144.

34. (b) Bible distribution

Colportage Association. By 1872 it was employing thirteen men, and, four years later, forty-five; by the end of the century eighty hawkers were employed. Tracts, Bibles, books and magazines were sold and given away and, besides the colporteurs knocking on doors, one novel form of distribution was used. This was the Bible carriage, which seems to have been in use in about 1875 – and more were planned.

In 1880 Spurgeon made a speech at the anniversary of the Religious Tract Society in which he supported their work with an eloquence that could not have been new to his audience and went out of his way to praise the society for publishing books other than religious ones. He put tracts first, but obviously hoped that they would lead on to more wholesome reading:

... but there is a servant girl yonder, and she has got a novel: see how she is taken up with it; see the tears in her eyes – some young fellow did not get married after all – something dreadful, an awful murder happened, and it

THE HAPPY FAMILY.

A LETTER

TO HENRY AND ELIZA·GRANT,
FROM THEIR FATHER,

WHILE ON A VISIT IN LONDON.

LONDON:
RELIGIOUS TRACT SOCIETY;
DEPOSITORY, 56, PATERNOSTER ROW, AND 65,
ST PAUL'S CHURCHYARD.

34. (c) A typical mid-Victorian religious tract

finishes up beautifully. I say if I can get that book away, and give her *Jessica's First Prayer*, I shall be doing her good.[20]

There is a touch of unreality about Spurgeon's recommendation of Hesba Stretton's novel. Whatever its merits, it is very doubtful whether many readers would have preferred its milk-and-water prose to stories of action and romance. The fact that he was so certain about this underlines the fallacy inherent in the impulse to tract-making and distribution. There was never any reason at all to suppose that a majority of people preferred the plain, straightforward morality of the tract to the pleasures of ballads, chapbooks and novels. Why, then, did this rather curious evangelical endeavour last for over two centuries?

Part of the answer lies in the Protestant tradition of Bible-reading, and in the related idea that personal religion depended to a great extent upon one's reading of the Scriptures and suitable religious

20. C. H. Spurgeon *et al.*, *Booksellers and Bookbuyers in Byeways and Highways* (1882), p. 43.

"It's all in the Coupling."

YOU may be a good husband, a kind father, a regular Church-goer, straight and honest; but all this, though right in its place, is not enough. Your own good works and righteousness will never take you to heaven. Just as the furniture of the railway carriages, however rich, elegant, and substantial, will never avail to move the train.

The one essential is this coupling between carriage and engine,—it's all in the coupling. "Faith" is that coupling. "He that *believeth* on Me hath everlasting life." "He that hath the Son, hath life." He who is united to Christ is a living soul. "He that hath not the Son of God, hath not life."

There is no power in the coupling-link itself; its importance all comes from what it *does*. So, faith is a simple thing; its only value is that it is God's plan,—by which a seeking soul is linked with a seeking Saviour;—by which a *guilty* soul is linked with a perfect Saviour;—by which a *condemned* sinner is linked with his accepted Substitute, who died in his stead on Calvary. Again,

"He that believeth on *Me* hath everlasting life."

Have you, reader, living, personal contact with Jesus, by thus trusting Him? If so, the link is on the hook, you have touched Him; and "as many as *touched*, were made perfectly whole."

It's either one thing or the other. I *have* trusted the Lord Jesus, or I've not. The coupling is either on or off. Don't say, "I hope it's on." Make sure. You may be uncertain about a good many things, but uncertainty about *salvation* is fatal. You say, "What am I to do?" "Do nothing." "What am I to believe?" Believe that the Lord Jesus Christ has died in your stead, and given Himself for your sins, that you might never perish.

Though the coupling is fastened on a huge, massive hook, it might break. But Christ can *never* fail to keep the soul that trusts Him.

Though faith is necessary, it is not faith that saves, but Christ. It is not the link that pulls, but the engine. Once more, it is not a *thing* to which faith anchors; it is a living Person, "the Son of God Who loved me, and gave Himself for me."

The Holy Spirit flashes His light upon my soul. I thought that I was good; I see my sinfulness, guilt, lost condition. Like a man who was reading to his wife one night from the Bible. Suddenly he stopped: "Wife," said he, "if this is true, we're all wrong." A few nights after reading on, "Wife," he exclaimed, "if this is true, we are lost." Having come down to that point, it was not long before he looked up, and almost shouted, "Wife, if that's true, then you and I may be saved; for Christ Jesus, has given His life for me."

"Payment God will not twice demand,
First at my bleeding Surety's hand,
And then again at mine."

publications. The poor could not be expected to read the Bible – its sheer volume might well have daunted them – but a start could be made with the short religious piece which had the great advantage of being quickly read. In addition – and this was an important point – the contents could be made both religious and relevant to the times. This was killing two birds with one stone, and the fact that it was often badly aimed did not inhibit the efforts of societies, organizations and individuals from producing and distributing tracts in ever-increasing numbers.

Another fallacy lay in the fact that those who wrote tracts and those who received them had a totally different notion of what was relevant. On the one hand there were the concepts of rank, duty and decorum in a Christian society; on the other, poor living conditions and getting enough to eat. The latter points of view were rarely, if ever, articulated, but were very real for all that. The simplistic religious consolation offered was not enough to bridge the gap between the two sides. How could it have been? The wonder is that the futility of tract distribution went on for so long. One explanation could be simply that contributing to the cost of tract production and buying them at wholesale rates to give away offered a satisfactory way of doing good at a reasonable cost. Tracts provided the satisfaction of giving something away; they could not, like cash, be used to purchase strong drink; and they might – to put it no higher – have a positively good effect.

This was not a matter of hypocrisy, but rather of self-satisfaction. Of those who gave away these publications, how many could have known how the other half lived? Certainly many of them *cared* – and showed their care by offering words of comfort and religious cheer. This was not enough, although I think that many distributors might have thought it was; and they went on thinking this, encouraged by evangelists like Hannah More and C. H. Spurgeon, who certainly made no money out of writing or disseminating tracts, but had wonders done for their respective reputations by these humble pamphlets. Rarely can so misguided an effort have gone on for so long with so little result – other than the satisfaction of a few.

CRITICAL BIBLIOGRAPHY

Facsimile reprint editions have made available again many books which have long been out of print and hard to find. Some of these new editions are mentioned in the following pages, though by no means all; and new titles continue to come onto the market.

My guiding principle in writing this bibliographical guide has been utility. While I believe that the subtleties and delights of bibliomania – discussion of original state and variant bindings, the detection of cancelled half-titles, the pursuit of rarity for its own sake – have a definite and honoured place in humane activities, my object here has been very different. It has been to provide a guide to the subject, and by so doing to define it. I cannot, of course, lay claim to any completeness, and no specialist will have to be too assiduous to find lacunae. My more modest hope is that I have produced a guide that the general reader will find useful.

THEMES AND EXAMPLES

Much, though not all, recent work on popular literature has been done outside Britain. Nearly all of it, besides possessing an intrinsic interest, indicates the dimensions of the subject and the ways in which it can be tackled.

ALBERT JOHANNSEN, *The House of Beadle and Adams and Its Dime and Nickle Novels. A Story of Vanished Literature* (2 vols.; Norman, Oklahoma, 1950; supplementary volume, Norman, Oklahoma, 1962). A richly illustrated and detailed survey of a nineteenth-century New York firm which specialized in cheap fiction. It is a model of the way in which such work should be carried out and deserves to be very much better known in this country, not only for its bibliographic and critical method, but also because it throws a good deal of light upon the literary relations of Great Britain and the United States at this period.

JAMES D. HART, *The Popular Book. A History of America's Literary Taste* (New York, 1950). Also traces a theme which has much relevance for this country.

JOHN DUFFY, *Early Vermont Broadsides*, (Hanover, New Hampshire, 1975). The best reproductions of broadsides I have come across. Scholarly and perceptive notes.

French writers have been active in this field. MICHEL RAGON, *Histoire de la littérature ouvrière du moyen age à nos jours* (Paris, 1953). A sensitive study, full of insights. Very good on Deloney and his novels.

ROBERT MANDROU, *De la culture populaire aux 17ᵉ et 18ᵉ siècles* (Paris, 1964). Thorough and workmanlike. It is to be regretted that no similar study has as yet been written in this country.

GENEVIÈVE BOLLÈME, *Les Almanachs populaires aux XVIIᵉ et XVIIIᵉ siècles* (Paris, 1969), and *La Bibliothèque bleue* (Paris, 1971). The latter is an account of popular literature in France during the eighteenth and nineteenth centuries.

There is an impressive and copiously illustrated collection of three essays by JEAN MISTLER, FRANÇOIS BLAUDEZ and ANDRÉ JACQUEMIN, *Epinal et l'imagerie populaire* (Paris, 1961). Several of the facsimiles are in colour, and this book gives a very good idea of the popular prints produced in this town in north-eastern France.

Similar, but slighter, is YURI ORAYANNIKOV, *The Lubok: 17th–18th Century Russian Broadsides* (Moscow, 1968). Although the book is in Russian, there is an English text by A. Shkarousky-Raffe; but the chief virtue of this book will be found in the illustrations in monochrome and colour, which vividly recall this forgotten literature and occasionally show a marked similarity to French popular prints.

WILLIAM A. COUPE, *The German Illustrated Broadsheet in the Seventeenth Century* (2 vols., Baden-Baden, Vol. 1 1966, Vol. II 1967). These cover the subject in a very scholarly way. 145 broadsides are reproduced in facsimile in Vol. II.

JULIO CARO BAROJA, *Ensayo sobre la literatura de cordel* (Madrid, 1969). This is a serious study of a Spanish and South American phenomenon, 'literature on a string' – ephemeral publications offered for sale hanging on strings.

An outstanding contribution to the popular literature of Spain is made in F. J. NORTON and EDWARD M. WILSON, *Two Spanish Verse Chapbooks* (Cambridge, 1969). In its application of bibliographic techniques to the study of chapbooks this book is extremely important. Professor Wilson's Taylorian Lecture, published as *Some Aspects of Spanish Literary History* (Oxford, 1967), is also very informative.

PREDECESSORS

Popular literature has attracted few historians. The founding father is generally held to be CHARLES NISARD, whose *Histoire des livres populaires ou de la littérature du colportage* was published in Paris in two volumes in 1854, and reissued '*corrigée avec soin et considérablement augmentée*' ten years later. This is a book of considerable value. A facsimile reprint of it is available today.

In Britain, attempts at this kind of history were very much less ambitious. Amongst the essays in ISAAC D'ISRAELI, *Amenities of Literature* (1840), was one entitled 'Books of the People'. This was a pioneer study and represented the first attempt, so far as I am aware, on the part of any writer in this country to put the subject into an historical perspective.

A somewhat longer essay upon this theme is CHARLES KNIGHT, 'The Beginnings of Popular Literature', in *Once Upon a Time* (2 vols., 1854). Time has not justified the note of optimism struck by the author, but because his working life was largely taken up with the provision of cheap literature in one form or another, Knight's sketch is well worth reading.

WILLIAM CHAMBERS, *Historical Sketch of Popular Literature*, Proceedings of the Royal Society of Edinburgh, Vol. 5, 1863 (published 1866). An interesting study by a publisher active in this field.

JOHN POWNALL HARRISON, 'Cheap Literature – Past and Present', in *Companion to the British Almanac* (1873). Concerned mostly with nineteenth-century popular fiction, it nevertheless discusses the subject more widely within an historical context.

EARLY POPULAR LITERATURE

Comparatively little material from this period has survived. Copies of broadsides, ballads and jestbooks can be found in the British Museum and comparable collections, but for the most part one has to rely upon reprints of scarce items and bibliographical catalogues. Basic books are few in number and variable in quality. See, for instance, W. C. HAZLITT, *Hand-book to the Popular, Poetical and Dramatic Literature of Great Britain* (1867), and *Remains of the Early Popular Poetry of England* (4 vols., 1864–6).

BROADSIDES

Some of the earliest broadsides are listed in ROBERT LEMON, *Catalogue of a Collection of Printed Broadsides in the Possession of the Society of Antiquaries of London* (1866). This is an indispensable reference tool, covering the period from 1496 to 1862. It records one hundred items from the fifteenth and sixteenth centuries. The earliest records a licence granted by Henry VII to Thomas Andrews of South Mimms, permitting him to collect alms and charitable gifts in churches, as all his property had been destroyed by fire. This of course is not 'literature', but the catalogue as a whole is a rich source of material and lists many unique items.

BALLADS

A number of sixteenth-century ephemeral sheets are reprinted in
JOSEPH LILLY (ed.), *A Collection of Seventy-nine Black-letter Ballads
and Broadsides* (1867; 'Second Issue', 1870). The book is prefaced
with an extremely valuable introduction.

JESTBOOKS

W. C. HAZLITT (ed.), *Old English Jest-books* (3 vols., 1864) contains
reprints of fifteen titles. A facsimile edition issued by Burt Franklin of
New York in 1964 meant that this extremely scarce work was once
more available. It has also meant that its defects are apparent to a new
generation of readers. Editorially this is a sloppy piece of work, and
Hazlitt felt obliged upon occasion to tamper with texts. Unfortunately,
for a number of jestbooks this remains the only accessible version.

Very much better is HERMAN OESTERLEY (ed.), *Shakespeare's Jest
Book* (1866). This is an edition of *A Hundred Mery Tales* based upon
a perfect copy of the 1526 edition printed by John Rastell, which the
editor found in the Royal Library of Göttingen University. Scrupulously edited, it is a very satisfactory version. The introduction errs on
the side of austerity.

P. M. ZALL, *A Hundred Merry Tales and Other Jestbooks of the Fifteenth
and Sixteenth Centuries* (Lincoln, Nebraska, 1963). This is the
handiest introduction to the subject. Despite its rather light-hearted
approach the introduction is extremely perceptive, and the modernized
texts give a good idea of the flavour of this kind of literature.

JOHN WARDROPER (ed.), *Jest upon Jest* (1970). An anthology gathered
from jestbooks from the reigns of Richard III to George III.

RIDDLES

JOHN WARDROPER (ed.), *Demaundes Joyous* (1973). A facsimile
edition, with an introduction, transcript, notes and bibliography, of
the only known surviving copy of the first English riddle-book,
published in 1511.

STUDIES AND SURVEYS

Critical and historical studies are few. Outstanding is F. J. FURNIVALL, *Captain Cox, His Ballads and Books* (1871). A survey, written with verve and expertise, of popular reading in the reign of Queen Elizabeth I. Absolutely fundamental reading, and hardly dated.

LOUIS B. WRIGHT, *Middle Class Culture in Elizabethan England* (North Carolina, 1935 and several subsequent editions). Authoritative, fully documented view of what Elizabethans read for pleasure and profit. The chapters on popular taste are superb.

Early novels are discussed in J. J. JUSSERAND, *The English Novel in the Time of Shakespeare* (1890), and M. SCHLAUCH, *Antecedents of the English Novel* (Warsaw and London, 1963). The former is sympathetically written and has stood the test of time well. Professor Schlauch's book, written from an orthodox Marxist standpoint, is both erudite and refreshing, and occasionally provocative.

Less scholarly, but required reading, is W. C. HAZLITT, *Studies in Jocular Literature* (Popular Edition, 1904).

K. R. H. MACKENZIE (ed.), *The Marvellous Adventures and Rare Conceits of Master Tyll Owlglass* (1860). Useful mainly for the bibliographical appendix.

Dealing very much more seriously with Till Eulenspiegel and other themes is C. H. HERFORD, *Studies in the Literary Relations of England and Germany in the Sixteenth Century* (Cambridge, 1886). An original work in which a vast amount of learning is worn lightly and presented readably.

ALMANACS

EUSTACE F. BOSANQUET, *English Printed Almanacks and Prognostications. A Bibliographical History to the Year 1600* (the Bibliographical Society, 1917). This has not been superseded, having remained a standard work for over half a century. There are 35 superb facsimiles of rare almanacs, and the introduction is entirely admirable.

See also A. HEYWOOD, JR, *Three Papers on English Almanacs* (Manchester, 1904).

BALLADRY

The literature of balladry is enormous. Three collections of early material are especially important:

FRANCIS CHILD (ed.), *The English and Scottish Popular Ballads* (5 vols., Boston, Mass., 1882–98; a facsimile reprint is available). See also B. H. BRONSON, *The Traditional Tunes of the Child Ballads* (4 vols., Princeton, New Jersey, 1950–72).

THOMAS PERCY (ed.), *Reliques of Ancient English Poetry Consisting of Old Heroic Ballads, Songs and Other Pieces of Our Earlier Poets* (3 vols., 1886). Edited by Henry B. Wheatley, this is the best edition of a work first published in 1765.

JOHN W. HALES and FREDERICK J. FURNIVALL (eds.), *Bishop Percy's Folio Manuscript :* Ballads and Romances (3 vols., 1867, 1868); Loose and Humorous Songs (1867). These four volumes reprint – somewhat reluctantly in the case of Volume 4 – the manuscript from which Percy worked. A superb piece of nineteenth-century scholarship. Percy took many liberties with the text – Hales and Furnivall present it verbatim.

See also: A. JOHNSTON, *Enchanted Ground* (1964) – there is an excellent chapter on Percy and other eighteenth-century collectors of early ballads; SIR WALTER SCOTT, *Periodical Criticism*, Volume 1, *Poetry* (Edinburgh, 1835) – interesting essays on eighteenth-century collectors of early ballad and related literature.

WILLIAM CHAPPELL, *Popular Music of the Olden Time* (2 vols., 1855, 1859). This remains a standard work.

EDMONSTOUNE DUNCAN, *The Story of Minstrelsy* (1907). Less ambitious than the previous item, but extremely useful.

JOSEPH STRUTT, *The Sports and Pastimes of the People of England* (1838). Good on minstrels and on popular amusements generally. It first appeared in 1801, and was reprinted in 1810. This is the first edition to include an index, which was compiled by William Hone.

ROBERT BELL (ed.), *Ancient Poems, Ballads and Songs of the Peasantry of England* (1857). Derives from an earlier work edited for the Percy Society by J. H. Dixon in 1846. The notes at the head of each ballad are particularly useful in showing how oral ballads passed into print.

JOSEPH RITSON (ed.), *Ancient Songs and Ballads* (third edition, revised by W. C. Hazlitt, 1877). Valuable for the same reason as the last item. It is also enhanced by Ritson's admirable introductory essay.

Writings about ballads are many. Among them are the following: FRANCIS B. GUMMERE, *The Popular Ballad* (New York, 1959). A reprint of a book first published more than fifty years ago, and still useful.

G. H. GEROULD, *The Ballad of Tradition* (New York, 1957). Still a fresh and pertinent study, over forty years after its first appearance.

Three articles by C. H. FIRTH are of especial value: 'The Ballad History of the Reigns of Henry VII and Henry VIII', in *Transactions of the Royal Historical Society*, Third Series, Vol. II (1908); 'The Ballad History of the Reigns of the Later Tudors', in *Transactions of the Royal Historical Society*, Third Series, Vol. III (1909); 'Ballads and Broadsides', *Shakespeare's England*, Vol. II, 1916, 1966): bibliographical notes are appended to this essay, which was reprinted, without illustrations, in Firth's *Essays Historical and Literary* (Oxford, 1938).

More recent studies include M. J. C. HODGART, *The Ballads* (1950). A lucid and knowledgeable survey.

LAJOS VARGYAS, *Researches into the Mediaeval History of Folk Ballad* (Budapest, 1967). Rather more esoteric, but useful.

V. DE SOLA PINTO and A. E. RODWAY (eds.), *The Common Muse* (1957), is a good introduction to the popular ballad. It was issued in two editions with and without what Hales and Furnivall (above) called 'loose and humorous songs'. The full edition was reissued in paperback (Penguin Books) in 1965.

For a fuller, though selective, listing of material on ballads, see LESLIE SHEPARD, *The Broadside Ballad* (1962).

HEROES

Robin Hood ballads were collected in the eighteenth century.

JOSEPH RITSON (ed.), *A Collection of All the Ancient Poems, Songs and Ballads Now Extant Relating to That Celebrated English Outlaw* (2 vols., 1795; several times reprinted). A facsimile of the 1823 (one-volume) edition is available.

J. M. GUTCH (ed.), *Robin Hood* (2 vols., 1847). This book was inspired by Ritson's research.

W. J. THOMS (ed.), *A Collection of Early Prose Romances* (3 vols., 1828 and subsequent reprints). Indispensable for the sources of early fiction.

LAURA A. HIBBARD (Laura Hibbard Loomis), *Mediaeval Romance in England* (new edition, New York, 1963). A number of legendary English heroes who figure in popular literature are discussed.

W. C. HAZLITT, *National Tales and Legends* (1899). Less scholarly, but this is a re-telling of traditional stories with some notes.

ARTHUR DICKSON, *Valentine and Orson* (New York, 1929). Traces the fortunes of a medieval romance which eventually became the subject of a chapbook.

RONALD S. CRANE, *The Vogue of Guy of Warwick from the Close of the Middle Ages to the Romantic Revival* (Publications of the Modern Language Association of America, Vol. XXX, 2; New Series, Vol. XXIII, 2; 1915). The best study of this kind.

THE UNDERWORLD

For criminals and vagabonds in the popular literature of the period, see FRANK AYDELOTTE, *Elizabethan Rogues and Vagabonds* (1913; new impression, 1967) and RONALD FULLER, *The Beggars' Brotherhood* (1936). Both are excellent.

TRADITIONAL TALES

Three books are especially useful in tracing comparative plots and themes:

THOMAS KEIGHTLEY, *Tales and Popular Fictions: Their Resemblance and Transmission from Country to Country* (1834).

W. A. CLOUSTON, *Popular Tales and Fictions, Their Migrations and Transformations* (2 vols., Edinburgh and London, 1887).

W. A. CLOUSTON, *The Book of Noodles* (1888).

FOOLS

ENID WELSFORD, *The Fool* (1935). A well-documented study of fools in literature.

FAIRIES

K. M. BRIGGS, *The Anatomy of Puck* (1959). An admirable guide to fairy beliefs. In addition there is a full bibliography which covers the subject very well indeed.

GIANTS

Giants crop up sometimes in the popular literature of this early period.

H. J. MASSINGHAM, *Fee Fi Fo Fum. The Giants in England* (1926).

F. W. FAIRHOLT, *Gog and Magog. The Giants in Guildhall* (1859).

THE SEVENTEENTH CENTURY

There are more survivals from this period than from the earlier one. Broadside ballads in particular have been extensively collected and studied. This is less true of popular prose literature which, in the form of pamphlets and small books, tends to be scattered throughout library catalogues. Much of this material still awaits detailed investigation.

BALLAD COLLECTIONS

Amongst the most important collections of broadside ballads are the following:

THE ROXBURGHE BALLADS (British Museum). The best edition (in nine volumes) is *The Roxburghe Ballads*; Vols. 1–3, ed. W. Chappell (The Ballad Society, 1871–80); Vols. 4–9, ed. J. W. Ebsworth (The Ballad Society, 1883–99). A facsimile, complete in eight volumes, is in print.

Less satisfactory are two earlier gatherings from this collection: John Payne Collier (ed.), *A Book of Roxburghe Ballads* (1847); Charles Hindley (ed.), *The Roxburghe Ballads* (2 vols., 1873, 1874).

THE PEPYS BALLADS (Magdalene College, Cambridge): Hyder E. Rollins (ed.), *The Pepys Ballads* (*1535–1702*), (8 vols., Harvard, 1929–32). Professor Rollins was an outstanding ballad scholar. See below for further books by him.

THE EUING BALLADS (Glasgow University Library): *The Euing Collection of English Broadside Ballads*. Introduction by John Holloway (University of Glasgow, 1971).

There are also the collection of ballads made by Francis Douce (four volumes, in the Bodleian Library, Oxford) and a two-volume ballad collection in Manchester Reference Library. These collections are unpublished.

HYDER E. ROLLINS

Mention has been made above of Hyder E. Rollins. Amongst his editorial contributions to ballad study are the following:

'The Black-letter Broadside Ballad', in *PMLA*, 34 (1919), pp. 258–339.

Old English Ballads 1553–1625 (Cambridge, 1920).

A Pepysian Garland. Black-letter Broadside Ballads of the Years 1595–1639. Chiefly from the Collection of Samuel Pepys (Cambridge, 1922).

A Handfull of Pleasant Delites ... by Clement Robinson and Divers Others (Harvard, 1923).

Cavalier and Puritan. Ballads and Broadsides Illustrating the Period of the Great Rebellion 1640–1660 (New York, 1923). A useful complement to this book is C. V. WEDGWOOD, *Poetry and Politics Under the Stuarts* (Cambridge, 1960) – knowledgeable, witty, provocative. See also C. H. FIRTH, *The Ballad History of the Reign of James I*, in *Transactions of the Royal Historical Society*, Third Series, Vol. V, 1911).

The Pack of Autolycus or Strange and Terrible News ... as Told in Broadside Ballads of the Years 1624–1693 (Harvard, 1927). All the Rollins editions are scrupulously edited and are essential reading. Several are available in reprinted editions. Of all his publications, it seems to me that *The Pack of Autolycus* gets most clearly to the seventeenth-century view of things.

BALLAD ANTHOLOGIES

ANDREW CLARK (ed.), *The Shirburn Ballads 1585–1616* (Oxford, 1907).

F. BURLINGTON FAWCETT (ed.), *Broadside Ballads of the Restoration Period ...* (1930).

THOMAS WRIGHT (ed.), *Political Ballads Published in England During the Commonwealth* (Percy Society, Early English Poetry, Vol. 3, 1841).

A pioneer anthology is W. W. WILKINS (ed.), *Political Ballads of the Seventeenth and Eighteenth Centuries* (2 vols., 1860). Covers the period from Charles I to George II. The annotations are extremely good.

In general, the publications of the Ballad Society at the end of the nineteenth century are helpful, and one must pay tribute to F. J. Furnivall, who provided the stimulus for so much work carried out by the Society.

I have already referred to Leslie Shepard, *The Broadside Ballad* (1962), and I must stress again that its bibliography, though selective, is enormously helpful.

BIBLIOGRAPHY OF BALLADS

Critical bibliographies and discussion of seventeenth-century ballads are not common. It is indeed a sad reflection upon the state of popular-literature studies that a reissue of HYDER E. ROLLINS, *An Analytical Index to the Ballad Entries (1557–1709) in the Registers of the Company of Stationers of London* (North Carolina, 1924; Hatboro, Pennsylvania, 1967), was being sold off cheaply in New York some years ago. This is a fundamental research tool, and Rollins did his work with immense care. More than three thousand ballad titles are listed; there is an index of first lines and of names and subjects. The compiler's comments are always perceptive, and the brief bibliography he provides is suggestive of further lines of reading and study.

Marginally less useful, but still very impressive, is *Bibliotheca Lindesiana. Catalogue of a Collection of English Ballads of the XVIIth and XVIIIth Centuries* (2 vols., 1890). Since this was originally issued in a very limited edition, the facsimile reprint published in New York is particularly welcome. Over 1,400 ballads are listed, and most useful of all is a list of printers, publishers and booksellers.

Two bibliographical essays are important: each has indicated in a decisive fashion new directions for ballad studies. The first is CYP-RIAN BLAGDEN, 'Notes on the Ballad Market in the Second Half of the Seventeenth Century', in *Papers of the Bibliographical Society of the University of Virginia*, Volume 6 (1953–4). A discussion of the mechanics of ballad printing and of relationships between printers. This essay is not only original in concept and splendidly executed, it also highlights the difference in approach of the older ballad editors (Rollins, of course, excepted) and a sophisticated observer of the book trade in the seventeenth century.

The second essay is LEBA M. GOLDSTEIN, 'An Account of the Faustus Ballad', in Transactions of the Bibliographical Society, the *Library*, Fifth Series, Vol. XVI, No. 3 (September 1961). This traces the history of the Faustus ballad, and in doing so draws upon a wide range of evidence. Like the Blagden essay, it is expertly done.

A very much older book, which can only by courtesy be termed bibliographic, is JOHN ASHTON, *Humour, Wit and Satire of the Seventeenth Century* (1883). I mention this partly because it does contain a useful appendix: 'Bibliographical Reference to the Source whence This Book was Compiled', and partly because it does manage to convey the flavour of what men and women at this period read for pleasure. An illustrated anthology, it contains much out-of-the-way material; moreover, it provides a convenient bridge between the broadside ballad and other forms of popular literature.

JESTBOOKS

Jestbooks continued to find favour with readers, and those reprinted by Hazlitt (see p. 269 above) show the sort of material they contained. P. M. ZALL (ed.), *A Nest of Ninnies* (Lincoln, Nebraska, 1970), contains extracts from twelve seventeenth-century jestbooks, an introduction and some notes. Extremely competent, it follows the compiler's earlier book on the jocular literature of the fifteenth and sixteenth centuries.

Continuities are further emphasized in J. O. HALLIWELL (ed.), *Tarlton's Jests and News out of Purgatory* (1844). Tarlton was a well-known comic actor on the Elizabethan stage, and these pamphlets, with obscure bibliography, appeared in various editions between 1590 and 1638.

Another jestbook reprint is REV. A. DYCE (ed.), *Kemps Nine Daies Wonder* (1840). The original was published in 1600 and appears in this edition expertly edited by Dyce, who was one of the finest scholars of his day.

The reprints just mentioned were published respectively by the Shakespeare Society and the Camden Society. A good deal of fugitive literature was issued in the nineteenth century, usually in limited editions, by such societies – notably the Percy Society. An indispensable guide to societies and their publications is HENRY G. BOHN, *Appendix to the Bibliographer's Manual of English Literature* (1864). This volume formed the concluding part of Bohn's revision of Thomas Lowndes's original work.

The most satisfactory edition of any jestbook is E. A. HORSMAN (ed.), *Dobsons Drie Bobbes* (Oxford, 1955). The original was published in 1607; this edition has a long introduction, including some detailed bibliographical notes, a glossary, facsimile title page, MS facsimile and two folding plates.

E. A. HORSMAN has also edited *The Pinder of Wakefield* (Liverpool, 1956). This is a jestbook first published in 1632; in this new edition the editor has contributed a short introduction and some notes.

WITCHCRAFT

J. H. MARSHBURN, *Murder and Witchcraft in England, 1550–1640, as Recounted in Pamphlets, Ballads, Broadsides and Plays* (Norman, Oklahoma, 1971). Provides ample illustrative material, together with bibliographical details of scarce publications. An excellent book which suggests, by implication, further lines of search.

Linked to some extent with Marshburn's study is an older book, M. A. SHAABER, *Some Forerunners of the Newspaper in England, 1476–1622* (Pennsylvania, 1929). A pioneer work which has not yet been superseded. Especially good on ballads and popular news.

AUTHORS

Amongst collected editions of popular authors, F. O. MANN (ed.), *The Works of Thomas Deloney* (Oxford, 1908), is outstandingly good.

Very much less satisfactory is the reprint of John Taylor's works. Between 1869 and 1878 the Spenser Society issued eight separate volumes of his writings. These have recently been reprinted in facsimile, but this is no substitute for the critical edition of Taylor that is required. Scolar Press reissued *All the Workes of John Taylor the Water Poet* (1630) in 1973.

CRITICAL BIBLIOGRAPHY

REPRINTS

A number of scarce tracts have been reprinted and are to be found in such collections as JOHN PAYNE COLLIER (ed.), *Illustrations of Early English Popular Literature* (2 vols., 1863) and *Illustrations of Old English Literature* (3 vols., 1866). There is also CHARLES HINDLEY (ed.), *The Old Book Collector's Miscellany* (6 vols., 1871-3). It may be necessary, and can often be rewarding, to look through these eleven badly arranged, indifferently edited volumes to find a little known seventeenth-century popular tract.

Very much more satisfactory is EDWARD ARBER (ed.), *An English Garner* (8 vols., 1895-7), though even here the material is not systematically arranged.

ALMANACS

CYPRIAN BLAGDEN, 'The Distribution of Almanacs in the Second Half of the Seventeenth Century', in *Papers of the Bibliographical Society of the University of Virginia*, Vol. Eleven (1958). This is a perceptive study and breaks fresh ground.

FICTION

Similarly, C. W. R. D. MOSELEY, 'Richard Head's "The English Rogue", a Modern Mandeville?', in the *Yearbook of English Studies*, Vol. I, (1971), indicates new paths in the study of popular literature.

ROGER THOMPSON (ed.), *Pepys' Penny Merriments* (1976). Chapbooks collected by Pepys at the end of the seventeenth century, many of which were frequently reprinted during the eighteenth.

Inevitably these notes reflect the lopsided state of studies in seventeenth-century popular literature. There has been a preoccupation with ballads and a neglect of prose. This balance needs to be redressed so that popular literature as a whole can be looked at in more critical terms than has hitherto been possible.

THE EIGHTEENTH CENTURY

The popular literature of this period has received the attention of
antiquarians of the Victorian age, but more scholarly work is, in
general, lacking. The eighteenth century lies between two great
centres of contemporary historical activity, and its social history, let
alone any serious account of its popular literature, has remained
largely unwritten. There are exceptions to this generalization, at least
so far as social history is concerned, for both Edward Thompson and
George Rudé have made important forays here; but the study of the
ballads and chapbooks of the eighteenth century has remained in the
doldrums.

APPROACHES

The starting point is a book which, despite having appeared more than
fifty years ago, has remained the standard work in the field. A. E.
DOBBS, *Education and Social Movements* (1919), is a superlative study
of the background to books and reading from 1700 to 1850. It was
originally conceived as part of a history of English popular education;
the remainder was never written.

A. S. COLLINS, *Authorship in the Days of Johnson* (1927), contains a
chapter on the growth of the reading public which is valuable.

Wider perspectives are opened up in LEO LOWENTHAL, *Literature,
Popular Culture and Society* (New Jersey, 1961), which has a chapter
(written in collaboration with Marjorie Fiske) entitled 'The Debate
over Art and Popular Culture: English Eighteenth Century as a Case
Study'.

JAMES SUTHERLAND, *A Preface to Eighteenth-century Poetry* (Oxford,
1948), III, 'Readers and Writers'.

BIBLIOGRAPHY

The standard - indeed, sole - bibliographical guide to eighteenth-
century popular literature is a book by the present writer, *Chapbook
Bibliography* (second edition, 1972). This attempts to list all the
relevant books and articles on the subject. Inevitably it falls short of

absolute completeness, but the omissions are few. There is an index of printers and publishers. See also the following works by the present writer:

'The Diceys and the Chapbook Trade', in Transactions of the Bibliographical Society, the *Library*, Fifth Series, Vol. XXIV, Number 3 (September 1969). This is a discussion of an important firm of printers, and attempts an assessment of their work.

The Penny Histories (Oxford, 1968). A study of chapbooks as children's literature. Several chapbooks are reproduced in facsimile, and there is a bibliography.

Popular Education in Eighteenth Century England (1972). Appendix 2 deals with the structure of the chapbook trade, and the role of chapbooks in education is discussed.

A useful background bibliography is ARUNDELL ESDAILE, *A List of English Tales and Prose Romances Printed before 1740* (the Bibliographical Society, 1912).

CHAPBOOKS

A good deal of eighteenth-century material has survived, mostly chapbooks, and the best collections are to be found in the British Museum, the Bodleian Library, Cambridge University Library, many of the national libraries and some of the larger provincial ones. Harvard College Library has an exceptionally fine collection, the catalogue of which is essential for research: *Catalogue of English and American Chapbooks and Broadside Ballads in Harvard College Library* (Cambridge, Mass., 1905). Over 2,400 items are listed, and indexes cover subjects, titles, publishers, printers and booksellers. A facsimile reprint edition was issued some years ago. New York Public Library also has a good collection: see HARRY B. WEISS, *A Catalogue of the Chapbooks in the New York Public Library* (New York, 1936). There are more than 1,100 entries, together with indexes of authors, publishers, printers and booksellers. No other collections have such admirable printed catalogues.

JOHN ASHTON, *Chap-books of the Eighteenth Century* (1882), gives a fairly good idea of what chapbooks were like. Title pages, woodcuts and specimens of texts are all put down without any apparent plan.

Nonetheless, this book has tremendous charm and is the best introduction to the subject. It has been reprinted at least twice.

Less visually attractive, and without illustrations, is R. H. CUNNINGHAM, *Amusing Prose Chap-books Chiefly of the Last Century* (1889). It gives the texts of twenty-five chapbooks.

HARRY B. WEISS, *A Book about Chapbooks* (privately printed, Trenton, New Jersey, 1942). This edition consisted of 100 copies but is now available in a facsimile reprint. The first general introduction to the subject, and the first attempt to provide a systematic bibliography of references, it is still eminently worth reading. Mr Weiss has made many contributions to the subject (see the present writer's *Chapbook Bibliography*), and his work is characterized by originality and learning. Esoteric as, for example, 'American Editions of "Sir Richard Whittington and his Cat"' (New York, 1938) may sound, it is in fact a delightfully humane and scholarly essay.

A nineteenth-century book which has inexplicably not been reprinted is *A Catalogue of Chap-books, Garlands, and Popular Histories, in the Possession of James Orchard Halliwell, Esq.* (for private circulation, 1849). This is something more than a list of Halliwell's collection; the annotations are extremely informative, and the Preface demonstrates clearly that Halliwell regarded chapbooks as more than antiquarian trifles.

One of the reprints edited by CHARLES HINDLEY, which later formed part of *The Old Book Collector's Miscellany*, was *The Life of Long Meg of Westminster* (1871). Hindley reproduces the 1635 edition together with a chapbook version, so that it is possible to see how a popular story was adapted for publication in a chapbook.

BALLADS

Ballads for this period are very much harder to find, and the best source is the collection formed by Sir Frederick Madden, which was purchased by Cambridge University Library in 1886. It is probably the largest and most important of its kind, covering the period from 1775–1850 particularly well, though there are some earlier and later pieces. There is a card index of titles or first lines. In all there are twenty-six folio volumes, and the Under Librarian tells me that they have 'a rough analysis of the contents of each volume by county, place and printer'. In general, eighteenth-century ballads are worth looking for in the libraries mentioned above as having chapbook collections.

Outstanding in the reprinting of ballad texts is MILTON PERCIVAL, *Political Ballads Illustrating the Administration of Sir Robert Walpole* (Oxford, 1916). This is a model of scrupulous editing. The introduction is quite the best thing that has been done on the political ballads of the period. Never reprinted, it is now an extremely scarce book. See also W. W. WILKINS, *Political Ballads of the Seventeenth and Eighteenth Centuries* (1860), described on p. 276 above.

JOHN HOLLOWAY and JOAN BLACK (eds.), *Later English Broadside Ballads* (1975). An indifferent and disappointing collection.

POPULAR FICTION

R. D. MAYO, *The English Novel in the Magazines, 1740–1815* (Evanston and London, 1962). A scholarly book with an extensive list of novels and novelettes with their places of publication. See also ALISON ADBURGHAM, *Women in Print* (1972).

PRINTS

Catchpenny Prints (New York, 1970) reproduces 163 popular prints originally published by Bowles and Carver. A unique collection.

See also C. F. VAN VEEN, *Cents Prenten/Catchpenny Prints* (Rijksmuseum, Amsterdam, 1976). Exhibition Catalogue with superb illustrations.

THE NINETEENTH CENTURY

The sources of nineteenth-century popular literature are manifold, mixed and, on occasion, curiously elusive. Street ballads are to be found in the British Museum (Baring-Gould and Crampton Collections), in national, university and provincial libraries. There are also reprints which are helpful. Popular fiction, however, does present certain difficulties. So far as sensational 'penny dreadful' fiction is concerned, the Barry Ono Collection in the British Museum is marvellous, but its sheer volume provokes all kinds of questions about authors and publishers. In regard to romantic popular fiction and cheap editions of the classics, very little is known about firms like Milner & Sowerby of Halifax or Nicholson of Wakefield, whose lists were extensive.

Neither have the publishers of non-fiction yet been investigated. It is true that some attempts have been made to examine the achievement of the Society for the Diffusion of Useful Knowledge, but later publishing enterprises in the field of cheap non-fiction have not yet been surveyed, let alone evaluated. The following bibliographical notes, then, besides listing some of the most useful reference works, will also indicate areas where basic work requires to be done.

STREET BALLADS

The present writer's *Chapbook Bibliography* (second edition, 1972) lists a number of works relating to the nineteenth-century street ballad.

CHARLES HINDLEY wrote a number of books on the subject and, although they tend to be rambling and ill-arranged, they have a value because the author preserved material and recorded facts which would otherwise have been lost. *The Catnach Press* (1869) is a collection of facsimiles of books and woodcuts of James Catnach, the most famous printer of ephemeral sheets and chapbooks in the nineteenth century. *Curiosities of Street Literature* (1871) is a large volume containing facsimile reproductions of street ballads. It was originally issued in a limited edition, but two facsimile reprints have appeared in the past few years. *The Life and Times of James Catnach* (1878) and *The History of the Catnach Press* (1887) followed. These four books by Hindley provide the best introduction to nineteenth-century street literature. With the proviso that they are essentially antiquarian compilations and in no sense critical studies, they are recommended.

LESLIE SHEPARD, *John Pitts, Ballad Printer of Seven Dials, London, 1765–1844* (Private Libraries Association, 1963), follows largely in the Hindley tradition. This beautifully produced, copiously illustrated book deals exhaustively with a contemporary and rival of Catnach. A considerable amount of new material is presented in it. Shepard's *The History of Street Literature* (Newton Abbot, 1973) is well illustrated and includes a glossary of terms and a bibliography.

JOHN ASHTON, *Modern Street Ballads* (1888), is an excellent anthology. So too is W. HENDERSON, *Victorian Street Ballads* (1937).

CHARLES MANBY SMITH, *The Little World of London* (1857), contains an essay entitled 'The Press of the Seven Dials'. It is of unusual interest because the author was himself a printer.

Recent contributions to the subject have included the following:

J. GOODMAN (ed.), *Bloody Versicles, the Rhymes of Crimes* (Newton Abbot, 1971).

V. E. NEUBURG, 'The Literature of the Streets', in H. J. DYOS and M. WOLFF (eds.), *The Victorian City* (2 vols., 1973), Vol. I, pp. 191–209.

R. PALMER (ed.), *A Touch on the Times. Songs of Social Change 1770–1914* (Penguin Books, 1974).

MARTHA VICINUS, *Broadsides of the Industrial North* (Newcastle, 1975) is helpful. The same writer's *The Industrial Muse* (1974) is informative and scholarly.

J. S. BRATTON, *The Victorian Popular Ballad* (1975). Profound and illuminating.

Street ballads rarely come onto the market these days. When they do, prices are high, and because of their scarcity booksellers find it worthwhile to add details to the bare description of what is offered for sale. In Catalogue 124 (1973) of Peter Murray Hill (Rare Books) Ltd, item 6 was 'BALLADS. A fine collection of 64 ballad sheets'. The collection consists of bawdy and amorous ballads; and the bookseller's notes which, together with a detailed description, take up one page, are a minor contribution to the bibliography of the subject.[1]

FICTION

For Pierce Egan's life and work, see J. C. REID, *Bucks and Bruisers: Pierce Egan and Regency England* (1971).

LOUIS JAMES, *Print and the People 1819–51* (1976), provides a well-illustrated introduction to the popular literature of this period.

The key book, however, is LOUIS JAMES, *Fiction for the Working Man: 1830–1850* (Oxford, 1963; Penguin University Books, 1974). This is a judicious, well-documented study which puts popular fiction into both an historical and a critical perspective. The full bibliography of sources represents the best guide to the subject that has yet been attempted. Appendix II comprises a list of publishers who issued penny fiction between 1830 and 1850. Appendix III is entitled

1. I am grateful to Denis Crutch for drawing my attention to this item.

'Check-list of Penny-issue Novels Partially Listed in or Omitted from Montague Summers's *Gothic Bibliography*'.

When it was first published by the Fortune Press, London, in 1940, MONTAGUE SUMMERS, *A Gothic Bibliography*, was something of a landmark. Its 620 pages attempted a bibliographical survey of the whole field. There was an index of authors and an index of titles, with substantial 'Addenda' to both. It is an erratic, often infuriating, book, but it is indispensable and remains a monument to one of the most eccentric scholars of this century. The same author's *The Gothic Quest* (1941) is extremely good, though often idiosyncratic, on some of the earlier writers of romantic fiction.

Also valuable is SIR WALTER SCOTT, *The Lives of the Novelists* (Everyman's Library, undated). See also ALISON ADBURGHAM, *Women in Print* (1972).

Very much more scholarly than either is J. M. S. TOMPKINS, *The Popular Novel in England 1700–1800* (1932).

EDITH BIRKHEAD, *The Tale of Terror* (1921). A somewhat earlier book on the subject which is still worth reading.

Superbly opinionated and compulsively readable, Q. D. LEAVIS, *Fiction and the Reading Public* (1932, 1965), remains essential reading.

E. S. TURNER, *Boys Will Be Boys* (new and revised edition, 1957; Penguin, 1976), is a much lighter account of popular fiction. Although, as the title suggests, it is mostly about boys' papers, it is nonetheless worth reading, and the illustrations are remarkably evocative of a lost literature.

MARGARET DALZIEL, *Popular Fiction 100 Years Ago* (1957), is critical in intent and has a list of mid-nineteenth-century cheap periodicals.

ODYSSEY PRESS, New York, issued a number of novels in a series entitled 'Popular American Fiction'. *Tempest and Sunshine*, by Mary Jane Holmes, together with *The Lamplighter*, by Maria Susanna Cummins, were reprinted in a paperback in 1968. T. S. Arthur was among the authors whose work was either announced or reprinted.

For bibliography, apart from Louis James and Montague Summers, there are two important items:

DOROTHY BLAKEY, *The Minerva Press 1790–1820* (the Bibliographical Society, 1939), is a major work, detailed, thorough, reliable. Its scholarship is impeccable.

W. L. G. JAMES, *Catalogue of the Barry Ono Collection* (1958), a card index available on request in the North Library of the British Museum.

A recent important contribution to the subject is D. KAUSCH, 'George W. M. Reynolds: A Bibliography', in Transactions of the Bibliographical Society, the *Library*, Fifth Series, Vol. XXVIII, no. 4 (December 1973), pp. 319–26.

P. HAINING, *The Penny Dreadful* (1975), offers a selection of extracts from cheap sensational fiction. Although not a scholarly work, it does have the great merit of making available a good deal of material which is otherwise hard to find. There are a number of illustrations.

There are areas of nineteenth-century popular fiction hardly covered at all. Two of the most important are cheap editions of novels by English and American authors and the penny romantic novel.

Amongst firms which specialized in cheap reprints were Milner & Sowerby of Halifax and W. Nicholson of Wakefield. An article by H. E. WROOT, 'A Pioneer in Cheap Literature. William Milner of Halifax', which appeared in the *Bookman* (March 1897), provides a starting point, but both firms await more detailed investigation.

Nothing seems to be known about W. B. Horner & Sons, London and Dublin, who published new novels at a penny each on the first and third Tuesdays in each month during the last two decades of the century, despite the fact that sales were phenomenal, with 450,000 copies of some titles quoted. In addition to specific information about the publishers I have mentioned, we need to know a good deal more about other firms and individuals who were involved in mass publishing. Edward Lloyd is an obvious example. Authors, too, are hard to track down, although some can be found in the pages of Allibone's *Dictionary of English Literature* in five volumes, and Montague Summers's bibliography is helpful. Cheap fiction formed an important element in the stock-in-trade of the smaller stationers' shops and circulating libraries in the back streets and unfashionable areas of large cities, and we know little about establishments of this kind. Finally, readership – who bought novels, who borrowed them? Questions like this underline the need for more knowledge about aspects of publishing and the book trade.

CHEAP NON-FICTION AND CLASSICS

The starting-point here is the Society for the Diffusion of Useful Knowledge, whose papers are in University College Library, London. There is a good account of the society in R. K. WEBB, *The British Working Class Reader 1790–1848* (1955). The autobiography of CHARLES KNIGHT, *Passages of a Working Life* (3 vols., 1864, 1865), is an invaluable document. HAROLD SMITH, *The Society for the Diffusion of Useful Knowledge 1826–1846, A Social and Bibliographical Evaluation* (Dalhousie University, School of Library Service, Occasional Paper No. 8, Halifax, Nova Scotia, 1974) demonstrates the value of bibliographical techniques for the study of social history.

WILLIAM CHAMBERS, *Memoir of Robert Chambers with Autobiographic Reminiscences* (sixth edition, Edinburgh, 1872). A longish book, 364 pages; indispensable but, alas, not indexed! See also the same author's *Story of a Long and Busy Life* (Edinburgh, 1882) – shorter, not indexed, readable and very informative.

SIMON NOWELL-SMITH, *The House of Cassell 1848–1958* (1958), is extremely good on John Cassell, founder of the firm, and his publishing activities.

With regard to cheap editions of the classics later in the century, I am not aware of any work which has been done. Besides those series mentioned in the text, there was 'The Penny Poets', edited by W. T. Stead and published in London at the 'Review of Reviews' Office; and George Newnes initiated their 'Penny Library of Famous Books' with *The Vicar of Wakefield* in 1896. The best – indeed, the only – guides to these series are the odd volumes which can still occasionally be found second-hand, in which lists of titles and prices are to be found. Publishers' catalogues and advertisements in their own books are of some importance, and will be discussed under 'The trade' (see pp. 295–7).

THE ORAL TRADITION

This is the most tenuous concept of all in popular literature, and for this reason the notes which follow are offered tentatively rather than in any definitive sense.

GENERAL

JAN VANSINA, *The Oral Tradition* (Chicago, 1965; Penguin University Books, 1973), is subtitled 'A Study in Historical Methodology'. Scholarly, authoritative, it has a good bibliography.

Lighter in tone is G. E. EVANS, *Where Beards Wag All. The Relevance of the Oral Tradition* (1970). Evans also wrote 'Aspects of Oral Tradition', an article published in *Folk Life*, Vol. 7 (1969).

An excellent brief introduction to the subject is DONALD MCKELVIE, 'Aspects of Oral Tradition and Belief in an Industrial Region', published in *Folk Life*, Vol. 1 (1963).

Very much older is 'The Elders of Arcady', an essay by AUGUSTUS JESSOP, reprinted in his *England's Peasantry* (1914). It is particularly good on country memories and traditions.

BALLADS

WILLA MUIR, *Living with Ballads* (1965), breaks fresh ground. A perceptive book, full of insights.

L. C. WIMBERLY, *Folklore in the English and Scottish Ballads* (Chicago, 1928), is a valuable analysis, perhaps a little outdated.

A. L. LLOYD, *Folk Song in England* (1967), is a marvellously rich book. There have been two paperback reprints.

RUTH A. FIROR, *Folkways in Thomas Hardy* (Pennsylvania, 1931). Not in any way outdated, this is a fine study of the oral tradition and the use made of it by a creative artist. (See also *The Collected Poems of Thomas Hardy, passim.*)

For a much earlier period, G. R. OWST, *Literature and Pulpit in Medieval England* (second revised edition, Blackwell, 1961), remains definitive.

PENNY READINGS

The literature of penny readings is meagre. A paper on the subject was read by Samuel Taylor to the annual meeting of the Social Science Association in 1858. Penny readings are also mentioned in the Annual Reports of the Yorkshire Union of Mechanics' Institutes for the years 1862 and 1864.

CHARLES SULLEY, *Penny Readings* (1861). Sulley was editor of the *Ipswich Express* and, according to J. E. Carpenter (see below), he founded the movement in Suffolk in the 1850s.

J. E. CARPENTER, *Penny Readings in Prose and Verse* (new edition, 9 vols., 1865). The standard collection. Volume 1 has an introductory note on 'The Penny Reading Movement'.

Another collection of extracts is TOM HOOD, *Standard Penny Readings* (new edition in 3 parts, 1871). There are prefaces to parts 1 and 2, and both are worth reading.

For the view of the twentieth century see H. P. SMITH, *Literature and Adult Education a Century Ago : Pantopragmatics and Penny Readings* (Documentary No. 3, Oxford, 1960); also OLIVER EDWARDS – urbane as always – 'All for a Penny', an article published in *The Times* (24 November 1966).

See also WINIFRED PECK, *Home for the Holidays* (1955); p. 170 mentions the survival of penny readings into the twentieth century.

J. F. C. HARRISON, *Learning and Living 1790–1860* (1961). He seems to be the only recent historian to have taken notice of the penny-reading movement.

SURVIVALS

For the strength and persistence of the oral tradition, see IONA and PETER OPIE, *The Lore and Language of Schoolchildren* (Oxford, 1959), and *Children's Games in Street and Playground* (Oxford, 1969).

TRACTS

COLLECTIONS

Religious tracts have survived in considerable numbers. They are to be found in the British Museum; the Methodist Archives; the Society for Promoting Christian Knowledge Archives, SPCK House, London; and in other libraries. There is, so far as I am aware, no census of tract collections, and the subject awaits investigation. Fortunately there is no shortage of material, although, unluckily, the Lutterworth Press (formerly the Religious Tract Society) lost its copies of early publications when its premises were bombed during the Second World War. For a general view of tracts, see the present writer's *Popular Education in Eighteenth Century England* (1971), Chapter 6.

MS GUIDES

Wesleyan Tract Society Minutes, 1822–1850. Bound MSS, John Rylands Library, Manchester University.

SPCK Minutes 1829–1850. Bound MS volumes, SPCK House, London.

PUBLISHERS

Cheap Repository Tracts

G. H. SPINNEY, 'Cheap Repository Tracts: Hazard and Marshall Edition', in Transactions of the Bibliographical Society, the *Library*, Vol. 20, Fourth Series (1939).

MARY ALDEN HOPKINS, *Hannah More and Her Circle* (New York, 1947). Both this and the preceding are admirable.

For a nineteenth-century view of Miss More and her tracts, see ANNA BUCKLAND, *The Life of Hannah More* (undated, ?1860); a much less critical view, but interesting.

SPCK

W. K. LOWTHER CLARKE, *Eighteenth Century Piety* (1944), has some useful notes on tracts. The same author's *A History of the SPCK* (1959) is authoritative and highly readable.

RTS

GORDON HEWITT, *Let the People Read* (1949), is a brisk, brief history of the Religious Tract Society and its outgrowths.

An earlier work, WILLIAM JONES, *The Jubilee Memorial of the Religious Tract Society* (1850), has a great amount of detail.

The best account of RTS tracts is to be found in *The Christmas Box or New Year's Gift*, originally published by the Society in 1825. A reprint dated 1889–90, issued by Field & Tuer, contains a twenty-two-page introduction by S. G. Green which is full of good things.

Methodists

FRANK CUMBERS, *The Book Room* (1956), is a short account of Methodist publishing. Two earlier works are also useful:

J. CROWTHER, *An Apology for the Liberty of the Press among the Methodists* (second edition, Halifax, 1810). A piece of polemic urging that tracts should be disseminated by hawkers and chapmen.

G. J. STEVENSON, *City Road Chapel and Its Associations* (1872). This is good on the Methodist milieu and its personalities.

DISTRIBUTION

Tracts were distributed to the poor by their 'betters'; they were given away free by the faithful; in some cases they were offered for sale. For aspects of tract dispersal see the REV. R. COOKE, *Colportage: Its History and Relation to Home and Foreign Evangelisation*, ed. Mrs W. Fison (Margaret Fison) (1859). Chapter VII deals specifically with Great Britain, but the entire book is of value, not least because it offers a sustained contemporary view of religious tracts and what it was hoped they would achieve.

C. H. SPURGEON, S. MANNING and G. H. PIKE contributed to *Booksellers and Bookbuyers in Byeways and Highways* (1882); the Earl of Shaftesbury wrote a preface. This little book offers a splendid insight into why it was thought worth-while to promote tract distribution. Spurgeon himself had been instrumental in founding the Colportage Association in 1866. See his *The Metropolitan Tabernacle: Its History and Work* (1876).

THE TRACT WORLD

Two books recreate vividly the rather narrow evangelical world of the end of the nineteenth century and the beginning of the twentieth, in which tracts flourished.

WILLIAM KENT, *The Testament of a Victorian Youth* (1938), tells of a boy growing up in South London. Descriptions of chapels and preachers are remarkably well done: the author's style matches his theme.

KENNETH YOUNG, *Chapel* (1973), presents an affectionate view of a way of life that has all but vanished.

THE BIBLE

Attempts were made to circulate Bibles as widely as possible. The British and Foreign Bible Society was active in this endeavour, and their jubilee volume contains revealing facts and figures. L.N.R. (L. N. Ranyard), *The Book and Its Story* (forty-first thousand, eighth edition, 1855).

See also J. M. WEYLLAND, *The Man with the Book: or, the Bible among the People* (twenty-first edition, undated, *c.* 1891).

Evangelists

The literature of evangelism is enormous, and much is of doubtful quality. JAMES DUNN, *From Coal Mine Upwards* (1910), is the autobiography of a man who worked, Bible in hand, for the London City Mission, after a varied career including service with the Army Work Corps in the Crimea.

WILLIAM POTTER, *Thomas Jackson of Whitechapel* (1929), is the biography of a Methodist minister in Whitechapel. Both books add an essential dimension to any consideration of evangelical popular literature.

LITERACY AND READERS

LITERACY

J. W. THOMPSON, *The Literacy of the Laity in the Middle Ages* (California, undated; reprinted New York, 1963), is an important basic work.

J. W. ADAMSON, *The Illiterate Anglo-Saxon* (Cambridge, 1946), contains an essay, 'Literacy in England in the Fifteenth and Sixteenth Centuries'. Originally a paper read before the Bibliographical Society in 1929, it is still worth reading.

Lawrence Stone has surveyed the relationship between literacy and education in two magisterial contributions to *Past and Present*: 'The Educational Revolution in England, 1560–1640' (No. 28, July 1964); and 'Literacy and Education in England 1640–1900' (No. 42, February 1969). Both are essential reading.

The development of literacy in the eighteenth century is discussed in the present writer's *Popular Education in Eighteenth Century England* (1971). This book dissents from the currently held view that figures for literacy can be established by counting signatures in parish registers, and attempts to assess growing literacy in terms of an increasing volume of popular literature.

MICHAEL SANDERSON, 'Literacy and Social Mobility in the Industrial Revolution in England', in *Past and Present* (No. 56, August 1972), is a trenchantly argued essay which relies heavily upon statistical evidence drawn from parish registers. Impressive, but not altogether convincing.

A good general account is C. M. CIPOLLA, *Literacy and Development in the West* (Penguin, 1969). Short, readable, and with a helpful bibliography.

READERS

General surveys of readership are to be found in R. K. WEBB, *The British Working Class Reader 1790–1848* (1955), and RICHARD D. ALTICK, *The English Common Reader* (Chicago, 1957). These two books complement each other. Webb's is the shorter, while Altick's, subtitled 'A Social History of the Mass Reading Public 1800–1900', is very much more detailed and includes a bibliography.

The autobiographies of working men often have something to say about books or reading. The following seem especially revealing:

W. E. ADAMS, *Memoirs of a Social Atom* (2 vols., 1903).

SAMUEL BAMFORD, *Early Days* (1849).

THOMAS CARTER, *Memoirs of a Working Man* (1845).

JOHN CLARE, *Autobiography*. Printed in *The Prose of John Clare*, ed. J. W. and A. Tibble (1851).

THOMAS COOPER, *The Life of Thomas Cooper* (1872).

THOMAS HOLCROFT, *Memoirs of Thomas Holcroft* (1816; Oxford, 1926).

WILLIAM HONE, *Autobiography*. Printed in *The Life and Times of William Hone*, by F. W. Hackwood (1912).

WILLIAM HUTTON: the best edition of his autobiography, which first appeared in 1816, is *The Life of William Hutton and the Hutton Family*, ed. Llewellyn Jewitt (undated, *c.* 1880).

JAMES LACKINGTON, *Memoirs, etc.* (1803).

WILLIAM LOVETT, *The Life and Struggles of William Lovett* (1876).

FRANCIS PLACE, *Autobiography*. Substantial extracts from the MS volumes in the British Museum are printed in MARY THALE, *The Autobiography of Francis Place* (Cambridge, 1972).

Also relevant to the theme of books and readers are the following accounts of self-taught men. Originally published in the nineteenth century to encourage the young, these books now have a rather quaint air which does not, however, detract entirely from their value as source material:

W. ANDERSON, *Self-made Men* (second edition, 1865).

G. L. CRAIK, *The Pursuit of Knowledge under Difficulties* (2 vols., 1831–2).

ANON., *Biography of Self-taught Men* (1852).

THE TRADE

HAWKERS, PEDLARS, CHAPMEN

There is no comparable work in England to RICHARDSON WRIGHT, *Hawkers and Walkers in Early America* (Philadelphia, 1927). To some extent outdated, it should not still be lacking its counterpart in this country.

The nearest thing to Wright's work is FELIX FOLIO, *The Hawkers and Street Dealers of the North of England Manufacturing Districts . . . Their Dealings, Dodgings, and Doings* (second edition, Manchester, undated ?1860). There is a good deal of information in it which is not easily found elsewhere.

HENRY MAYHEW, *London Labour and the London Poor* (4 vols., 1851–64), is a vast storehouse of information about street-sellers in the metropolis. Volume 1 is particularly good on those who sold ballad sheets and books.

CRITICAL BIBLIOGRAPHY

DAVID LOVE, *The Life, Adventures and Experiences of David Love* (Nottingham, 1825), is the autobiography of a pedlar.

WILLIAM GREEN, *The Life and Adventures of a Cheap Jack*, ed. Charles Hindley (New edition, 1881). According to the editor, Green spent many years as a street-seller.

A similar book is WILLIAM CAMERON, *Hawkie: the Autobiography of a Gangrel*, ed. J. Strathesk (Glasgow, 1888). This is the life story of a Scots pedlar.

KAREN F. BEALL, *Cries and Itinerant Traders, a Bibliography/Kaufrufe und Strassenhändler, eine Bibliographie* (Hamburg, 1975). This will be the standard work for many years to come.

CATALOGUES

One of the most important sources of information about popular literature is the publisher's catalogue giving details of titles and, usually, prices. Ranging in size from a single sheet to forty-eight pages, they offer a unique view of what was available. The earliest I have come across is a broadside issued by William Thackeray of Duck Lane, London, during the last decades of the seventeenth century. It advertises 'small books, ballads and histories'. More than half the items are ballads, but several chapbooks – variously called 'small godly books', 'small merry books', 'double books' and 'histories' – are listed. No prices are given, and at the top of the sheet is the information that 'any Chapman may be furnished with them or any other Books at Reasonable Rates'. The broadside is reproduced, somewhat reduced, between pages 20 and 21 of LESLIE SHEPARD, *John Pitts* (1969).

Glasgow University Library possesses a 104-page catalogue issued by Cluer Dicey and Richard Marshall in 1764. There is another Dicey catalogue, incomplete, in the Bodleian Library, Oxford, with MS annotations by Bishop Percy. The range of Dicey's publications is considerable, and the majority have not survived.

LESLIE SHEPARD, *The History of Street Literature* (1973). This contains a facsimile reproduction of an 8-page catalogue issued by James Catnach in 1832, offering songs, song books, carols and a selection of children's books at a halfpenny or a farthing each.

In the Mitchell Library, Glasgow, there is a 48-page catalogue of songs issued by H. P. Such of the Borough, in south-east London, towards the end of the nineteenth century. It is of special interest because Such was one of the last street-ballad printers in the capital.

The firm of Milner & Sowerby, founded by William Milner, did a great deal of advertising. Their earlier volumes usually had 'A list of cheap books' printed on the insides of the front and back covers and on the fly leaves. In their later volumes it was the custom to bind up a catalogue with each book. Thirty-two pages seem to have been the favoured length, and these lists are a mine of information about titles, series and prices. Some of the catalogues have notes on the authors. This kind of source material is invaluable, but has to be looked for. A large number of Victorian publishers included catalogues with their publications, and they represent a rich field for investigation.

PICTURES

SIGFRED TAUBERT, *Bibliopola* (2 vols., Hamburg and London, 1966), contains splendid illustrations in colour and in black and white of bookshops, wandering print-sellers, circulating libraries, and even of the more orthodox side of bookselling!

DAVID KUNZLE, *The Early Comic Strip* (Berkeley, 1973). 'Narrative strips and picture stories in the European broadsheet from *c.* 1450-1825.' The popular background as seen by contemporaries.

INDEX